MW00632492

# HER OWN HERO

# Her Own Hero

*The Origins of the Women's Self-Defense Movement*

Wendy L. Rouse

NEW YORK UNIVERSITY PRESS

New York

NEW YORK UNIVERSITY PRESS
New York
www.nyupress.org

An earlier and partial version of the introduction was published (with Beth Slutsky) in the *Journal of the Gilded Age and Progressive Era* 13, no. 4 (September 2014): 470–499, copyright 2014, Cambridge University Press; reprinted by permission.

An earlier and partial version of chapter 2 was published in the *Pacific Historical Review* 84, no. 4 (November 2015): 448–477; copyright 2015, Pacific Coast Branch, American Historical Association, and the University of California Press; reprinted by permission.

References to Internet websites (URLs) were accurate at the time of writing. Neither the author nor New York University Press is responsible for URLs that may have expired or changed since the manuscript was prepared.

Library of Congress Cataloging-in-Publication Data
Names: Rouse, Wendy L., author.
Title: Her own hero : the origins of the women's self-defense movement / Wendy L. Rouse.
Description: New York : New York University Press, 2017. | Includes bibliographical references and index.
Identifiers: LCCN 2017003624 | ISBN 9781479828531 (cloth : alkaline paper)
Subjects: LCSH: Self-defense for women—United States—History. | Self-defense—Social aspects—United States—History. | Women—United States—Social conditions. | Women—Political activity—United States—History. | Women's rights—United States—History. | Feminism—United States—History. | Social movements—United States—History.
Classification: LCC GV1111.5 .R68 2017 | DDC 613.6/6082—dc23
LC record available at https://lccn.loc.gov/2017003624

New York University Press books are printed on acid-free paper, and their binding materials are chosen for strength and durability. We strive to use environmentally responsible suppliers and materials to the greatest extent possible in publishing our books.

Manufactured in the United States of America

10 9 8 7 6 5 4 3 2 1

Also available as an ebook

# CONTENTS

# ACKNOWLEDGMENTS

This project grew not only from my research and interest in Progressive Era history but also from my personal history in learning and teaching women's self-defense. I began studying martial arts at ten years of age and had the privilege of training under the direction of some amazing teachers. My first instructor, Bart Wilson, instilled in me a sense of confidence and taught me a love of Japanese karate. At Sacramento State University, I continued my training in the martial arts through the study of Okinawan karate with Joan Neide, a professor of kinesiology and teacher of Uechi-ryu. Joan has had a profound influence on so many students over the years, fostering in us all a deep respect for the history of martial arts. She provides an example of excellence in teaching and remains a mentor to her students, past and present. I also wish to thank Uechi-ryu teacher Robert Van Der Volgen, who is also an amazing instructor modeling a patient style of teaching and a dedication to gender equity in the martial arts. I have learned so much over the years from fellow martial artists and advocates of women's self-defense whose commitment to their own training and teaching provided an inspiration for much of this research. Thank you especially to Nikki and Renee Smith for opening my eyes to various approaches to self-defense training by introducing me to the vast networks of women martial artists advocating empowerment models of self-defense through organizations such as Pacific Association of Women Martial Artists (PAWMA).

This book evolved through years of research, paper presentations, and discussions. I owe a huge debt of gratitude to all the individuals who commented on conference presentations, read drafts, provided feedback, and suggested revisions for the various incarnations of this manuscript. I especially want to thank Beth Slutsky, a great colleague and friend who was involved in this project from the beginning. Thank you also to Cecilia Tsu, Jennifer Terry, Sarah Gold McBride, Barbara Molony, Kimberley Jensen, and Renee Laegreid, who commented on initial presentations of this work and helped shape the future direction of my research. Tony Wolf and Emelyne Godfrey were amazing in responding so enthusiastically to my numerous inquiries, tapping into their expertise in the history of women's martial arts around the world. Thank you also to Martha McCaughey, Martha E. Thompson, and Jocelyn Hollander for their insightful research and careful reading and recommendations for the conclusion of this book. Their ongoing scholarship and advocacy on behalf of the empowerment model of women's self-defense are inspirational. I also want to acknowledge my colleagues Maria Alaniz, Wendy Ng, Erica Boas, and Carlos Garcia in the Department of Sociology and Interdisciplinary Social Sciences at San Jose State University for supporting this research. Research grants from the College of Social Sciences helped make this project possible.

Thank you also to the scholars, archivists, and research librarians who helped locate essential resources. I especially want to thank Catherine Palczewski, professor in the Women's and Gender Studies Program at the University of Northern Iowa; Robert Cox at the Department of Special Collections and University Archives at the University of Massachusetts Amherst; Lauren Sodano at the George Eastman Museum in Rochester, New York; Coi E. Drummond-Gehrig at the Denver Public Library; Nyle Monday at the San Jose State University Library; and Kim Stankiewicz of the Polish Genealogical Society of America.

I am also grateful to the individuals who helped edit and improve various chapters of the book in their original form as journal articles, including Alan Lessoff and Jonathan Geffner at the *Journal of the Gilded Age and Progressive Era* and Dave Hedberg, Luke Sprunger, Brenda Frink, Katherine Nelson, and Cathy Valentine at the *Pacific Historical Review*.

The editorial staff at NYU Press was professional and supportive throughout the publication process. I especially want to thank Clara Platter for believing in this book from the beginning. Thank you also to Amy Klopfenstein for all her assistance along the way. I am grateful to the anonymous readers who gave so freely of their time, offering insightful observations and helping me to reconceptualize the significance of my findings and place them in a much broader context.

Finally, I wish to thank my parents, Sherry Sweeney and Denis and Jennifer Sweeney, for encouraging and supporting me in all aspects of my life. Thank you to the rest of my family—Bridget Kearns, Michelle Forrester, Catriona Harris, Amanda Sweeney, Patricia Sweeney, Emily Spece, Lance Spece, and Diane Rouse—for doing what family does best in alternately mocking and supporting me. It is good to know we are always there for each other. I am most indebted to Allison Romero for the inspiration, enthusiasm, and joy that she freely shares with the world. I won't remember anything else.

This book is dedicated to my grandmother Lina Rouse, who patiently listened to me talk about the research over the years but was not able to see the final book. She never failed to love us no matter what passions we pursued and she continues to send her love to us all from the other side.

# Introduction

This book examines the emergence and development of a women's self-defense movement during the Progressive Era as women across the nation began studying boxing and jiu-jitsu. The women's self-defense movement arose simultaneously with the rise of the physical culture movement, concerns about the strength and future of the nation, fears associated with immigration and rapid urbanization, and the expansion of women's political and social rights. However, the meaning and transformation wrought through self-defense training varied from individual to individual. Women were inspired to take up self-defense training for very personal reasons that ranged from protecting themselves from stranger attacks on the street to rejecting gendered notions about feminine weakness and empowering themselves. Women's training in boxing and jiu-jitsu was both a reflection of and a response to the larger women's rights movement and the campaign for the vote. Self-defense training also opened up conversations about the less visible violence that many women faced in their own private lives.[1]

At first glance it appears that the majority of women who participated in this Progressive Era self-defense movement were white women from the middle and upper classes. An interest in physical culture was especially popular among society women in the early twentieth century. The national obsession with physical culture at this time was somewhat linked to larger racialized and gendered concerns about the future of the Anglo race and indeed the future of the nation.[2] Women's athletics were promoted as essential to ensuring the health of the nation's future wives and mothers, with educated, native-born white women enjoying greater opportunities to learn jiu-jitsu and boxing through physical education courses in high school or college. After graduating from college, some women organized their own athletic social clubs where they continued their physical pursuits. Wealthier women could afford to hire professional boxers and wrestlers to give them private instruction. Japanese jiu-jitsu instructors also marketed their services to eager men and women desiring to learn the Japanese art of self-defense. Increasingly, women took classes in self-defense at gymnasiums. A few women became experts in self-defense themselves and began teaching other women.

The women who trained in boxing and jiu-jitsu were predominantly middle- or upper-class, native-born, and Anglo. However, working-class, immigrant, and nonwhite women also learned self-defense. Some of the interest in self-defense spread from the top down as reform-minded upper-class women advocated on behalf of women of the working class. Anne Morgan, for example, insisted on the necessity of self-defense for the protection of workingwomen and organized jiu-jitsu classes for shopgirls in New York City.[3] Similarly, a department store in Newark, New Jersey, hired former boxer Charles Weiner to teach its female employees self-defense against men who might harass or assault them on their way to work.[4] Upper- and middle-class women saw this work as a natural extension of their role as members of the civilized Anglo race. Casting off the notion that they themselves needed male protection, these women assumed the role of protector of women of less civilized races and classes. In so doing, they were able to gain some degree of authority and power within the confines of existing gender and racial boundaries.[5]

Yet boxing had emerged from and was a large part of the culture of the working class.[6] Lower-class women, therefore, most likely learned self-defense in less formal and less public ways than their upper-class counterparts. Young women growing up in the working class may have learned boxing from relatives or friends in their own homes. Some of the working-class women who learned boxing in the early twentieth century went on to train more formally, with a few even pursuing careers as exhibition or competitive fighters. These women were motivated perhaps more by economic motives than simply by a desire to learn self-defense.

Whether the participants were rich or poor, the self-defense movement appears to have been overwhelmingly an urban movement. Most of the formal classes were held in large cities such as New York, Philadelphia, Los Angeles, San Francisco, and Chicago. The impetus and demand for self-defense courses seemed to be partly inspired by concern for women's safety in the urban jungle. Anxiety over the presence of more women on the city streets led to concerns over their physical safety. Self-defense training seemed essential to protecting women from attacks by the strange men they might encounter as they navigated through public space.

The fact that the majority of women who studied and advocated self-defense were urban, Anglo women from the middle and upper classes is significant. These women were trapped in an oppressive legal, economic, and political system that ignored white men's violence against them. Anglo men were depicted as women's natural protectors and as exemplars of morality and civilized behavior. Immigrants and men of color were more often stereotyped as dangerous kidnappers, rapists, and murderers. However, this only obscured the reality, deflecting blame for violence against women onto nonwhite, nonnative men. But the truth was that native-born Anglo men were the primary perpetrators of harassment and violence against women on the streets. Recognizing this and rejecting the notion that women needed white men to serve as their protectors, some women rebelled against the constraints of white femininity and trained to defend themselves against attackers. Unable to fully accept the notion that women would be capable of fighting back and unwilling to relinquish their view of themselves as women's natural protectors, white men reenvisioned and justified self-defense as a way for white women to protect themselves from potential attacks by nonwhite men only when they were not present to do so themselves. Thus, objections against women studying boxing and jiu-jitsu dissipated as long as women's self-defense was framed as a means of protecting white women's sexual purity from threats by nonwhite men and therefore in effect preserving white women's bodies for white men. The potential masculinizing effects of women's athletic conditioning were mitigated through the creation of less intense, sanitized versions of boxing and jiu-jitsu lessons for women that focused primarily on preserving their feminine beauty while promoting normative cultural conceptions of heterosexual, white femininity. The objectification and sexualization of female self-defense practitioners served to minimize fears about the potential disrupting influence of women's training in the fighting arts on traditional gender and sexual norms. Outward displays of normative femininity and the construction of female fighters as objects of heterosexual desire further minimized critiques of women's self-defense.

Women who more dramatically stepped outside the box, pursuing a rigorous course of self-defense training, fully acknowledging women's capacity for violence, or rejecting the notion that women were inherently vulnerable and requiring male protection, were marginalized by mainstream society as nonconformist physical freaks, masculinized deviants, or deluded by unrealistic feminist notions. Yet these women who transgressed the boundaries of normative gender relations paved the way for future generations of female athletes and embraced a model of women's self-defense that in some ways foreshadowed the empowerment model adopted by second-wave feminists.

The first two chapters of this book examine how women came to study boxing and jiu-jitsu, respectively, and the larger cultural and political debates about those two fighting systems. The remaining three chapters focus specifically on the significance of the first women's self-defense movement and its ability to transform the individual lives of women on the street, in the political arena, and in the home.

Chapter 1 surveys the roots of the women's self-defense movement in the physical culture movement of the late nineteenth and early twentieth centuries. Justified as a way of maintaining a healthy, younger-looking physique and preparing women's bodies for motherhood, women's athletics became increasingly popular around the turn of the century. Women across the country eagerly began practicing a range of sports, from tennis and cycling to the more controversial sport of boxing. Eugenicists contributed to the craze by raising the specter of race degeneration and by pointing to declining birthrates among elite Anglo families, the expanding population of nonwhites, and increasing miscegenation between the races. Ensuring the survival of the Anglo race included a commitment to improving the physical health of middle- and upper-class men and women. The physical culture movement became a national obsession that was promoted by the nation's leading academics and politicians as necessary not only for the health of the nation but also for the perpetuation of the Anglo race. Pioneering women used the new obsession with the nation's health to justify their participation in traditionally male sports. This chapter explores aspects of race, masculinity, and boxing to set the stage for women's entry into the male world of combat sports. Female boxers challenged notions of masculinity and femininity through their training in the quintessential "manly art." In the process, they broke down gender barriers and shattered preconceptions about feminine frailty. Enduring personal attacks, some female boxers chose to emphasize their femininity in an effort to deflect criticism about the masculinizing effects of boxing. Female athletes who exhibited outward displays of acceptable white, heterosexual femininity found more social acceptance. The physical culture movement encouraged the transgression of class boundaries as men and women of the upper classes studied sanitized elements of working-class fighting sports, and working-class men and women found a degree of fame and upward mobility in exhibition boxing or prizefighting. Working-class female exhibition fighters, however, found their bodies objectified, sexualized, and commercialized by promoters who often were more interested in turning a profit than in promoting equality in athletics for men and women.

Chapter 2 turns to jiu-jitsu by exploring the history of how American men and women came to train in the Japanese martial art. This chapter considers the broader historical context of American jiu-jitsu training within the framework of the larger debate about imperialism, manliness, and the future of the white race. The rising military power of Japan and an increase in Japanese immigration to the United States combined to create a fear of the Yellow Peril. This fear led to a national debate about boxing and jiu-jitsu in an attempt to determine which fighting system (and by extension which race and nation) was ultimately superior. The debate played out in the popular press as well as in gymnasiums across America as Japanese jiu-jitsu experts literally battled it out against American boxers and wrestlers. A variety of responses to jiu-jitsu were evident in the discourse that followed, ranging from exoticizing, vilifying, and feminizing the art to an eventual appropriation of aspects of jiu-jitsu. As American men wrestled with jiu-jitsu's effectiveness in relation to Western styles of fighting and its meanings for American manhood, American women seized opportunities to justify their own experimentation with jiu-jitsu.

Chapter 3 explores how women who trained in boxing and jiu-jitsu used their newfound knowledge to lay claim to public space. Increasingly, women began to recognize the usefulness of self-defense as a means of physical empowerment against potential attackers. Working-class women had already learned to negotiate the perils of the city streets. However, the existence of more upper- and middle-class women in public, where they were subjected to the sexual gaze of men, generated anxiety over potential threats to women's respectability. Envisioning themselves as the purveyors of the advances of white civilization, some middle- and upper-class Protestant women justified their movement into the public domain as a way of civilizing and uplifting the less advanced classes and races. To these middle- and upper-class women, self-defense represented a means of exercising their right to safely walk down the street free from harassment and sexual assault. These women also advocated self-defense training for working-class women as a way of protecting them from the advances of sexual predators or unscrupulous men who threatened the moral reputation of young working women. Newspapers reported numerous examples of women successfully using their self-defense skills to thwart violent attacks on the street and in their workplaces. The sinister threats that awaited them in the stereotyped forms of the flirtatious masher, the foreign white slaver, and the black rapist endangered their physical safety and sexual respectability. Beneath the hype, however, the fact that the practitioners and advocates of women's self-defense were predominantly upper- and middle-class native-born white women, and their attackers native-born white men, revealed an undercurrent of discontent that suggested a fissure in white racial solidarity. Self-defense equipped women with the skills to fight for their rights and paved the way for other women by asserting their right to exist and thrive in the public domain.

Chapter 4 continues the discussion by examining the broader cultural and political implications of women's self-defense and considering the explicit connections between the physical and political empowerment of women during the Progressive Era. Women's self-defense training disrupted existing gender stereotypes and countered the myth that men were women's natural protectors. Women's rights advocates recognized the significance of this new bodily empowerment and linked it to larger campaigns to challenge the oppressive patriarchal structure. The radical suggestion that women were capable of serving as their own protectors in effect both emerged from and was influenced by larger campaigns for women's rights. Advocates for women's self-defense training in England and the United States insisted that all women could defend themselves and should learn self-defense not only to protect themselves physically but also to prepare themselves psychologically for the political battles they would face in the public and private spheres. Militant English suffragettes increasingly used their bodies to convey discontent and resist oppression through marches, pickets, and hunger strikes. Self-defense training offered some women yet another way to embody the political as their bodies became vehicles for resisting gender violence. Although only a few radical American suffragists explicitly sought to emulate their English counterparts by specifically training in self-defense, the English model led to important discussions in the United States about women's use of violence and the myth of the male protector.[7] American suffragists experienced much less physical violence than the English suffragettes. However, their own experiences with harassment and violence challenged American suffragists to reconsider their views about women's right to empower their bodies and use force when necessary. These discussions further shaped the views of women's rights activists and later feminists about the potential of self-defense training to help liberate them from their subservient status. Yet, and perhaps more important, even average women, with no direct association with suffrage organizations, expressed a newfound sense of liberation through physical training in boxing and jiu-jitsu. Although not all of the women who trained in boxing and jiu-jitsu had explicit political motives, women's self-defense figuratively and literally disrupted the existing power structure. By physically embodying the political, these women stretched the limits of the definition of the "New Woman."

Beyond the social and political implications, the self-defense movement led to conversations about the violence that women faced in their own homes. On an individual level, some advocates believed that the discussion of women's self-defense could have revolutionary implications for women who suffered in abusive relationships. Nowhere was the myth of the male protector more blatantly dismantled than in the homes of women who were subjected to violence perpetrated by the men they loved. This is the subject of chapter 5. Despite the popular rhetoric about the dangers that women faced from shadowy strangers on the street, self-defense advocates understood that women were most likely to be attacked by a relative or an intimate partner. Most often they would face violence not on the city streets but in the privacy of their own homes. The discourse surrounding women's self-defense helped pierce the silence about the true sources of violence against women. The women's self-defense movement thus came to symbolize the fight against gender oppression in public and in private.

Progressive Era women who trained in and advocated self-defense found a way to make the political physical by empowering their bodies through self-defense. Few scholars, however, have specifically examined or even acknowledged the efforts of this generation of women in pursuing boxing and jiu-jitsu as a means not only of self-defense but also of expressing their personal and political power. Through self-defense training, women deconstructed femininity and myths about inherent feminine weakness, constructing instead a new image of women as powerful and self-reliant. Their bodies then become sites of resistance against an oppressive system. Whether or not women consciously pursued self-defense for these reasons, their actions embodied feminist politics.[8] Although their individual motivations may have varied, their collective action echoed through the century. The women's self-defense movement demanded women's emancipation from the constricting barriers that prevented them from exercising their full rights as citizens and human beings.[9]

1

# The Womanly Art of Boxing

Strict gender boundaries in the mid-nineteenth century confined white middle- and upper-class women to the domestic sphere. These women faced severe societal sanctions that limited the degree and type of their activity. However, by the late nineteenth century, women increasingly pushed the limits of these boundaries by pursuing expanding employment and recreational opportunities in cities across the nation, eventually resulting in a shift in popularly accepted gender norms. Similarly, shifting gender expectations for men focused on a new, more overtly masculine and in many ways more confining model of manhood. A gendered and racialized movement to strengthen the bodies and characters of American men emerged from concern over the weakening state of white masculinity and larger anxieties over the survival of the Anglo-Saxon race. The birth of the physical culture movement and the emphasis on physical fitness in strengthening the mothers and wives of the nation expanded the opportunities for women, especially middle- and upper-class Anglo women in their role as civilizers, to participate in a wider range of activities. Yet even as attitudes began to shift in the early twentieth century, women still encountered gendered restrictions on the types of activities polite society permitted them to engage in. Limits on women's physical activities resulted from apprehension over the masculinizing effects of sport and fear of the potential emasculation of Anglo men. Women were encouraged to pursue less intense activities such as golf, tennis, and croquet, which were suggested as ways to improve women's health without compromising their femininity or undermining their roles as wives and mothers. More physically demanding sports were reserved for men. Boxing was definitely off-limits.

Still, some women determined to test the boundaries by choosing to train in boxing, which in many ways represented the epitome of American masculinity in the nineteenth century. The common usage of the phrase the "manly art of self-defense" suggests the degree to which participation in this type of physical training was gendered. Interest in a variety of sports among the general population emerged from an increasing concern about physical culture and a belief in the necessity of athletic training to maintain one's health and reverse the effects of overcivilization. Boxing was among the more rigorous of sports and was advocated mostly for young men. Early female practitioners of boxing found themselves the target of intense criticism from detractors who attacked their femininity. Some instructors responded to the apprehension caused by women's boxing by creating a less aggressive and less combative type of boxing that allowed women to retain their feminine qualities. Ultimately, this less aggressive form of women's boxing was tolerated by the general public, to some degree, if only as a means of strengthening Anglo women's bodies for their role as wives, mothers, and civilizers of the race. Other women rejected the gendered restrictions on the extent of their physicality and pursued competitive boxing as a means of directly defying their critics. The physical culture movement also encouraged some transgression of class boundaries as upper-class men and women studied sanitized elements of working-class fighting sports, and working-class men and women found a degree of fame and upward mobility in exhibition boxing or prizefighting.

## Constructing White Masculinity

The rapid industrialization and urbanization of America in the late nineteenth century generated a great deal of anxiety about the impact of these changes on daily life. Psychologist G. Stanley Hall and neurologist George M. Beard were concerned that white masculinity had entered a state of crisis. They believed that industrialization and urbanization or excessive civilization threatened to physically and mentally debilitate men, turning them into effeminate weaklings and ultimately threatening the survival of the race. As more men moved away from farms and shops in small rural communities and into factory and office jobs in cities, their autonomy and self-control diminished. Rather than working for themselves, they now worked for a wage under a new boss. The less physically demanding labor weakened their bodies and their muscles. Long hours indoors separated from nature further damaged their mental and physical health. Beard feared the effects of an illness he termed "neurasthenia," or nervous exhaustion, which included symptoms that ranged from headaches to impotence and was caused primarily by the demands of modern civilization. He believed that as more middle- and upper-class men took less physically demanding jobs in business, the overuse of mental power stunted their physical power and led to effeminacy.[1]

G. Stanley Hall, influenced by Beard's theories, argued that human development mirrored the path of civilizations. Young children began life essentially as savages and eventually developed into civilized adults. Hall believed it was possible to counter the effects of overcivilization by encouraging boys' natural impulses to act as savages; through rugged, active outdoor play, boys could express and eventually expel these barbaric tendencies before evolving to a more advanced stage of civilization in their adult life. Providing opportunities for this evolution in childhood ensured a healthier, less anxiety-prone adulthood. Hall's ideas about child development were influential, and some educators and leaders believed this type of active physical training was the key to preserving the masculinity of American men and indeed the nation-state.[2]

Organizations emerged to allow boys to express their inner savage while helping to mold and shape them into civilized men. In the cities, the YMCA catered to working-class youth by providing opportunities for recreation and male comradeship. The Playground Association of America built playgrounds and formed organized playgroups for inner-city youth. Summer camps became popular among boys of the upper and middle classes. These camps encouraged rugged outdoor play that helped foster a love of nature and of physical activity. Year-round clubs such as the Woodcraft Indians and the Sons of Daniel Boone also formed with a focus on helping boys forge a connection to the outdoors and providing an outlet for their "primitive instincts." Paramilitary clubs such as the Boys' Brigade and the Boy Scouts focused on inculcating discipline, promoting rugged outdoor recreation, and cultivating character. Physical culture and organized sports offered an additional opportunity to shape boys into men.[3]

Periodicals produced by prominent bodybuilders such as Eugen Sandow and Bernarr Macfadden provided young men with visible models of an ideal manly physique. Eugen Sandow became famous as a bodybuilder in Germany. In the 1890s, he toured the United States, demonstrating his abilities in a series of strongman shows. Sandow's popularity and fame spread as he became the model of male physical perfection, and he later published several popular books and magazines on body-building that further spurred the interest in physical culture. Similarly, Bernarr Macfadden began publishing his magazine, *Physical Culture*, with its focus on nutrition and fitness, in 1899. The magazine was known for its photographs of near-nude athletic men, depicting the muscula-ture of an ideally developed body. The new emphasis on physicality and obsession with creating the ideal body was linked to a rejection of intel-lectualism and an emerging emphasis on the virile man of action who was celebrated more for his experiences than for his intellectualizing.[4]

As president of the United States from 1901 to 1909, Theodore Roo-sevelt proved an influential advocate of the physical culture movement and its celebration of the man of action. Beginning in his youth, Roos-evelt aggressively engaged in a variety of active pursuits. The purpose, he insisted, was not only to combat his own ill health but also to strengthen his resolve as a man. The muscular Christianity movement that flour-ished among American Protestants beginning around 1880 shaped Roosevelt's thinking. Proponents of muscular Christianity insisted on the necessity of a strong body to fulfilling one's Christian duty, which, according to this thinking, included civilizing and Christianizing the world. In advocating competitive physical culture, the predominantly white Protestant advocates of muscular Christianity sought to counter physical weakness and effeminacy to strengthen not only men but also the nation and the church.[5]

Roosevelt adopted elements of muscular Christianity in the develop-ment of his own philosophy about exercise and manliness. In a letter to Edward Sandford Martin, Roosevelt explained his views on fighting and manhood. He hoped to instill in his boys both an obligation to de-cency and the idea "that they ought not to shirk any quarrel forced upon them." He explained to his son Ted that "he could be just as virtuous as he wished if only he was prepared to fight." Roosevelt believed that "the man who merely possesses these traits, and in addition is timid and shirks effort, attracts and deserves a good deal of contempt. He attracts more, though he deserves less, contempt than the powerful, efficient man who is not at all virtuous, but is merely a strong, selfish, self-indulgent brute." Roosevelt noted that the message he learned from his own father was that a man should be both decent and manly.[6] He thus adopted the Victorian definition of manliness that exalted both physical strength and integrity of character. Roosevelt took it a step further in making a connection between strong manhood and strong nations by insisting that men, like nations, must physically prepare themselves to take on any challenger. These ideas influenced Roosevelt's adherence to imperialistic policies.[7]

Nativists insisted that the rapid influx of "new immigrants" from southern and eastern Europe and Asia represented the potential weakening of the Anglo-Saxon race and the internal demise of the nation. In 1870, southern and eastern Europeans accounted for 2.5 percent of all immigrants. By 1890, that figure had risen to 35 percent.[8] Charles Darwin's discoveries about evolution were used by social Darwinists to justify a form of racial inequality that positioned Anglo-Saxons on top in a biologically defined racial hierarchy. This hierarchy was reinforced and legitimized through the 1911 report of the Dillingham Commission, a U.S. congressional committee formed to investigate the causes and effects of immigration to the United States.[9] The commission's report differentiated new European immigrants from their predecessors from northern and western Europe as inferior and indeed not quite white. Marginalized and positioned in a state of what scholars have referred to as "in-betweenness" these new immigrants were classified as neither black nor white. Although they did not endure the same type of hard racism as that experienced by people of color, the new European immigrants did experience discrimination and racialized violence. While many Progressive reformers, including Theodore Roosevelt, optimistically believed that the ascension of the new immigrants' descendants into the ranks of whiteness was possible through the process of Americanization and education, the presence of these newcomers still elicited concern among ardent nativists.[10]

Nativists worried about the potential threat the new immigrants posed to labor and the American standard of living, but they particularly fretted about these immigrants' perceived mental defects and criminal tendencies. Social Darwinism and genetic theory were manipulated to argue that the new immigrants were far inferior to the old Protestant Anglo immigrant stock. Eugenicists relied on Mendelian theory to prove that mental illness and criminal dispositions could be inherited, leading to the conclusion that the procreation of the less fit should be discouraged. Madison Grant argued that intermarriage between the races resulted in degeneration of the superior Nordic race from northern Europe. In the United States this thinking led to more calls for immigration restriction and laws against miscegenation and, at the more extreme end, involuntary sterilization of individuals deemed mentally or morally deficient. Racist and nativist attitudes fueled anti-immigrant violence and demands for exclusionist legislation, culminating in the Immigration Act of 1924 (the Johnson-Reed Act).[11]

The debate over the new immigrants coincided with the migration of African Americans into northern cities and the westward movement of Anglo-Americans into regions occupied by Native American and Mexican families. Nativists, who also worried about the mingling of these nonwhite races with whites in these environments, feared that miscegenation threatened the future purity and stability of the Anglo-Saxon race.[12] Hall, Beard, and Roosevelt believed in the necessity of strengthening the physical bodies of white men in part because they feared race suicide and the weakening of the Anglo-Saxon race. The increasing birthrates of immigrant and non-Anglo populations compared with the declining birthrates of the native-born Anglo population suggested to them that the Anglo middle and upper middle classes were slowly committing a form of race suicide. Roosevelt encouraged American men and women of the middle and upper middle classes to procreate and do their part to strengthen the white race. The physical strengthening of Anglo-Saxon men went hand in hand with this desire to protect the nation and preserve the race.[13]

In light of all these factors, the importance of the physical culture movement seemed clear to men like Roosevelt. His speech "The Strenuous Life" (1899) warned against the dangers of a life of ease and idleness. Overcivilization, timidity, and laziness threatened to reduce the strength of the nation internally and on the international stage.[14] Roosevelt had begun studying boxing in college at Harvard and continued to practice sparring into his adult life. He attributed his improved health and vigor to his embrace of the strenuous life. Even as he criticized the degradation and brutality of prizefighting, Roosevelt proclaimed his love of the manly art and advocated boxing for American boys and men. By the turn of the century, the athletics obsession had spread nationwide as men worked to outwardly shape their bodies to reflect their inner manliness.[15]

## Boxing and Making Boys into Men

As the "manly art," boxing stood as the symbol of Anglo-American masculine toughness. Prizefighting, as practiced by men of the lower classes, had long been associated with violence and masculinity, and the ability to physically defeat an opponent symbolized the pinnacle of manliness. Successful competition fighters attained respect and a degree of social mobility in what historian Elliott Gorn has described as "a distinctly working-class version of the American dream."[16] Prior to the mid-nineteenth century, Anglo middle-class men created an ideal masculinity that focused on their roles as economic provider, husband, and father. Sports and especially prizefighting were deemed immoral distractions to be avoided, and boxing was considered barbaric and uncivilized. However, as the physical culture movement took hold, more middle-class men began to pursue sport as a means of better preparing their bodies for their moral duties as husband, father, and citizen. Boxing grew in popularity as evidence of manly courage and physical toughness. Men of all social classes gathered to watch bloody prizefights and cheer on the combatants, although the extremity of the violence seemed too uncivilized for white men of the upper classes to participate in the action. Instead, the aggressive natural instinct for blood sport and the need to develop a man's physical strength were channeled into a less extreme form of sparring or "scientific boxing" for gentlemen. This allowed them to develop the physical abilities of the boxer and cultivate a martial spirit without damaging their bodies or their moral character through prizefighting. A single definition of masculinity with a focus on aggressiveness, martial valor, and toughness emerged among white men across social classes.[17]

G. Stanley Hall insisted that some fighting was natural for boys, pointing out that "an able-bodied young man, who can not fight physically, can hardly have a high and true sense of honor, and is generally a milk-sop, a lady-boy, or a sneak. He lacks virility, his masculinity does not ring true, his honesty can not be sound to the core." Hall concluded, "A scrapping boy is better than one who funks a fight." Hall himself was an avid spectator of prizefights, yet he insisted on the need to channel boys' natural instincts toward aggression and fighting into training in a more civilized form of boxing: "At its best, it is indeed a manly art, a superb school for quickness of eye and hand, decision, force of will, and self-control . . . the surest of all cures for excessive irascibility and has been found to have the most beneficent effect upon a peevish or unmanly disposition." Hall argued that every boy should be taught boxing during adolescence or earlier to limit the effects of too much feminine sentimentality.[18]

Many white American men took these warnings to heart and aggressively pursued boxing as a means of improving their strength and manliness. DeWitt Van Court of the Los Angeles Athletic Club promised to transform the disposition of weak boys through boxing. Van Court argued that "for these little, timid boys—mother's pets—who cry at sight and run away when you touch them, boxing is a real cure. It changes them entirely. Teach them how to use their fists, and then give them a few antagonists they can lick at first. That's all that's necessary to take the timid streak out of them."[19] In the magazine *Outdoor Life*, Chauncey Thomas wrote, "If we are to thrive as a people we Americans must have more boxing and less baseball, more leather and less lace, more drilling and less dancing, more artillery and less alimony, more men and fewer Miss Nancys." Thomas also made the connection between strong men and strong nations: "A nation's history is carved by the weapons of its enemies, and this soft Thing, a sissy, a Mamma's boy, cannot stand against the heavy-handed men of virile, non-effeminate nations." The solution, according to Thomas, in order for America to regain its manhood, was for men to take up boxing.[20] Among white working-class men, boxing represented the embodiment of manliness.[21] Now men of all classes recognized the appeal of boxing in transforming their weak feminine bodies and dispositions.

## Womanly Women

If industrialization, urbanization, and the new immigration combined to weaken white manhood, the New Woman and her movement into the traditionally male-dominated public sphere seemed to represent an equally ominous threat. Hall believed that too much feminine influence in the raising of boys threatened to interfere with their development into masculine men. Boys grew up under the watchful eyes of their mother at home and female teachers at school. Male-only recreational clubs and physical training were necessary to counteract the effects of feminization. Despite these attempts to segregate boys from female influence and to create separate male spaces, female intrusion into other areas of male life posed additional threats in the eyes of American men. The number of women in the workforce nearly doubled from 1900 to 1920 (reaching almost 40 percent by 1920). Increasingly, women moved into traditionally male areas of sport, as well.[22]

Some women eagerly adopted physical culture, insisting that men were not alone in the need to improve their physical health. If athletics offered a potential cure for men afflicted by neurasthenia, then surely nervous and anxiety-prone women would benefit from recreation and sports. The YWCA emerged from the YMCA to provide recreational opportunities for women in the cities. The Camp Fire Girls and Girl Scouts offered social adventures in the outdoors for girls just as similar organizations did for boys. Organizations for young women in the workforce such as the Working Girls' Clubs also emphasized the necessity of physical culture.[23]

However, women were not always encouraged to pursue a course of physical training. In the late nineteenth and early twentieth centuries, critics focused on the potential danger of athletics to the reproductive and emotional health of women. A well-known objection to women's participation in athletics was the possible threat to their ability to bear and raise children. In 1873, Harvard's Dr. Edward Clarke contended that too much mental exertion through physical activity and education could deplete and debilitate young women, ultimately rendering them sterile. Clarke argued that women were especially weakened by the process of menstruation and advised abstinence from exercise and mental activities during this time. He went so far as to recommend bed rest during menstruation to take "care of the reproductive system that is the cradle of the race." Ironically, he argued that while this treatment "toughens a girl and makes a woman of her," it "will emasculate a lad."[24] Other physicians and psychologists agreed with Clarke and recommended a similar regimen of severely limited mental and physical exertion for young women. Pioneering female physicians weighed in on the debate as well, with some accepting the idea espoused by many male physicians that supposedly innate biological differences justified separate spheres and limited activity for women. Focusing on women's maternal roles, these doctors agreed that women should restrict their mental and physical activity, especially during menstruation and puberty, to protect their more delicate minds and bodies. Other female doctors, however, began to challenge this view of feminine weakness and suggested that women should not be considered invalids. Instead, they argued that exercise was necessary for women's health.[25]

Dr. Mary Putnam Jacobi conducted a study that refuted the accepted claims of the medical profession and directly challenged Clarke's assertion that women were physically weakened by menstruation and therefore should subscribe to a regimen of rest. Jacobi earned her medical degree in the United States in 1864 and a second degree from a medical college in Paris in 1871. She opened a practice in New York City and became a professor at the Woman's Medical College of the New York Infirmary. Jacobi's research, based on interviews with hundreds of women, refuted Clarke's idea that women were weakened by their reproductive system. Instead, she insisted on the similarities between men and women and the need for both to maintain their health through a continuous regimen of physical and mental education. Jacobi advocated coeducation along with a system of physical education for girls, arguing that systemic exercise was even more important for girls than for boys, since girls were less likely to get exercise "spontaneously."[26] Jacobi's initial essay refuting Clarke's claims was published along with a series of essays supporting coeducation in a book edited by Anna C. Brackett. In "The Education of American Girls," an essay from the same book, Brackett responded to contemporaries like Clarke who insisted that exercise could be too strenuous for girls; Brackett argued that "there are . . . forms of exercise which are not judicious by their very nature; but I find myself at a loss to name any one which girls desire, or in which they indulge, that would properly fall under this class, unless it be sewing and washing."[27] Brackett insisted on the necessity of building up women's endurance through regular exercise such as walking four or five miles a day.

As physical culture grew in popularity and more women engaged in a variety of activities, attitudes toward female athletics began to change.

Physicians, psychologists, and educators argued that women should engage in light to moderate exercise to protect their health. G. Stanley Hall contended that the primary role of women was to serve as wives and mothers. Hall did, however, vigorously advocate physical education for women, insisting on extensive activity for young girls and then more limited physical training for females at puberty and beyond. The purpose of physical training in youth, according to Hall, was to strengthen girls for motherhood. Physical activity was encouraged in adulthood, as long as it remained moderate and noncompetitive, to maintain a woman's strength, but Hall warned against anything that might sap women of the energy necessary to carry out their biologically ordained duties. Much of Hall's thinking was related to eugenics arguments concerned with ensuring the continued survival and strength of the Anglo-Saxon race.[28]

Anglo-American women adopted a similar racialized argument to justify their entry into traditionally male sports. Like Hall and his contemporaries, white women embraced a racial hierarchy backed by the pseudoscience of social evolutionary theory. Positioning themselves alongside Anglo men on the ladder of civilization, Anglo women envisioned themselves as the most civilized and therefore the most evolved of all the races. Female reformers relied on these evolutionist discourses to justify their reform work, especially as it related to civilizing the primitive masses both at home and abroad by schooling them in middle-class domesticity. Thus, white women's public reform work outside the private sphere posed no threat to gendered expectations about white womanhood and was permitted as an extension of their civilizing mission and their role as preservers of the Anglo-Saxon race. Similarly, then, women's rights advocates justified women's higher education and physical education as necessary to the fulfillment of their private and public duties. Athletic training was essential to preparing women's bodies for their roles as wives and mothers and in perpetuating the race.[29]

However, most advocates of this new physical culture movement for women, even those who emphasized its necessity to the future of the Anglo race, did not believe that women should participate in all sports equally. Instead, they relied on gendered arguments to justify their claims that women's exercise should be restricted. According to medical professionals, approved sports included croquet, rowing, horseback riding, archery, golf, and tennis.[30] More strenuous sports were reserved for the male sex. Specifically objecting to women's basketball, football, and athletics, a female writer insisted in 1903 that "a woman in a very short skirt and bloomers, with her hair streaming in the breeze and kicking a large ball over a field, is a sight to make angels weep . . . there is no particular need of making a guy and show of one's self." The writer predicted that "the next thing we will have will be women boxers and prize-fighters; they logically come next."[31] In 1906, Yale graduate Dr. Dudley Allen Sargent, director of Harvard's Hemenway Gymnasium and founder of a school to train physical educators, expressed fear that "the time may come when effeminate man will succumb to virile woman." To prevent that possibility, Sargent argued for separate spheres in the realm of athletics: "Let woman rather confine herself to the lighter and more graceful forms of gymnastics and athletics," which emphasized "good carriage, perfect poise, self-command and exquisite grace and refinement." Only men would participate in the "rougher sports," and women should serve as the "sympathetic admirer of men and boys in their efforts to be strong, vigorous and heroic." In this way "mental and physical education" would focus on the development of "the manly man and the womanly woman."[32]

Regardless of the heady debates of intellectuals over the costs and benefits of female physical culture, women eagerly participated in an increasingly wider range of athletics. By the 1910s, women were taking part in a variety of individual and team sports from bicycling to basketball. At the same time that more women began attending female colleges, programs of physical education were integrated into the educational system. The strong, athletic woman was becoming synonymous with the more modern and educated New Woman.[33] Anna de Koven, writing for *Good Housekeeping* in 1912, insisted on the importance of exercise for women of all ages as essential to their development. De Koven noted that much had changed for women in the early twentieth century, arguing that "the hoydenish tomboy, who was the despair of the mother of the past generation, is to-day just the normal girl whose keen love for outdoor sports is the pride of the family." In response to critics who insisted on the dangers of strenuous sport for women, de Koven insisted that "no sport is too reckless, too daring, or too strenuous for the more experienced among athletic American women."[34] Physical fitness had become an important defining characteristic of the New Woman.

## The Boxing New Woman

Despite the gradual acceptance of women's athletics, some extremely strenuous sports, such as boxing, remained generally taboo for women. Men and women of the middle and upper classes had condemned male prizefighting as an immoral and unnecessary display of bloody violence. Nineteenth-century moral reformers and even prominent suffrage leaders such as Susan B. Anthony objected to the violence and degradation of prizefighting. Polite society considered it improper for females to witness the spectacle of a boxing match, let alone participate in one.[35] Women's dispositions were believed to be too gentle and sensitive for them to observe or take part in such a brutal event.

Some women, however, dismissed these ideas about women's natural dispositions and pursued their own strenuous course of physical culture by training in the manly arts. A few women even fought as prizefighters, thereby directly challenging existing gender norms.[36] Hattie Stewart defied notions of the doll-playing gentle young girl when she explained that as a child she most enjoyed fighting boys. As a teenager, she channeled her love of active physical play and fighting into club swinging and boxing. Eventually, Stewart determined to try her hand at prizefighting. She performed in a number of highly publicized boxing matches in the 1880s and 1890s against other female boxers. She also toured the country performing in boxing exhibitions at a range of entertainment venues along with her husband, who was also a professional boxer. She later went on to teach boxing for women in Virginia. Stewart took pride in being referred to by promoters and the press as the female John L. Sullivan.[37]

Women, like Stewart, who transgressed gender boundaries found themselves the target of critics who directly attacked their femininity. Opponents of female boxing feared that the athletic woman would develop overly masculine qualities and ultimately become more manlike.[38] Their arguments focused on deep-seated concerns about the masculine nature of boxing and its potential to defeminize women and disrupt the "natural order." In 1901, the Reverend Dr. William Short of St. Peter's Episcopal Church addressed graduates from the Mary Institute, a school for girls in St. Louis, denouncing what he perceived as "masculine affections" in women. He insisted that women who attempt to exercise the "privileges and powers of man, social, political, and otherwise, . . . are directing their efforts to develop in woman a sort of self-assertiveness and independence and to break down certain barriers of distinction between the sexes." He further argued, "This imitation of mannish manners and masculine methods is simply vulgar." Short condemned athletic clubs that trained girls in boxing as unladylike and "bordering on the indecent."[39]

Opposition to female boxing on the grounds that it was inappropriate for ladies dominated public opinion.[40] In 1911, when Dr. Everett Beach, high school athletic director in Los Angeles, decided to ban boxing for girls at Los Angeles High School, he justified his decision by stating, "It was not the aim of the instructors to turn out a generation of feminine fighters, and there was no desire to develop an unnaturally combative disposition, 'which would interfere with the natural laws of the home.'" After the ban, two female students, Fern Powell and Lauretta Davlin, expressed their intense disappointment. Both girls had been training in boxing for several months and found themselves "still infatuated with the sport." However, Beach insisted the ban was intended for their benefit. "Suppose a pretty girl's nose was broken while boxing," he said. "It probably would mean permanent disfigurement, and might seriously injure her social prospects."[41] Thus, Beach defended his decision by arguing that he was protecting young women's physical bodies and feminine dispositions from the dangers of violent sport.

Individuals who shared the opinions of Beach sought to confine women to athletics they deemed gender appropriate and use the law, if necessary, to enforce any transgressions. Some states had antiprizefighting laws on their codebooks, but the enforcement of these laws varied with public sentiment. Boxing matches between women so upset public sensibilities that the police were sometimes forced to intervene. Hattie Leslie, for example, was arrested for competing in a highly publicized prizefight with Alice Leary in Buffalo, New York, in 1888 after an outcry of concern from an outraged public. Although Leslie was never convicted, the male fight organizers received fines and prison sentences for their role in promoting the fight.[42] When Helen Hildreth fought Johnny Atkinson in New York in 1916, police broke up the match after the first round for violating the Frawley Boxing Law.[43]

Concern over female boxing also reflected fears of the emasculating effects on men of women's participation in male sports. More often, concern over female prizefighting and public attacks on the physically active woman revealed underlying fears of homosexuality. Psychiatrist Richard von Krafft-Ebing's book *Psychopathia Sexualis* (1886) labeled homosexuality a psychological disorder and a form of perversion. Furthermore, Krafft-Ebing defined women who pursued "manly sports" as mannish lesbians and therefore as pathologically disordered. Krafft-Ebing argued, "The masculine soul, heaving in the female bosom, finds pleasure in the pursuit of manly sports, and in manifestations of courage and bravado."[44] Sexologist Havelock Ellis suggested that in the inverted woman there is "often some capacity for athletics."[45] Feminism, athleticism, and lesbianism were all dangerously linked in Ellis's mind. The fear of an association between female athleticism and lesbianism became more common in popular discourse in the 1920s and took on more hysterical tones by the 1950s.[46]

The view of female boxers as masculine deviants was clear in their portrayal in the popular press. The public expressed simultaneous amusement and hostility toward female boxers, and promoters discriminated against female boxers at the same time they exploited them to earn a profit. Meanwhile, the press tended to celebrate the physical accomplishments of the male boxer while constructing female fighters as physical freaks.[47] Female boxing was depicted as "unnatural" and the woman boxer as a disrupter of traditional gender roles. Matches between women were described as "disgraceful," "barbaric," "savage," "loathsome," "brutal," and "disgusting." Often depicted as grotesquely deformed masculine deviants, female boxers were frequently described as animalistic or savage.[48] Heavyweight champion boxer Jack Dempsey said that athletic women "are losing the lines that I used to know as feminine. I have to look twice at some of them to make sure they are not boys."[49]

The construction of female boxers as sexual "others" was often also accompanied by a construction of these women as racial "others." Athletic young women, especially boxers, were sometimes cast in racialized terms. Previous generations prized passivity and fragility as ideals of femininity. Lighter skin tone as a result of limited exposure to the sun and a leisured lifestyle served as indicators of class status. However, the new generation of more athletic women were engaging in a variety of activities that seemed to challenge this ideal of womanhood. In reference to the athletic New Woman, Minna Thomas Antrim wrote in 1911: "So, with muscles tense and blood aflame, she plays the manly role. What cares she that her face and arms are Indian brown . . . ?"[50] Although Antrim concludes that athleticism is a trait ultimately to be admired in women for its ability to mold them into strong wives and mothers, her choice of words demonstrates the ways in which physically fit females were in a sense recast as nonwhite "others." This racialized construction was even more pronounced when applied to working-class female prizefighters. Physical descriptions of their unnatural, almost barbaric muscularity, darker skin tones, and assertive presence served to distance working-class female athletes from their delicate, demure, pale-skinned (and, by implication, more civilized) middle- and upper-class sisters. By the 1910s, psychologists such as G. Stanley Hall authorized some degree of primitivism as a cure for overcivilization.[51] However, the acceptable limits of that primitivism varied considerably by age, race, class, and gender.

Concerns about the racializing and masculinizing effects of sport were apparent in media depictions of female boxers. Reporters often described professional boxer Gussie Freeman as very manly and never failed to mention her height and weight (five feet ten inches and 180 pounds). One reporter took it a step further by seemingly questioning Freeman's sexuality by noting that she had never been kissed by a man. This comment was intended to point out her "unnatural" and "unfeminine" status as a female boxer. Enduring criticism about her physical size and masculine habits, Freeman told the reporter with a note of sadness in her voice, "I wish I was more like a woman. I don't like to be so much like a man, but I can't help it. I must make a living, and I am not fit for anything but the kind of work I do." When the reporter probed into her love life, Freeman admitted, "No man has ever kissed me. Those who thought of doing so learned long ago that it was dangerous to attempt it. I tell you I am not like other women." Freeman freely admitted that she did not fit traditional gender stereotypes and lived her life as she wished. However, the reporter reflected the fears of mainstream society in insisting that masculine women like Freeman posed a threat to manhood: "It begins to look as though the weaker sex will become the stronger and man [will] have to step aside in all avocations that have been exclusively his own, leaving to the heretofore lord and master little more than the drudgery of the kitchen or the nursery."[52] The female boxer thus was blamed for weakening the manliness of American men. White men's fears of emasculation in the home were linked to larger fears about their emasculation by non-Anglo men at home and abroad. The increasing number of non-Anglo men mixing with Anglo women in the United States heightened the possibility of interracial relationships and therefore race degeneration. The growing economic and military strength of non-European nations likewise posed a threat to American dominance on the world stage. Women studying the manly art of boxing seemed to further undermine white masculinity.

In an apparent attempt to assuage the fears of anxious Anglo men, an article by Minna Thomas Antrim in *Lippincott's Monthly* in 1911 addressed the issue of the masculine, athletic girl by seeking to deconstruct some misconceptions and reposition her firmly within a white, heterosexual framework. Antrim assured her readers that they should not worry about the athletic girl's refusal to talk of marriage. She insisted that the skeptical need not fear because "it is the vital girl that Sir Eligible is choosing these days. He is her bachelor-brother first, her 'pal' next, and finally, if the gods speed his wooing, her husband and the proud father of her robust children." Antrim noted that the athletic girl who takes to sports like golf is developing stronger muscles "for later duties" because "strong girls make stalwart mothers."[53] Thus, despite her masculine tendencies as demonstrated by her proclivity for outdoor sports, the athletic New Woman presented no real threat to Anglo masculinity or indeed to normative heterosexuality. Her athletic training served only as conditioning for marriage and preparation for her role as mother. In this sense, then, boxing for women was justified as an essentially feminine activity, and Anglo women who pursued athletics were fulfilling their duty to the nation and the white race.

Athletics for women were gradually permitted as long as female athletes remained within the bounds of acceptable white, heterosexual femininity and recognized that the goal of their pursuit of physical fitness was to strengthen them in their roles as wives, mothers, and preservers of the race. Champion boxer Robert Fitzsimmons wrote a book on physical culture and self-defense in which he stressed: "Muscle building brings beauty to women." He warned, however, that women should not "make physical freaks of themselves" since "a woman cannot stand too much training in any one direction at the expense of the rest her body as well as a man can. Her physical make-up is not constructed for it."[54] Fitzsimmons advocated the benefits of a softened version of boxing training for women.

Some female boxers chose to emphasize their femininity in response to societal constraints and criticisms about the masculinizing effects of boxing.[55] When interviewed about their practice of the sport, these women chose to talk about their roles as wives and homemakers to minimize the association with masculinity. Vera Roehm, a vaudeville actress and famous boxer, used the established argument about a woman's "natural role" as wife and mother to justify women's boxing. Roehm, who was known as a "physical culture expert, boxer, and all-around athlete," told a reporter, "While no doubt women should be truly feminine, and cling to the maternal instinct, I really believe that she should be more athletic and physically stronger than she has ever been heretofore."[56] Roehm appealed to stereotypical gender norms by arguing, "A man wouldn't have a chance in the world in the ring with a woman. . . . You see, all she would have to do would be to use her eyes, and other feminine wiles, and the poor man would be helpless. And the sight of a woman in gymnasium costume might distract his attention." She further insisted, "The innate chivalry of a man would prevent him from hitting a woman hard—especially if she smiled at him." Taking the gender stereotypes even further, Roehm suggested that women would most likely never participate in professional boxing competitions against each other because "almost any woman, if hit a good hard wallop, would get mad and bawl . . . most likely, if they got mad they would forget all about science and start pulling hair." The suggestion here that boxing matches between women would degenerate into bouts of hair pulling was a common theme in articles that attempted to denigrate female boxers or minimize the threat of women's boxing. She also insisted that boxing, as purely an exercise for women, accentuated "grace, agility and poise."[57]

By the early 1920s, Roehm was marketing a mail-order health and beauty course called "Womanly Charms," which, she promised, would reveal secrets to "radiant health, rare poise and grace, and a perfect figure." Through her course she told women, "Men will admire you. Women will envy you. You, yourself, will feel like a different woman—a

Figure 1.1 Harry Mellon Rhoads, "Female Athletes in Gym, Probably in Denver," ca. 1900–1920. Harry M. Rhoads photograph collection, Denver Public Library, Western History Collection, Rh-611 Engle #50143 DPLW.

happier, prettier, more carefree one with that pleasing personality which always becomes part of such a woman."[58] Roehm's emphasis on non-competitive boxing exercises to maintain one's feminine beauty seemed ironic given that she chose to pursue an active, rigorous boxing regimen and engaged in sparring bouts against famous male boxers. One reporter noted that these bouts "weren't tame affairs, either. Miss Roehm is minus one tooth, which was knocked out by Leach Cross."[59] Roehm's use of gendered arguments based on women's "natural role" as wives and mothers to justify boxing as exercise for women may have been strategic given that most people would not have supported female competitive boxing. However, Roehm clearly believed in a subdued and gendered form of boxing for most women.

By the early 1900s, feminized versions of boxing and fighting arts emerged as acceptable adaptations for women athletes to pursue. Physical educators sought to protect the reputation and health of women by creating a less controversial style of athletics that reflected an image of respectable femininity.[60] Boxing was heralded as having a wide range of health and practical benefits for respectable women. An article in the *New York Times* in 1904 announced that the "Boxing Girl" had arrived. Anticipating the comments of critics, the author de-emphasized the inherent violence in women's boxing training and focused instead on the potential health and beauty benefits of exercise of any kind. Physical fitness leaders reinvented and painted women's boxing in a much more feminine light. The author of the *Times* article insisted that by training in gyms and at home, women avoided the brutality of competitive fighting. The article highlighted the health advantages of boxing for women by explaining that the exercise tones and strengthens muscles while combating weight gain.[61] Instructors promised that this type of boxing, with its lighter approach, was especially suited for society girls because it "does not mean 'slugging.' Neither does it mean a black eye or bloody nose for our maiden." Through shadowboxing, bag work, and light sparring, boxing developed poise and balance.[62] In this way, proponents of women's boxing claimed that the brutality of the sport had been replaced with science and skill.[63] The focus on the femininity of the exercises was used to justify women's participation in an activity previously limited to the male sphere.

The emphasis on its ability to enhance feminine beauty further justified boxing as an activity for women. The popular conception of the New Woman focused on creating a new ideal for women's bodies that emphasized thinness and muscularity.[64] As an advocate and practitioner of this new form of boxing for women, Harriet Edwards Fayes of New York explained in 1915 that boxing "beats dancing as a [weight] reducer." She also insisted that boxing is "the most splendid exercise for increasing the circulation of the blood. I feel 20 years younger since I learned to box."[65] An article in the *San Francisco Chronicle* in 1913 mentioned the popularity of boxing for society girls interested in reducing their weight and preserving their beauty.[66]

Some advocates of boxing for women took the argument one step further in insisting on boxing as a solution to feminine bad habits. Instructors argued that boxing could serve to *cure* women of unbecoming behaviors. Just as DeWitt Van Court of the Los Angeles Athletic Club

Figure 1.2 "New York Women Pay $25 Apiece for Boxing Lessons," *Tacoma Times*, March 8, 1915, 2.

insisted on boxing's transformative power in turning boys into men, he also recommended boxing for women as a cure for "bad temper," "feminine hysterics," and a "catty disposition." In addition to making "the matron look years younger," the practice of boxing "in a short time eliminates the disposition toward hysterics."[67] This argument played into stereotypes of the hysterical and emotional woman and offered boxing as a potential treatment in managing these supposedly unique feminine afflictions.

As more women attended college, young women of the middle and upper classes enjoyed additional opportunities to participate in respect-

Figure 1.3 "The Maid and the Mitts," *San Francisco Call*, December 2, 1906, 9.

able feminine sports. Women's colleges offered a range of competitive and recreational sports, and participation in leisure and sport activities served as a visible indicator of these women's social status.[68] In July 1915, young women attending the summer school of Tulane University in New Orleans participated in a boxing competition. Students from Mississippi challenged those from Louisiana to a competition to determine the physical superiority of the women of the South. The match was supervised and refereed by Carl Andrews Hanson, Tulane's physical director. Other than Hanson, the audience included only female students.[69] Negative publicity following the event sparked the suppression of a second match the following day and the creation of a general ban on all future female boxing matches. The matches reputedly moved underground in response to the ban and the criticism. Sayers McDonald, "a leading society girl of Mississippi" and the undisputed champion of the matches, responded to critics by defending the right of women to engage "in this splendid form of exercise." McDonald appealed to traditional gender roles while also challenging those same roles to justify women's participation in the sport. She was quoted as saying: "Boxing makes them graceful, self-reliant and tends to make stronger women."[70] A reporter insisted that "the bouts were conducted without any semblance of roughness and the best of good feeling prevailed among the contestants. . . . The exercise tends to develop grace and confidence and as conducted at Tulane is robbed of all objectionable features."[71] Adopting a similarly gendered argument, another writer asserted that boxing training would prepare women to be better wives and mothers who would be "physically fit to bear children and spank them when needed."[72]

Even beyond college, boxing proved a popular activity among many society women, who justified their training as a way to improve their health and prepare their bodies for motherhood. In 1915, Nixola Greeley-Smith described how New York society women were eagerly taking up the manly art of boxing: "New York women are boxing mad. Those who wondered what we were going to do after we got tired of tangoing and fox-trotting need worry no longer. They know the answer now. We are going to box!"[73] The lighter, feminized version of boxing offered by many instructors was marketed directly to this middle- and upper-class audience of white society women.

Figure 1.4 "Boxing to Be a Fad for Women," *Chicago Daily Tribune*, October 26, 1902, 48.

## Holding Their Own: Professional Female Boxers

Some women rejected sanitized versions of boxing created specifically for women and determined instead to train with an intensity that proved their equality with male boxers and their effectiveness as professional fighters. One reporter noted that many of the society women took up their training in earnest and soon became extremely efficient in the sport: "Men in society would be surprised to know how many of the graceful, charming women they know and meet at social functions could take them on with the regulation boxing gloves and make dummies of them in a couple of rounds."[74] Mrs. Tommy Daly, the wife of a champion Canadian boxer, took up boxing herself after training alongside her husband. She was described as a strong and capable fighter: "She hits straight and clean from the shoulder, throwing her body with her punch, and her blow has weight behind it. Of course, she could not appear in evening clothes, because her forearms are bruised from blocking punches."[75] The mention of Daly in evening clothes served as a simultaneous reminder of and rejection of her femininity, tellingly demonstrating the ways in which female boxers challenged the constraints of their gender. Daly proudly defied existing gender norms by engaging in a rougher version of competitive boxing than the shadowboxing or light sparring practiced by her upper-class counterparts.

Another way that boxing women flouted gender norms and stereotypes was through outward displays of the traditionally male-associated traits of aggression and brutality. Nellie Higgins and Maude Swanson, two female exhibition fighters in Buffalo, New York, developed a rivalry that became particularly intense. Ultimately, they determined to fight out their issues in a public boxing match. Higgins and Swanson crossed the border into Ontario, Canada, to compete in a formal fight that would determine once and for all which was the superior fighter. According to witnesses, they fought with "savagery and hatred," with both women bleeding from the face.[76] A 1912 fight between Mabel Williams and Myrtle Havers in Saginaw, Michigan, proved equally brutal. Havers endured a volley of jabs to her face, culminating in a right eye that was badly bruised and swollen shut. Nevertheless, she returned fire, and the ten-round fight ended in the seventh round when Havers knocked out Williams with a stiff uppercut.[77]

Female boxers also rebelled against the status quo while proving their fighting prowess by publicly competing against men. Caroline Bauman studied boxing in New York City with Eddie Toy. Reporter Nixola Greeley-Smith described Bauman as a professional boxer in an effort to distinguish her from the scores of society women who took up less strenuous and noncompetitive forms of boxing.[78] Bauman fought several public fights against both women and men. After Bauman defeated her instructor in a match in February 1915, one male reporter explained that the feminine victor "wasn't puffed up" over the win but "took her victory like a good man."[79] Another reporter described Bauman as strong and capable of holding her own against male boxers.[80] Ignoring the critics who told them that their bodies and natures were not intended for violence, female competition fighters like Bauman continued to pursue these "masculine methods" with much interest and intensity, effectively challenging the "natural laws of the home."

Competitive boxing provided some opportunity for social mobility for working-class women.[81] This form of fighting, which was rougher than the sparring practice of middle- and upper-class society women, may have been more socially acceptable for women from the lower socioeconomic strata in part because they were viewed as physically stronger and therefore less delicate than the leisured women of the upper classes.[82] Still, these athletic women found themselves the target of attacks against their "unfeminine" behavior. The association of female boxers with prostitutes in the public display of their bodies no doubt dissuaded many women from pursuing competitive boxing.[83]

Gussie Freeman was not deterred by these arguments, however, and pursued a prizefighting career in an attempt to free herself from poverty. Freeman was raised in a poor German immigrant family on Long Island, New York. To provide financial support for her family, she found employment at the age of twelve making rope at a ropewalk, where the intense physical labor required a great deal of strength and endurance. Freeman began her boxing career when her coworkers encouraged her to take on the challenge of professional boxer Hattie Leslie, who offered twenty-five dollars to any fighter who could knock her out in four rounds. Freeman lost the fight to Leslie but won an opportunity to go on tour with Leslie as a sparring partner. Attracted by the potential to improve her economic situation, Freeman gave up work on the ropewalk and went on tour around the country, performing in a number of boxing matches. Leslie's socioeconomic status and lack of education limited her employment opportunities, but boxing offered her a glimmer of hope. Freeman pursued boxing out of a desire to create a better life for herself, but after a year on tour she returned home disillusioned and feeling cheated out of her salary. Freeman, who went on to become a saloonkeeper, lamented, "If I only had some education . . . I would not be in this kind of business, but I must do something."[84] Freeman and other female boxers who were put on "exhibition" in this way no doubt felt robbed of their full worth and devalued as professional boxers. Spectators and promoters essentially reduced these women to a commodity to be bought and sold as entertainment.

Nellie Bennett, a former schoolteacher and the mother of five girls, also took up prizefighting out of economic necessity after the death of her farmer husband. Bennett was already working as a police officer at the DuPont powder plant in an attempt to support her family.[85] At age twenty-seven, Bennett competed in a fight against eighteen-year-old Bessie Martin in Oklahoma City. Prior to the match, public outrage demanded a ban on the bout, but the mayor and county officials insisted that there was no local ordinance against prizefighting. The fight took place before an audience of several hundred people, many of whom were women, who cheered on the fighters. Although the fight was officially a draw, Bennett took a severe beating.[86] For working-class women like Bennett, the necessity of earning money outweighed the physical costs of prizefighting.

The poverty of these female boxers sometimes was a topic of conversation and scrutiny in the popular press. Before meeting her husband, Minnie Rosenblatt Besser supported herself by working in a factory. Besser, who learned boxing from her husband, "Swipes the Newsboy," a professional boxer, took part in a number of exhibition bouts against famous female fighters such as Gus Looney, Hattie Leslie, and Hattie Stewart. Besser explained that her interest in boxing was linked to the need for economic stability, that it was a necessity rather than a choice.[87] The newlywed couple lived and trained in a tenement in New York City. A reporter recounting the couple's city hall wedding highlighted their lower-class status through condescending descriptions of their clothing and language. Besser was "not attired exactly as a bride should be . . . a natty little plaited cape tried hard to cover a rent in her bodice, but without success. A sailor hat was perched jauntily on her sunny curls." The reporter emphasized the lack of education of the newlyweds by attempting to re-create the pronunciation of Swipes's words: "We've been goin' togedder for about a year off an' on. She shook me two or three times, but I got her back, see? An' here she is, an' goin' to be my old woman."[88] In this manner, fighters like Besser faced simultaneous condescension and awe from the public and the press.

Female boxers who fought on the exhibition circuit found their bodies commodified.[89] Depicted in a range of seemingly incongruous ways from physical freaks to sexual objects, women boxers performed in a variety of venues from theaters and vaudeville shows to circuses and freak shows. The physical positioning of female boxers next to various "others" described as freaks served to classify and label these boxing women as aberrant social deviants.[90] The bodies of boxing women were scrutinized and objectified on the public stage. Described as a vaudeville farce, "The Roger Brothers in Wall Street" opened at English's Grand Park Empire in Indianapolis in April 1900. Previously performed in Boston, New York, and Philadelphia, the show featuring a variety of songs, dances, and comedic performances was apparently a hit with audiences. One popular portion of the performance featured a number of "physical culture" girls demonstrating their athletic abilities in fencing, boxing, riding, golf, football, and baseball. The *Indianapolis Journal* explained, "The 'physical-culture girl' is presented here in attractive form, and goes through a series of marching and dancing figures which serve admirably to show off this type of girl."[91] The performance of their athletic abilities for others rather than for themselves and the emphasis on the "attractive forms" of these women by the press illustrate their primary function as objects for public consumption.

The sexualization of female boxers was clear in descriptions that focused on their physical features. Described as a charming and a "bewilderingly pretty girl," Mrs. William E. Parker, the wife of professional boxer "Kid" Parker, became a professional boxer herself. Writers, however, focused mostly on her looks, mentioning her "fair skin, with the color coming and going in her cheeks in a way most distracting to the pulse, yellow hair, and the daintiest of figures. Her mouth has the curves of a baby, and she is, altogether, the picture of a charming young girl, with no touch of the professional."[92] She was described as "a woman of rare grace and beauty" characterized by "gentle femininity."[93]

The attire of women boxers was also heavily scrutinized, and descriptions often were tinged with accusations of sexual impropriety. When Helen Hildreth fought male opponent Johnny Atkinson before a large crowd in Harlem in 1916, a reporter recorded the response as Hildreth entered the ring and threw off her robe: "The spectators strained their necks several inches, for she was attired in white tights, the same as worn by women who take part in contortion acts on vaudeville stages."[94] Illustrations, photographs, and films also featured sexualized images of women boxing in their bloomers. In *Girls Biffed Each Other*, a drawing published in the *Police Gazette* in 1890, Mamie Herbett and Mabel

Brown are depicted in a brutal fistfight apparently inspired by a dispute over a beau. The winner of the prizefight would win the male suitor. The drawing depicted the two women in a desperate struggle, with the shoulders and neck of one of the fighters fully exposed as the strap of her bodice slid suggestively down her arm.[95] The public exhibition and especially the costume of the female boxer transformed her into an object of sexual desire exploited by promoters for monetary gain.[96]

## Conclusion

The fascination with physical culture and concern over the nation's fitness increased the popularity of boxing training for both men and women. The rhetoric emphasizing the importance of combating over-civilization and preparing men to take on the task of saving the race and building the nation contributed to the nationwide athletic craze. Anglo-American men feared the consequences to their own race caused by the rapid influx of new immigrants from southern and eastern Europe, the migration of African Americans to northern communities, and the intermingling of Anglo, Asian, Native American, and Mexican races on the frontier. Boxing was revived from its status as a reviled and barbaric sport of the masses and resurrected as a manly method of training American men in courage, perseverance, and toughness.

This reconstruction of masculinity paralleled a similar restructuring of femininity. The New Woman was expected to be healthy and strong enough to be an effective wife and mother. This was especially important to eugenicists concerned with protecting Anglo-Americans against race suicide. Athletic training of Anglo men and women was thus seen as essential to the well-being of the nation as a whole. The movement of women into a wide range of sports dismantled old constructions of the frail and weak female, reconstructing her as strong and capable. Some women seized the opportunity to train in the traditionally exclusively male field of boxing. Objections to the potential masculinizing effects of women's boxing and Anglo men's fears of emasculation were overshadowed by the potential benefits that Anglo women's boxing posed to the future survival of the race. White middle- and upper-class women expressed their fondness for recreation and leisure by pursing feminized and sanitized versions of boxing that focused more on building muscle and beauty than on fighting in and of itself. Working-class women found a degree of social mobility in exhibition boxing, and some even pursued careers in competitive prizefighting. Regardless of social class, women who took up some variation of boxing overwhelmingly expressed the sense of freedom they felt in their choice to mold their bodies into specimens of health and fitness.

Although women may have found some sense of liberation through boxing, this freedom was limited. The creation of feminized versions of boxing fitness classes for the middle and upper classes, while paving the way for women to train in the fighting arts, ironically also played into existing gender stereotypes about women's allegedly frailer physical natures. Even as female boxers developed the technical skills and physical abilities of male pugilists and proved their equality as athletes, they still failed to dismantle the hegemonic gender structure. Female competition fighters faced a wide range of discrimination in trying to penetrate the male world of boxing. Often trivialized as mere physical freaks or as sexualized objects of exhibition, female competitive boxers struggled to be taken seriously. Exhibition fighters showcased their physical talents and skills but often acquiesced to demands that they flaunt their sexuality for popular attention and economic gain. Female competition fighters discovered that the establishment profited off their ability to draw curious crowds of paying spectators but failed to take them seriously as fighters.[97]

In the end, then, the pursuit of the manly art provided an avenue for the New Woman to test the limits of her gender and dismantle existing stereotypes, although the contradictory results of her endeavor reveal the limits to her being viewed as an equal in male sporting culture. Ultimately, many female boxers would find a variety of alternative meanings in their pursuit of the fighting arts, from the political to the personal.

# Jiu-Jitsu, Gender, and the Yellow Peril

The introduction of and subsequent fascination with Japanese martial arts in the early twentieth-century United States generated much anxiety and debate about the merits of the American system of boxing as the most effective means of manly self-defense. Japan's rise as a world power, especially after its victory in the Russo-Japanese War, represented the military threat of an Asian nation. Jiu-jitsu symbolized the physical embodiment of the Yellow Peril. The efficiency and effectiveness of Japanese jiu-jitsu, as introduced to Americans in the early twentieth century, challenged preconceived notions of the dominance of Western martial arts and American constructions of race and manliness. The American press insisted that boxing and wrestling were more manly and honorable ways of fighting than the deadly and deceptive "bone-breaking" techniques of jiu-jitsu, yet educated upper-class American men like Theodore Roosevelt were enamored with the traditional fighting arts of the samurai. They found common ground in popular constructions of the samurai as the ideal scholar and warrior and sponsored demonstrations of jiu-jitsu in the United States. The fascination with Japanese martial culture also had the unintended effect of rendering Japanese Americans more visible in American society at the same time that it cast them as perpetual foreigners.[1]

Much to the chagrin of boastful proponents of American fighting methods, highly publicized contests pitting Japanese jiu-jitsu experts against American wrestling and boxing champions failed to determine once and for all which art was more effective. This failure to establish American fighting arts as superior threatened to upset the racial hierarchy in revealing the Yellow Peril as a real physical threat. As Americans wrestled with Japan and jiu-jitsu, they developed a variety of strategies for dealing with the new menace. The jiu-jitsu threat was ultimately subjugated and domesticated by exoticizing, vilifying, feminizing, and eventually appropriating aspects of it in order to reassert the dominance of

GIVING HIM THE JIU-JITSU.—From the *World* (New York).

Figure 2.1 "Giving Him the Jiu-Jitsu," *American Monthly Review of Reviews* 29, no. 3 (March 1904): 262.

Western martial arts, the white race, and American manliness.[2] Middle- and upper-class white women inspired by the physical culture movement and taking advantage of the rhetoric that attempted to feminize jiu-jitsu seized the opportunity to train in the defensive art themselves.

## The Yellow Peril

The concept of the Yellow Peril and anti-Asian sentiment in the United States predate the arrival of Japanese immigrants and the rise of Japan as a major world power. Chinese immigrants began arriving in large numbers, especially on the West Coast, in the 1850s after the discovery of gold in California, and they played a significant role in developing the mining, agriculture, fishing, railroad, and manufacturing industries of the West. By the 1870s, however, economic recession combined with increasing immigration led to virulent anti-Chinese sentiment. Anti-Chinese mobs targeted immigrant and American-born Chinese on the West Coast. Chinese American communities were terrorized by riots, arson, and lynching, especially throughout the 1870s and 1880s. Political organizations such as the Workingmen's Party of California formed and began to demand an end to Chinese labor. Composed of white labor leaders and working-class men, this new political party demanded boycotts of Chinese labor and the denial of civil rights, such as suffrage and access to the courts, to those Chinese immigrants already living in the United States. The Workingmen's Party lobbied the California legislature and the U.S. Congress to pass laws to restrict future immigration from China. In 1882, the United States passed the Chinese Exclusion Act, which barred the entry of Chinese laborers into the country (the act was extended in 1892 and again in 1902). The 1892 legislation, known as the Geary Act, required Chinese Americans to carry proof of their right to live and work in the United States through "certificates of residence." Chinese exclusion was not repealed until 1943, when China had become a U.S. ally during World War II. Thus anti-Chinese violence and harassment in the American West were institutionalized by the time of the arrival of a significant number of Japanese immigrants in the late nineteenth and early twentieth centuries. The fear of this second Yellow Peril generated a different kind of concern, since Japan wielded much more economic and military power than China.[3]

Kaiser Wilhelm II of Germany is credited with popularizing the term "Yellow Peril," using the phrase in 1895 to warn of the potential future threat of Asia toward European powers. Although the concept dated back at least to the fifteenth century, the term came into popular usage after 1895 and was widely used in the American press to refer not only to the military threat of Japan but also to the growing tide of immigrants from Asia.[4] In 1905, the Japanese victory in the Russo-Japanese War (the first major victory of a nonwhite nation over a European nation in the modern era) seemed to validate the kaiser's prediction and generated further hysteria about the threat of an Asian world power. At the request of the Japanese government, Roosevelt helped to negotiate a peace agreement ending the war. Roosevelt and the American public generally supported the Japanese in their efforts to resist Russian aggression, and he remained cautiously respectful in future relations with Japan in part because the emergence of Japan as a formidable military power worried him. As Americans sought to assert and maintain their status as a world power, anxieties over race and manliness rose to the surface and were especially visible in discussions of the Japanese martial art of jiu-jitsu.

Japanese immigrants began arriving in large numbers to California beginning in the late nineteenth century. Demand for workers on plantations in Hawaii, and later on farms in California, encouraged Japanese laborers to leave their homes and try their luck abroad. By 1900, nearly 30,000 Japanese had immigrated to the United States. Immigration peaked between 1900 and 1908, with an additional 127,000 Japanese entering the country during that period. Recruiters encouraged a secondary migration of Japanese from Hawaii to the mainland to compensate for a shortage of cheap agricultural labor in California. The 1910 census revealed 41,356 Japanese living in California.[5]

Even at the peak of immigration, Japanese Americans remained a very small minority in California, at less than 1 percent of the total population. However, their presence soon excited controversy statewide. As Japanese immigration increased in the 1890s, exclusionists began to call for restrictions on Japanese immigrants similar to those imposed on the Chinese.[6] In February 1905, the *San Francisco Chronicle* published an article predicting that after the success of the Japanese military in the Russo-Japanese War, the stream of immigrants from Japan would become a "raging torrent."[7] This Yellow Peril rhetoric generated further support for exclusionist efforts. By March, the California state legislature had passed a resolution calling for Congress to limit Japanese immigration. Within this climate, the Asiatic Exclusion League was created on May 14, 1905, when delegates from sixty-seven (mostly labor) groups met in San Francisco to organize against Japanese immigration. The league insisted that the Japanese represented an economic threat on account of their "low standard of civilization, living and wages." Branches of the league opened in a number of cities throughout the state. They lobbied for immigration exclusion and on the local level advocated boycotting of Japanese shops and restaurants while discouraging the employment of Japanese laborers.[8]

In 1906, the San Francisco Board of Education voted to segregate Japanese and Korean schoolchildren, sending them to the Oriental School in Chinatown where Chinese children had been segregated since 1885. News of the incident resulted in protests by the Japanese government. President Roosevelt intervened to keep the peace and promised to Japan that the Japanese in the United States would be treated with respect. This assertion was motivated less by a belief in the equality of the races than by a concern about Japan's growing military might as evidenced in the recently concluded Russo-Japanese War. In his annual message to Congress, Roosevelt argued that "to shut them out from the public schools is a wicked absurdity."[9] Roosevelt, however, recognized that the move to segregate Japanese schoolchildren was a manifestation of a larger concern about Japanese immigration. In an effort to address the needs of both parties, Roosevelt negotiated the Gentlemen's Agreement, under which Japan promised to ban new Japanese laborers from immigrating to the United States in exchange for better treatment for the Japanese already living here (including the right to attend integrated public schools). Despite this temporary resolution, anti-Japanese hostility in the West continued, leading to legislation to deny Japanese the right to own land through the California Alien Land Law of 1913. The exclusionists further celebrated their success with the Immigration Act of 1924, which banned immigration from Japan altogether.[10]

Roosevelt had a much more complicated attitude toward Japan than exclusionists who feared the Yellow Peril. On the one hand, he respected the Japanese people and seemed fascinated by Japanese culture and history. He especially admired the samurai culture and its Bushido principles emphasizing loyalty and honor.[11] Roosevelt was attracted to the idea of an elite and cultured warrior class of men dedicated to upholding manly virtues. Victorians idealized a concept of manliness that required men to exhibit a strong moral character and uphold ideals of physical and mental courage similar to those valued in Japanese samurai culture.[12] No doubt Roosevelt felt some affinity with the samurai in part because he could identify with them as members of the educated upper class. On the other hand, he recognized the dangers of Japan's military might and Japanese immigration in inciting anti-Japanese violence that could eventually trigger a war. In a letter to Senator Philander Chase Knox of Pennsylvania written in 1909, Roosevelt admitted that the Japanese were a "most formidable military power" who had "been bitterly humiliated to find that even their allies, the English, and their friends, the Americans, won't admit them to association and citizenship, as they admit the least advanced or most decadent European peoples." Roosevelt regretfully acknowledged the necessity of carrying out the American policy of Japanese immigrant exclusion to protect Japanese Americans from violent backlash and to protect the United States from a potential war with Japan. At the end of the letter, however, Roosevelt added in his own handwriting his recommendation that "the Japanese should be shown, what is the truth, that our keeping them out means not that they are inferior to us—in some ways they are superior—but that they are *different*; so different that, whatever the future may hold, at present the two races ought not to come together in masses."[13] Thus Roosevelt revealed his complicated view of the Japanese that vacillated between respectful admiration of their culture and fear of their military power and a paternalistic view of the Japanese as an unassimilable race in need of protection.[14] Roosevelt clearly saw the Japanese as different from other races and closer to Anglo-Saxons in racial advancement and civilization. In his mind, then, this would in part justify the adoption of elements of the Japanese fighting system.

Journalist Jack London's reports from Manchuria during the Russo-Japanese War similarly reflected racialized views, mixing a complicated respect and awe for Japan and a warning about the potential rise of Japan as a world power. London further contributed to the Yellow Peril hysteria by declaring that China, under the influence of Japan, represented the true cause of concern. London declared the "Japanese a race of mastery and power, a fighting race through all its history, a race which has always despised commerce and exalted fighting." A clear sense of admiration emerged as London detailed the successes of the Japanese in economic and military advancement: "From the West he has borrowed all our material achievement and passed our ethical achievement by. Our engines of production and destruction he has made his. What was once solely ours he now duplicates, rivaling our merchants in the commerce of the East, thrashing the Russian on sea and land." Still, London insisted on the moral superiority of the Anglo-Saxon race, noting that despite "the evil things we have done, there is a certain integrity, a sternness of conscience, a melancholy responsibility of life, a sympathy and comradeship and warm human feel, which is ours, indubitably ours, and which we cannot teach to the Oriental."[15] This positioning of

Anglo-Saxon men as a morally upright "right-seeking race," in contrast to Asian men who were depicted as bereft of integrity and conscience, served to heighten anxieties and tensions about the potential expansion of an Asian world power.

In addition to the racialization of the Japanese as morally inferior, American culture tended to construct Japanese masculinity in complex but ultimately unflattering ways. Newspapers, magazines, books, and movies presented contradictory images of Asian and Asian American masculinity in the late nineteenth and early twentieth centuries. On the one hand, Asian men were portrayed as feminine, weak, or even asexual. On the other hand, they were sometimes depicted as hypermasculine, sexual threats to white American womanhood. In either scenario, white, working-class manhood was represented as ultimately superior in both its physically strong manliness and its inherent chivalry.[16]

Ideas of race and manliness were intimately linked in Roosevelt's mind, and he believed that the pursuit of a physically active lifestyle was essential to combating weakness and effeminacy. Historian Gail Bederman has argued that Roosevelt advocated "imperialistic warfare and racial violence if necessary" to advance the interests of the nation and in effect prove the virility of American manhood.[17] Roosevelt admired the virility of Japan but argued that China was weak, and therefore unmanly, because of its failure to build up its military. He warned that a similar fate could befall America and American men if action was not taken to pursue a "strenuous life." Roosevelt warned that "the over-civilized man, who has lost the great fighting, masterful virtues," threatened to undermine the strength of the nation in fulfilling its duty to the world.[18] This duty included uplifting races that he had identified as weaker and less manly (such as the Filipinos) in a reflection of the "little brown brother" paternalist and racialized ideology. In Roosevelt's mind, Japan had already reached a high level of civilization, but other races required more assistance to rise up from primitivism.[19]

## Roosevelt and Jiu-Jitsu

These anxieties over race and manliness were further manifested in debates about Japanese martial arts. Roosevelt's interest in Japanese jiu-jitsu began when his close friend William Sturgis Bigelow, a Boston physician and collector of Japanese art, showed the president a series of jiu-jitsu grips practiced by Japanese police and soldiers.[20] Upon Bigelow's recommendation, Roosevelt hired John J. O'Brien in March 1902 to teach him lessons in jiu-jitsu.[21] Roosevelt praised the system as "marvelous," even though he admitted that he was having difficulty in learning it.[22] After a few weeks of study, however, he had to suspend his training to recover from a back injury he sustained while "turning a somersault on a pile of boulders" during a walk on a non-jiu-jitsu training day.[23]

Two years later, Roosevelt heard that a prominent judo instructor named Yoshiaki Yamashita was visiting the United States. Roosevelt invited Yamashita to Washington to teach him additional lessons in the art.[24] Writing to his son Kermit on March 5, 1904, Roosevelt said, "I am wrestling with two Japanese wrestlers three times a week. I am not the age or the build, one would think, to be whirled lightly over an opponent's head and batted down on a mattress without damage; but they are so skillful that I have not been hurt at all. My throat is a little sore, because once when one of them had a strangle hold I also got hold of his windpipe and thought I could perhaps choke him off before he could choke me. However, he got ahead!"[25] The president's enthusiastic descriptions of sprains and bruises suggested both his eagerness to learn the art and the reason he decided to back off on his own training. It is clear that Roosevelt respected and admired the effectiveness of Japanese martial arts. This reverence and willingness to learn more about Japanese fighting culture distinguished him from others who simply dismissed jiu-jitsu as a vicious and deceitful method of dishonorable fighting. A scornful attitude toward jiu-jitsu was especially common in the writings of the working-class press, which feared the growth of the Japanese as a world power, resented the presence of Japanese immigrants in the United States, and insisted on the superiority of Western fighting arts.

Despite Roosevelt's open-minded approach and admiration of Japanese culture, he tended to side with working-class critics in their conclusions. On February 24, 1905, he had written a letter to Kermit describing a match between champion middleweight wrestler Joseph Grant and Yamashita.[26] Roosevelt admitted that Yamashita's fighting skills were equal if not superior to Grant's. However, Roosevelt insisted, "With a

little practice in the art I am sure that one of our big wrestlers or boxers, simply because of his greatly superior strength, would be able to kill
any of those Japanese, who though very good men for their inches and
pounds are altogether too small to hold their own against big, powerful,
quick men who are as well trained."[27] Although Roosevelt acknowledged
the advantages of jiu-jitsu, and even admired the Japanese for their martial valor and skill, in the end he concluded that Western wrestling and
boxing, and in fact American men, were morally and physically superior
to the Japanese and their fighting system. Still, the Japanese and their
martial art worried men like Roosevelt as they pondered the future of
the United States and the potential threat of the new Yellow Peril.

Roosevelt's experimentation with jiu-jitsu signaled the beginning of
a public discussion among the general American population. Stories in
newspapers and popular magazines as well as the publication of several
teaching manuals fueled interest in the art of jiu-jitsu. Some praised the
efficiency and effectiveness of the system at the same time they suggested deeper concerns with the implications of the Eastern martial
art's potential dominance over Western fighting systems. Others clearly
saw the threat of the Yellow Peril in the deadly art of jiu-jitsu. Popular discourse about jiu-jitsu and the Japanese revealed a wide variety of
responses.

## Exoticizing Jiu-jitsu

The most common initial approach, especially among proponents of the
art, was to present a favorable but exoticized view of Japanese martial
arts.[28] This coincided with a general American obsession with Japanese
culture and goods.[29] John J. O'Brien, Roosevelt's first jiu-jitsu instructor, exoticized the art of jiu-jitsu for purposes of self-promotion. In his
book, *A Complete Course of Jiu-Jitsu and Physical Culture* (1905), O'Brien
claimed to be the first to introduce the system to the United States and
promised to reveal the secrets of the deadly art. John F. McDonald of the
American College of Physical Culture and Jiu-Jitsu introduced the book
by explaining to the reader, "This is the first time that all the secrets of
the Japanese national system of physical training and self-defense have
been given to Western people. Less than a generation ago you could
not have obtained this knowledge at any price. So religiously have the

principles of Jiu-Jitsu been guarded that no foreigner has ever before received official instruction from one who has taken the highest degree in the art." McDonald continued, "As a means of self-defense, Jiu-Jitsu is as potent at short range as the most deadly weapon that human ingenuity has devised." In constructing jiu-jitsu as foreign, exotic, and secret, O'Brien and his supporters helped to erect a shroud of mysteriousness around the art that both captivated and worried American audiences.[30]

White writers were not alone in their attempts to exoticize the art of jiu-jitsu. Japanese instructors recognized the value of appealing to Western stereotypes of the exotic foreigner to promote and market their services. Ads designed by Japanese jiu-jitsu instructors revealed the tendency to use white stereotypes of Japanese culture to their own advantage. Yae Kichi Yabe immigrated to the United States around 1892, and some accounts claim he studied at Yale for a time.[31] By 1904, he had opened the Yabe School of Jiu-Jitsu in Rochester, New York. His magazine and newspaper advertisements explained that "after being jealously guarded as a national secret in Japan for over 2,000 years the science of Jiu-Jitsu—the most wonderful and mysterious physical science in the whole world—will be taught for the first time in this country." Potential students would enjoy the privilege of training under the tutelage of Yabe, "who is conceded to be the most learned teacher of Jiu-Jitsu in all Japan" and "has been delegated to teach this ancient and sacred art to Americans." The ads claimed that training in the art would enable "a child of 14 years to overcome and render powerless a man of thrice his strength."[32] Yabe asserted that the practice of jiu-jitsu helped explain the superhuman strength and low death rates of the Japanese, as well as the material and military progress of the Japanese nation.[33]

The historical association of jiu-jitsu training with the samurai class was often highlighted in the promotional literature to authenticate jiu-jitsu as a practical fighting system, to identify it as an honorable means of self-defense, and to add an aura of mystery to the idea of training in the art. Bushido was a code of honor adopted by the samurai that insisted on obedience, loyalty, and duty. The idea of Bushido, which mirrored Western concepts of chivalry, and the ideal of the samurai as scholar-warriors were in part what attracted Roosevelt to Japanese martial arts. According to some scholars, the concept of Bushido appears to have grown more out of a late nineteenth-century search for

Japanese national identity during the Meiji Restoration rather than from centuries of samurai tradition as exaggerated in popular periodicals and books. Borrowing from nineteenth-century European medieval concepts of knighthood and chivalry, the Japanese government sought to inculcate martial values in the military and educational system by popularizing the idea of Bushido. Western nations learned about Japanese culture and the "ancient" tradition of Bushido at the same time a newly industrialized and modernized Japan stepped onto the stage as a major world power. As members of an educated upper class, Roosevelt and his contemporaries recognized the similarities with their own newly romanticized notions of European chivalry and found common ideological ground with the samurai and their "ancient" moral code.[34] Frequent reference to the "code of honor" of the "noble" samurai in the writings about jiu-jitsu suggested that fighting except in cases of self-defense was generally regarded as immoral. Yabe insisted that jiu-jitsu "trains both mind and body and fits the young generation to bear the responsibilities of manhood. No Japanese is worthy of the name of a jiu-jitsian who uses the art for any other purpose than enforcing justice or defending his honor and person."[35] Thus training in the art of jiu-jitsu involved not only the acquisition of physical skill but also adherence to a sort of moral code. This argument served as a counterpoint to those critics who would suggest that jiu-jitsu was an immoral system of fighting. Described as a "national secret" previously denied to foreigners and even to those outside of the samurai class, jiu-jitsu was now imbued with a larger significance that seemed to validate its authenticity as an effective and deadly art.[36]

The fascination with jiu-jitsu and exoticization of Japan had the effect of helping to render Asian Americans more visible in American culture. When a newspaper reporter visited Iitaro Kano's jiu-jitsu dojo in Seattle, he described his experience almost as if he was pulling back a veil to reveal the secret world of Japanese Americans: "These Japanese boys in their wrestling club are entirely different from the types we see on the streets or at work. In contact with Americans the Japanese tries to be as American as possible. Here he is pure Japanese, with the clothes of Western civilization hung on a nail, the torturesome shoes kicked into a corner and his half-naked brown body glistening under the costume of his country."[37] The writer played on a "perpetual foreigner" theme in constructing Asian Americans as foreign, exotic, and separate from American society. Although clearly exoticzing these Japanese American men and boys, the reporter's exposé helped to shed some light on the "secret" world of Japanese America for white Americans.

Another story describing a Japanese American valet reflected the perpetual foreigner stereotype. Ichihara Iizuka, a Japanese American valet who was attacked while walking home to his boardinghouse in Philadelphia, gained notoriety when he used jiu-jitsu to throw one of the three attackers over his head. The robber rose to his feet and quickly fled the scene before police apprehended him. The newspaper reporter described Iizuka's actions as heroic while at the same time noting that Iizuka had detailed the incident in perfect English.[38] The fact that the reporter seemed surprised by Iizuka's English-speaking abilities revealed a common misconception among white Americans that all Japanese living in America retained their essential "foreignness" and failed to assimilate or learn to speak English. Although Iizuka had lived in the United States for twenty-two years and was married to a white woman, the reporter assumed that he was essentially a foreigner, thus reflecting the perpetual foreigner stereotype.[39]

Some entrepreneurs recognized that interest in jiu-jitsu and Japanese culture opened up new opportunities. Japanese instructors found their services in demand as white Americans sought an "authentic" training experience in traditional Japanese martial arts. Tsunejiro Tomita and Mitsuyo Maeda, who came to the United States in 1904 to teach judo, gave numerous public demonstrations and opened a training club in New York City. Maeda eventually moved on, traveling the world competing in highly publicized wrestling matches.[40] Japanese immigrants to the West Coast of the United States also found much interest in jiu-jitsu. The Nippon School of Jiu-Jitsu at 1281 Market Street in San Francisco was one of many jiu-jitsu schools that opened their doors to white Americans. The instructors widely promoted the school in local newspapers beginning in 1905, with advertisements that bragged that "expert Japanese instructors" would teach students Japanese self-defense.[41]

The interest in jiu-jitsu helped to render Asian American women more visible at the same time that it worked to counter the stereotype of the passive Asian female. In Harlem in 1905, a Japanese American woman named Hisaso Sota (alternately spelled Misoa Soga or Moso Sota) challenged the stereotype by kicking an assailant in the knee and using jiu-jitsu to throw him to the ground. The display drew a crowd of several hundred onlookers, including a group of women who cheered Sota on and insisted that she beat the man, who was later identified as J. F. McCullum. When McCullum rose to his feet, Sota asked him if he had had enough. He replied "no" and lunged at her again. At this point, Sota thrust her arm under his throat and threw him to the ground again, this time pinning him with her knee as the crowd applauded.[42] Later, a fascinated reporter detailed the scene in the courtroom when the judge asked Sota to demonstrate the move for the court. The reporter noted that the 95-pound "little Japanese girl" reenacted the scenario for the court by sending the 165-pound Japanese interpreter Koyta Yoshmure flying through the air.[43] The demonstration evoked cheers from the court spectators and laughter from the judge, who fined McCullum for disorderly conduct. Sota's attacker was identified as a prominent athlete and boxer. The emphasis on McCullum's athletic training, Sota's small stature, and the weight differential between the two reinforced the idea that Sota was far from a passive Asian female.

Another woman who challenged stereotypes was Ai Kishi, who was traveling with the mikado's royal troupe of jiu-jitsu performers with the Barnum and Bailey Circus. At eighteen years of age, 110 pounds, and four feet eight inches in height, Kishi delighted audiences by throwing large athletic men with minimal effort.[44] She declared that it is just as important for women to know how to defend themselves as it is for men. In response to hundreds of letters from girls requesting lessons in self-defense, Kishi offered to teach lessons in defending against an attack, and she demonstrated several techniques that were detailed in text and pictures as tutorials for readers. The techniques she demonstrated were far from passive as she described breaking arms and snapping legs. Kishi explained to reporters that she had the knowledge and ability to kill an attacker if she were required to do so in a life-threatening situation. This declaration of Kishi's deadly abilities helped dispel myths about the passive Asian woman. One reporter insisted that she "is not a curiosity, neither is she a freak of human nature. She is simply educated in the art of self-defense and knows how to protect herself."[45]

## Vilifying Jiu-Jitsu

Although the promotional literature produced by advocates of jiu-jitsu was generally positive and in some ways helped to render Asian Americans more visible, the exoticized construction of Japan and jiu-jitsu revealed an alternate undercurrent of fear about the Yellow Peril that was especially prevalent among the white American laboring class. Many American journalists exoticized the art, depicting it as something mysterious and foreign but ultimately condemning it as devious and immoral and associating it with Yellow Peril themes. As the popularity of jiu-jitsu training spread, reporters began to write articles on the subject for popular consumption in working-class magazines and newspapers. Some critics proved outright hostile. A writer with the *Daily Capital Journal* in Salem, Oregon, declared jiu-jitsu a "fake." The author described an exhibition at West Point where American wrestlers were able to easily defeat Japanese jiu-jitsu experts. The writer attacked not only the technical merits of the art of jiu-jitsu but also the manliness and morality of the practice: "Jiu jitsu does not appear to be the manly art of self-defense, but rather a method of attack by springing upon an unguarded person and taking a peculiar hold upon his throat or by taking him unawares in some other vulnerable part of the person. The same thing might be accomplished by creeping stealthily behind a man and striking him down with a sandbag." The author continued to racialize the art by asserting, "It is to be hoped that the academies at West Point and Annapolis will waste no more time upon this heathen 'science.' What is needed there is wholesome physical and mental development, not the acquisition of tricks for unfair advantage."[46] The writer disparaged jiu-jitsu as a "heathen" fighting art not worthy for use by decent American men.

The adjectives used to describe jiu-jitsu further suggest the ways in which jiu-jitsu and the Japanese were racialized as inferior. The words "heathen," "tricks," "fiendish," "uncivilized," "barbaric," and "brutal" appeared frequently in descriptions of jiu-jitsu.[47] Similar language had been used in the past to describe Native American, African American, and Filipino men and their alleged propensity toward animalistic and savage violence.[48] This is in sharp contrast to descriptions of Western boxing and wrestling, which were presented as more restrained, responsible, and honorable ways of fighting. Charles Willard, a physical culture instructor in Baltimore, reflected this attitude when he argued that American fighting systems teach "one to be quick, graceful, strong, honorable, brave and merciful."[49] Former champion boxer and wrestler Frank S. Lewis wrote a book on self-defense in 1906 in which he insisted that Western self-defense "strengthens the mind and body and builds up a manly courage, that makes them [American boys] disdain to resort to atrocities as practiced by other nations." Lewis argued that boxing and wrestling were responsible for "the noble courage that elevates the English speaking people, and which stern, impartial and logical minds must recognize as the proudest attribute of our AMERICAN CHARAC-TER."[50] By associating boxing and wrestling with manly attributes of courage and character, Lewis clearly distinguished Western martial arts from Japanese fighting systems.

Such allusions to the moral superiority of Americans and thus by default the immorality of the Japanese became increasingly common. Japanese jiu-jitsu was often defined as "unmanly and cowardly."[51] One article insisted, "An American going into a [fighting] contest with a Jap would be handicapped unless he had made up his mind to forget humanity for a time."[52] Another writer argued that "Oriental carelessness for life" characterizes the study of jiu-jitsu.[53] The "fiendish tricks" of Japanese jiu-jitsu were constructed as less humane and less honorable than American methods of self-defense. In 1905, Horace Fogel, a Philadelphia sportswriter, insisted that the bone-breaking and strangling techniques of jiu-jitsu were uncivilized and barbaric and would not be tolerated in the United States. The writer compared jiu-jitsu matches to dogfights in their brutality. Fogel argued that boxing, in comparison, was a much safer and efficient method of self-defense: "Any third-rate pugilist can lay low the most expert jiu-jitsuist in less time than it would take to tell the story of it . . . those who have studied jiu-jitsu or seen two Japs in such a contest simply laugh at it." Fogel pointed out that "the Japs may have made a scientific discovery of how . . . to break every bone in your body and strangle you to death, but the civilized Americans and Europeans discovered centuries ago how to use their fists in self-protection." Fogel referred here to Roosevelt's insistence that American men pursue a physically active "strenuous life," suggesting that the bone-breaking techniques of Japanese jiu-jitsu were perhaps a bit too strenuous. Fogel implied that these dishonorable tactics lacked a sense of fair play and courage, one that was inherent in Western boxing. [54]

Weighing in on the discussion, John L. Sullivan, a heavyweight boxing champion, declared jiu-jitsu a fake. Sullivan referred to it as "Chop Suey fighting" and insisted that it was far inferior to the "old way," saying a "yellow man hasn't the staying power that a white man has, and a yellow race can't stand out against a white race. I'll put my money on the white man against all other colors—yellow, red, or black—and in a fight to a finish the white man has got to win. The Japs are fighting for their Emperor, who may be a nice sort of a gent all right, but the white man fights for his country and that's the kind of an inducement that will tell in the end."[55] Sullivan insisted on the superiority of Western martial arts and the physical power of the white race at the same time that he argued that a strong sense of democracy among Americans would guarantee their ultimate victory.

Japanese jiu-jitsu experts fought back against such racialized attacks by defending the efficiency of their fighting art and insisting on the inherent morality in jiu-jitsu training. Teiichi Yamagata was a former officer in the Japanese navy before moving to the United States to study and write. Yamagata, writing in *Leslie's Monthly* in 1904, did not deny the bone-breaking techniques and used them to illustrate jiu-jitsu's superiority over boxing. He argued, "Boxing has no real value when opposed to jiu-jitsu. To illustrate: no matter how swiftly and hard the boxer hits out, his wrist can be readily dislocated or broken by a blow delivered with the open hand of *jiujitsu-shi*." However, Yamagata pointed out that jiu-jitsu is intended to be used only for self-defense and that practitioners take an oath not to use the techniques unless absolutely necessary. The instructor closely observes his student, and "if not satisfied as to the coolness, prudence and honesty of his pupil, the more important secrets are not imparted."[56] Yamagata thus insisted on the code of honor inherent in the study of jiu-jitsu and used this to counter arguments intended to label the Japanese and jiu-jitsu as dishonorable.

## Feminization of Jiu-Jitsu

In addition to the racialized language that was used to exoticize and often disparage jiu-jitsu, a few critics adopted a gendered approach to attacking the Japanese and the system of jiu-jitsu. Although a much less common tactic, feminizing Japanese fighting arts further served to diminish the perceived threat of Japanese expansion. Books and articles often emphasized that the practice of jiu-jitsu in Japan was extended to men and women, implying that even weakly women could learn the techniques.[57] The emphasis on female practitioners of jiu-jitsu by some observers implicitly served to reduce it to a form of exercise rather than a deadly system of fighting.

Descriptions of the physical bodies of Japanese who studied jiu-jitsu versus American wrestlers and boxers further illustrated the tendency to feminize Japan and the Japanese. American men were often described as large and muscular while Japanese men were depicted as small and feminine. According to the *Salt Lake Herald*, a match between wrestling coach Harvey Holmes of the University of Southern California and a jiu-jitsu practitioner named Nagamatsu proved the superiority of American wrestling to Japanese jiu-jitsu. The author noted that Coach Holmes used a half nelson, double-arm lock and "speedily placed the little brown man hors du combat." The use of the racialized phrase "little brown man" served to emasculate and dismiss the Japanese and their fighting methods.[58] An article in the *Daily Press* of Newport News, Virginia, dismissed descriptions of the merits of jiu-jitsu in which "Japs, with soft muscles and no appearance of great strength would grapple with husky American giants and throw them down or toss them in the air." Instead, "the noble art of self-defense as practiced by the American boxer is best of all" because "it is sportsmanlike and a truly athletic game, tending to promote good hard muscles, sound wind, activity of limb, quickness of eye and hand and steadiness of nerve." In contrast, then, to the Japanese, American men were portrayed as more muscular, noble, and therefore manly through the study of Western martial arts. As the title of the article suggests, Japanese jiu-jitsu is "not true athletics" and therefore not worthy of the interest of American men.[59]

Japanese men were also feminized in descriptions of their martial arts training. An article in the *Seattle Times* used a racialized and gendered tone in describing a jiu-jitsu class. Explaining that the practitioners "squat on the floor like they would at home," the author contrasted them with "Americans," who "prefer the benches." The writer pointed out that "quite often the two men on that mat giggle like school girls."

Although the writer heralded jiu-jitsu "as a wonderful means of defense in case of attack on the street at night," ultimately, he concluded, "it seems doubtful if anyone but an expert could bring it into play save against the slowest and most dull-witted of thugs. A miss would be disastrous against any man with a hard right fist or a club." The author insisted on the utility of jiu-jitsu only as an exercise.[60] The description of adult men as giggling schoolgirls diminished the reputation of jiu-jitsu as an effective fighting system for American men. T. K. Hedrick, writing for *Wetmore's Weekly*, alluded to Japanese clothing and cowardice in an attempt to emasculate Japanese jiu-jitsu fighters: "We shall expect President Roosevelt to hand his Jiu-Jitsu instructors a swift kick in the Kimona, and chase them across the White House lawn with a rapid-fire battery of upper cuts and short-arm jabs. We are the people. We can lick any old yellow, red, blue or green peril that walks. Hurrah for the good American fist!"[61] By evoking this image of the president using boxing techniques and chasing kimono-clad Japanese men, Hedrick attempted to paint a picture of Japanese men as feminine and cowardly while representing Roosevelt as the embodiment of American manhood.

An article in the *Los Angeles Herald* in 1906 revealed a similar tendency to feminize the Japanese by dismissing jiu-jitsu as a fad whose time had come and gone. Like that of other authors quoted here, this writer's language reflected racialized tensions as he stereotyped the Japanese fighting system and the Japanese as deadly, deceptive threats to civilization. The fad had begun to die down as "the jewjit classes started to fall off and the great Japanese man killers went back to answering the tinkle of the hotel clerk's call bell." The author declared jiu-jitsu useless as a fighting art, especially when it was met with a right hook, and attempted to further attack the legitimacy of jiu-jitsu by feminizing it. "Jewjit might do for settling class rows at Vassar, but when it came down to deciding debates with cabbies, delivery men and half illuminated limber jacks, jewjit was about as effective as stabbing them in the ear with a slice of angel food."[62] Jiu-jitsu was therefore relegated to women's colleges with the suggestion that the Japanese could not harm real men.

To some degree, the initial gendering of jiu-jitsu as feminine made it more acceptable for women to train in the art. Nixola Greeley-Smith wrote in 1905 in the *Evening World,* a New York newspaper, that "few women are strong enough to master the art of boxing to the extent of making it of practical use . . . but the art of jiu-jitsu . . . if correctly applied will enable a 110-pound woman to overpower a giant, and may therefore be mastered by every woman." Greeley-Smith depicted jiu-jitsu as much less threatening than boxing in the sense that even a supposedly weaker woman could master it. However, the author noted the advantages of the techniques as a method of self-defense for women.[63]

The idea that women in Japan trained alongside men in the study of jiu-jitsu seemed to further inspire American women to take up the art of self-defense. An article on jiu-jitsu in *Leslie's Monthly* explained that the wives of the samurai trained in jiu-jitsu, making them "as redoubtable as the men." The author, Teiichi Yamagata, noted that the elite class of Japanese women who train in jiu-jitsu in modern times "are able to cope with any man who has only brute strength."[64] The editor of *Harper's Bazaar* wrote that jiu-jitsu has made Japanese women "the equals of men in health and vigor." The editor, who seemed surprised to learn about women defeating men in jiu-jitsu matches in Japan, concluded that "it certainly will not hurt any American woman to learn the secret of the smiling grace and suppleness of her Japanese sisters" and pointed out, "With *jiu-jitsu* in full swing, there will be no 'weaker-sex,' it is alleged."[65] Japanese women thus opened the doors for American women to train in jiu-jitsu.[66]

Just as boxing for women was promoted as a path to feminine health and beauty, jiu-jitsu was justified as a means of transforming a woman's body. In a public interview, Mademoiselle Dazie (Daisy Ann Peterkin), a vaudeville actress, openly advocated jiu-jitsu training for women. Peterkin, who studied jiu-jitsu for two years, claimed that it would help women get rid of scrawny arms and shoulders and develop symmetry and strength in their muscles. Peterkin also insisted that jiu-jitsu "gives a woman confidence in her power to take care of herself, and it will aid the underdeveloped woman to put a curve where she wants it and the woman of over-luxuriant figure to take off a curve or two."[67] Proponents advocated jiu-jitsu as an overarching system to help women maintain a healthy weight not only through exercise but also through diet and lifestyle.[68]

Harrie Irving Hancock published a series of books that reflected similar gendered ideas about women's jiu-jitsu training. His three books described exercises and techniques for men, women, and children desiring to study jiu-jitsu.[69] In *Physical Training for Women by Japanese Methods*, Hancock argued that jiu-jitsu could strengthen women's bodies at the same time it prevented obesity. More than that, however, he stressed the radical and anti-Victorian notion that physical training in martial arts challenged gender stereotypes of women as weak. "One of the phrases that should be stricken from the English language is, 'the weaker sex.' After a long experience in Japanese athletics the writer has no patience with women who consider that merely because of their sex they should be weaker than men. In Japan the women are not weaker, and in this country they have no right to be."[70] Hancock's call to action was significant in that he insisted that women eagerly embrace martial arts training as a way of expressing their newfound place in society, writing, "The day has gone by when women prize weakness as a dainty attribute of their sex, and the science of *jiu-jitsu* points out the path for the new physical woman to pursue."[71] In addition to encouraging American women to adopt Asian physical culture as a way to strengthen their bodies and bolster their sense of selves in society, Hancock offered classes in New York City to train men and women to become teachers of jiu-jitsu themselves.[72]

Jiu-jitsu training was also promoted as part of a holistic training of young girls in preparation for their role as mothers and caretakers. The 1913 Girl Scout handbook included a list of recommended activities for meetings. In addition to stressing that Girl Scouts should learn how to load and fire a gun, the handbook argued that girls should learn jiu-jitsu for self-defense.[73] The Girl Scout organization was modeled in part on Major D. Cossgrove's Peace Scout movement for girls in New Zealand. Although Cossgrove advocated jiu-jitsu training for girls as early as 1909, in the same sentence he argued that Peace Scouts should learn "nursing, care and management of infants, and invalid cookery."[74] The feminizing of jiu-jitsu helped open up opportunities for women to train in the art.

The growing acceptance of jiu-jitsu as a feminine art no doubt also helped justify its practice by refined and cultured Anglo women. Just as middle- and upper-class Anglo men expressed a curiosity and affinity for Japanese culture and fighting arts, Anglo women of the upper classes were similarly drawn to jiu-jitsu. Lillian Schoedler, a 1911 graduate of Barnard College and one of the top female athletes in the country,

Figure 2.2 William M. Van der Weyde, "Jiu-Jitsu for Women," ca. 1900 (a digital positive from an original negative). George Eastman Museum, Rochester, New York.

organized female graduates of more than fifty universities to form the Intercollegiate Alumnae Athletic Association. As president of the newly formed organization, Schoedler joined her fellow board members representing the colleges of Smith, Mount Holyoke, Bryn Mawr, Vassar, and Cornell. The organization's goal was to encourage exercise and recreation for female college graduates through basketball, swimming, bowling, handball, polo, tennis, hockey, and baseball. Schoedler also invited a jiu-jitsu instructor and her husband to train more than 200 members of the organization in the art of self-defense.[75] These college-educated white women recognized the importance of physical training as a representation of their status. Women's physical culture training, especially for middle- and upper-class Anglo women, was considered essential to maintaining their own health and by extension that of the white race. The perception of jiu-jitsu as a feminine art and the role of athletics in preparing women's bodies for their gender-prescribed roles as wives and mothers justified the training of white women in jiu-jitsu.

## Appropriation

Despite the arguments between proponents and critics and efforts to exoticize, vilify, and feminize the art, jiu-jitsu remained a serious threat to Western martial arts. Numerous demonstrations and matches between jiu-jitsu experts and championship wrestlers or boxers failed to resolve the debate over which art was most efficient.[76] Yet the effectiveness of the jiu-jitsu techniques could not be denied. For some, the solution was clear. It would be better for American men to learn the system than risk attack and defeat. This in fact was the approach taken by Roosevelt once he witnessed for himself the adeptness of jiu-jitsu fighters and recognized the advantages that this type of training could offer American men. He advocated the adoption of jiu-jitsu in the curriculum of the nation's top universities and military academies.[77]

Japanese success in the Russo-Japanese War and the sudden rise in Japanese military prowess were attributed in part to their training in jiu-jitsu. A poem by Tom Gregory, printed in the San Francisco Call, illuminated the underlying fear that Japanese military supremacy signaled a potential significant threat to American interests abroad. Gregory wrote that "when the little Japanese hunts the Russian from the seas . . .

The Policemen Are Given a Regular Practical Course in Jiu Jitsu of a Modified Form by Competent Instructors in the Art

This method of throwing the attacking criminal over the shoulder looks easier than it is

Bending the wrist in this fashion forces the criminal to open his hand and drop his knife

If the push under the chin is hard enough it may break the gangster's neck

Figure 2.3 "How Philadelphia 'Strong-Arm' Policemen Are Trained to Cope with Criminals and Gangsters Who Resist Them," *Popular Science Monthly* 93, no. 1 (July 1918): 14–15.

he'll turn around and out of Uncle Sammy take a fall—jiu-jitsu poor old Sammy in a very heavy fall."[78] According to Gregory, jiu-jitsu symbolized deceit, cunning, and the Yellow Peril threat to both American manhood at home and American military supremacy abroad.

Some advocates used this awe and fear of Japan to argue for the necessity of the American appropriation of jiu-jitsu. In his book *Jiu-Jitsu Combat Tricks* (1904), Harrie Irving Hancock insisted that the performance of the Japanese in the war with Russia was proof that jiu-jitsu was the best system of athletic training in the world.[79] An article in the *San Francisco Call* remarked on the "startling agility of the Japanese in their struggle with Russia" and reported that the "little brown men" had successfully implemented Japanese jiu-jitsu "upon a grand scale." Linking the military training of the samurai class with the practice of jiu-jitsu in Japanese schools, the author argued for the adoption of jiu-jitsu by Americans. Failure to do so suggested that Americans awaited a fate similar to that of the Russians.[80]

Public debate eventually acquiesced to the necessity of jiu-jitsu training for American soldiers and law enforcement. In an editorial in the *Argonaut*, a San Francisco newspaper, the editor lamented the loss of boxing as the primary means of "manly self-defense": "We have termed the art of boxing the manly art of self-defense, and even our own President is an expert admired of professionals." But jiu-jitsu had challenged that. The editorial continued: "The *jiu-jitsu* athlete has conquered our boxers, and we are swinging away from the old proud faith in the efficacy of the manly art . . . we stand little chance with our national art in a hand-to-hand contest with the art of Japan." The editor insisted that police must be able to cope with criminals skilled in the art because "boxing and courage are really useless against tricks which break backs, fracture skulls, and maim bodies with a finger's twist. Cold and stern necessity has put boxing into the rear." Still the author stressed the moral superiority of boxing:

> What English-speaking people will ever forget the great battles fought with fists? . . . After all, it is the national way, the race's mode of settling disputes. It is a very fair and honorable way. . . . We have despised other nations for their peculiar methods. The French *savate*, the Italian's knife— all the stealthy and underhand tricks to maim and kill—we have put aside and treated as unworthy of an American or an Englishman. Who shall say we are not the better for having felt the cleanliness of boxing, the good bodily health, the pride in our well-being, in our nerve, in our courage which has taken its final embodiment in the "manly art of self-defense?"

In the end, however, the editor concluded, "If *jiu-jitsu* is impregnable against our old attack, and our enemy knows its wiles and tricks, then we too, shall learn the new way, regretfully, of course."[81]

Roosevelt's insistence that American military cadets study and master the art of jiu-jitsu stands as proof not only of his belief in its effectiveness but also of his fear that failure to learn Japanese fighting techniques

Figure 2.4 "Cannon May Kill at Ranges of Five and Ten Miles; Machine Guns May Fire Six Hundred Shots in One Minute; But the Hand-to-Hand Struggle Still Lives in Modern War—and Our Boys Must Be Masters of the Art," *Popular Science Monthly* 92, no. 6 (June 1918): 808–809.

would put Americans at a military disadvantage.[82] In January 1905, Yamashita began teaching his art at the U.S. Naval Academy, a development that generated much debate. In February and March 1905, a joint board of army and naval officers met to consider the merits of jiu-jitsu training for American soldiers. Their report concluded that "it is not of great value as a means of physical development but knowledge of this system would inspire the individual with a degree of self confidence."[83] Later demonstrations suggested a preference for wrestling as the primary means of military training. Yamashita stopped teaching at the academy in June. Although President Roosevelt intervened to get him rehired for the following year, by the end of 1906, the U.S. Navy decided to terminate the jiu-jitsu program.[84] Later, World War I would revive interest in jiu-jitsu training for the U.S. military.

Critics of jiu-jitsu could not deny the efficiency of the techniques, especially as police departments began adopting aspects of jiu-jitsu in their training academies. Cadets learned a variety of wrist, shoulder, and elbow locks to subdue or disarm an opponent. Historical photographs also show the practice of jiu-jitsu throws for purposes of self-defense.[85] An article appearing in the *Ogden Standard* in 1913 described the adoption of jiu-jitsu techniques by the police forces of New York, Boston, Chicago, Detroit, and St. Louis. Praising jiu-jitsu's superiority for favoring brains over brawn, the author declared the system less clumsy than wrestling. At the same time that he praised the superiority of jiu-jitsu as a fighting art, he declared Japanese criminals crueler than white criminals. Thus although less harsh than writers of the previous decade, this author still racialized the Japanese as devious and immoral. The article went on to explain that jiu-jitsu is "not a gentlemanly art" and not a fair way of fighting by American standards. However, the author admitted that jiu-jitsu was especially effective in defending against a deadly attack. The author ended by explaining the tricks used in jiu-jitsu, such as falling to the floor when struck, which would cause the boxer to pause. The boxer then would find his foot seized and twisted until he fell to the ground. The author explained that the art of boxing is one of the oldest forms of fighting and that "Americans could fight that way, too, if they wished, but they do not wish. It doesn't sound fair. Even an enemy is not struck when down. American school boys in a fight stop when the other fellow hollers 'nuff.'"[86] It is clear here that the Japanese were perceived as more cunning and less trustworthy than American fighters. However, rather than rejecting jiu-jitsu outright, this author argued that through appropriation of aspects of the system, Americans ensured their ability to repel outside threats while also asserting their moral and physical superiority. The use of jiu-jitsu by law enforcement grew increasingly acceptable if only as a means of counteracting the dirty fighting of morally deficient criminals.

With American entry into World War I, the necessity of a well-trained military became an issue of general concern. An article in *Popular Science* published during the war insisted that American soldiers "must be masters of the art" of hand-to-hand combat. Accompanying illustrations detailed popular jiu-jitsu techniques used by the U.S. Army to disarm an opponent. This knowledge gave U.S. soldiers an advantage over the enemy through deadly grips borrowed from Japanese martial arts.[87] Arthur Elmer Marriott, who served as the physical director of the Army YMCA, taught a combined system of jiu-jitsu and Greco-Roman wrestling techniques to the soldiers of the Thirtieth Army Division stationed at Camp Sevier, South Carolina, and in 1918 published a manual that included photographs and written descriptions of the techniques. In the book's foreword, Benjamin S. Gross, who worked with the Welfare Department at Camp Sevier, reasserted the dominance of American manliness and fighting arts, insisting that the uniquely American sports of boxing, baseball, and football prepared American men for the realities of combat. In contrast, the German enemy, rarely "a patron of the manly sports," was far less capable of defending himself in hand-to-hand combat. Despite the dominance of American men on the battlefield, Gross apparently acknowledged the necessity of further preparation. British troops and officers had testified to the efficiency of jiu-jitsu techniques on the battlefield. In response, the American army hired individual jiu-jitsu instructors such as Marriott to add to the repertoire of the average soldier.[88] Jiu-jitsu's gradual acceptance by the military was justified as a means of defending against morally bereft and violently vicious enemy nations.

Preparedness was also necessary for American women. In an article titled "Every Woman Her Own Bodyguard," Edna Egan argued that women's self-defense training was now a wartime necessity, especially since men had been called to defend the country. While men were serving abroad, Egan argued, women would be unescorted, and therefore "every woman should be her own bodyguard."[89] The Scudder School in New York City apparently agreed with this approach. The private school for girls stressed that it served as a place where girls could "learn 'preparedness' in the broadest sense, with a view to patriotic service in case of war, and for service in all good causes in times of peace." The female students took a wide range of physical activity courses, including jiu-jitsu.[90] Professional boxer Helen Hildreth insisted in 1917 that physical culture training was women's patriotic duty: "They owe it to themselves and they owe it to their families. Now with the nation at war and with Uncle Sam mobilizing every resource, domestic as well as military, she owes it to her country."[91] Women who actively participated in preparedness campaigns recognized their duty to protect their nation, and learning self-defense was justified as a way for women to serve their country.[92]

The specter of wartime sexual assaults may have also helped garner some public support for the training of women in self-defense. A group of nurses at Camp Custer, Michigan, began taking boxing lessons in 1918 "on the grounds that they could protect themselves against such atrocities as the Germans have perpetrated in Belgium and France."[93] This reference tapped into fears generated by recent stories of brutal sexual assaults against women by invading armies. The emphasis on the German threat removed the association of American men with domestic violence or sexual assault. Women's self-defense training, then, was less threatening to American men and was rationalized as a measure to preserve the purity of their women during times of war.[94] By extension, the invading hordes of dangerous immigrant classes or black rapists represented a threat to women's bodily integrity in the absence of their natural Anglo-American male protectors. As we will see in the next chapters, this deflection tactic was commonly used to justify women's self-defense training and, in the process, concealed the reality of violence against women.

Following jiu-jitsu's general acceptance by law enforcement and military officials, its adoption in mainstream culture was gradually justified by modifying and mixing aspects of it with wrestling and boxing, and therefore sanitizing and domesticating it for use by American boys and men.[95] Wrestlers Farmer Burns and Frank Gotch offered mail-order lessons that promised to teach men and boys a combination of "holds, breaks, defenses, and tricks" of wrestling and jiu-jitsu.[96] This seemed especially ironic given that ten years earlier, Gotch had ridiculed the Japanese system, asserting that an American fighter could easily defeat a jiu-jitsu expert.[97] No doubt he still insisted on the superiority of the American systems, but it appears that by 1915 he had incorporated elements of jiu-jitsu in his own teaching and found it an important point to emphasize in his advertising.

World War I may have revived interest in martial training and values, but this interest continued well after the war. Allan Corstorphin Smith had studied Kodokan judo in Japan and later taught combat fighting to American soldiers at Camp Benning in Georgia from 1917 to 1918.[98]

# Could you hold your own?

You probably haven't had a real fight since you were very small. Settling a dispute with your fists is the last thing you'd think of. And yet, a time may come when you will *have to fight*.

Suppose you saw a rowdy in the act of insulting a woman. Could you look the other way? No, sir, you'd want to step right up and teach him the lesson he deserved. But *could* you? A quarrel might lead to the challenge "Come outside and fight." Could you do it and hold your own? Or suppose you were

Figure 2.5 "Could You Hold Your Own?," *Popular Science Monthly* 98, no. 1 (January 1921): 104.

Smith contended that the Western boxer, unfamiliar with jiu-jitsu techniques, could be easily defeated.[99] After the war, Smith marketed jiu-jitsu as essential for all American males who wished to be able to defend their honor. Smith's techniques as taught to the military promised to transform the average American boy into a man. These arguments mirrored earlier discussions of the benefits of boxing as a means of transforming boys into men. An extended advertisement for Smith's book in *Illustrated World*, written by the fictional Kirtland Bowen, told the story of how Bowen learned jiu-jitsu by reading Smith's book. A few days later Bowen explained that a friend, Dot Hadley, had invited him to a reception. Bowen apparently had a romantic interest in Hadley, but she failed to reciprocate the feeling. Bowen attributed this to the fact that Hadley considered him a "poor apology for a man." At the party, Bowen was surprised to see Hadley come running out of the ladies' dressing room after having had an encounter with burglars. She told Bowen that she was "going to get some of the boys." Bowen was humiliated that she "couldn't think of me as a man." He rushed into the dressing room and subdued the burglars with his newfound jiu-jitsu skills. Bowen concluded, "Certainly I shall never be troubled by people thinking I cannot take a man's part—if you notice a ring on Dot's finger, you'll know that she certainly feels otherwise." Bowen redeemed his reputation and his manliness through the study of jiu-jitsu as taught in Smith's book.[100] In the minds of white American men, the use of jiu-jitsu for such honorable purposes as defending one's own or another's honor helped to Americanize it and disassociate it from the devious Japanese. Thus, in advocating the use of jiu-jitsu's deadly techniques only for purposes of honorable self-defense, proponents seemed to tame and domesticate the exotic art for American consumption.

Stories about the use of jiu-jitsu to defend one's honor were intended to generate a feeling among boys and men that they needed to learn elements of Japanese martial arts in order to defend their manliness if necessary.[101] Advertisements in boys magazines promised to arm young men with the tactics and techniques of boxing, wrestling, and jiu-jitsu so they would be able to disarm an opponent twice their size.[102] Boxing instructor Marshall Stillman vowed to teach men and boys more than self-defense through his mail-order business.[103] As Stillman insisted in his advertisements:

Deep down in your heart you know that you if you were called upon tonight to defend a loved one, you couldn't play the part. That if a bully insulted your mother, sister or sweetheart, you couldn't teach him a lesson. That if you were attacked on a dark road you couldn't overcome your opponent. You're not a coward—but you don't *know how*. When the test comes, it isn't going to be just a question of whether you are brave or not, but whether you know how to box, how to disarm him, how to stop the kick he launches at you. Don't you see that in justice to those who look to you for protection, it is your duty not only to be *willing*, but *able* to play a man's part.[104]

Thus, Stillman offered to teach not only a deadly combination of wrestling, boxing, and "bone-breaking jiu-jitsu holds" but also the meaning of American manhood through his mail-order lessons.

By the early 1920s, women who were practicing these mixed martial arts that included elements of boxing, wrestling, and jiu-jitsu were clearly transgressing gender boundaries and delving into traditionally male spheres of physical culture. Allan Corstorphin Smith advocated training in his mixed martial art not only as a way of schooling men in manliness but also as a way of equipping women with the skills necessary to protect against a violent attack.[105] As we will see in the next chapters, the argument that women could train in boxing and jiu-jitsu for purposes of self-defense justified their dabbling in the manly arts. For many women, however, their training represented much more than physical culture or even self-defense.

## Conclusion

By the end of World War I, jiu-jitsu had come to be tolerated and ultimately was appropriated into American fighting culture as a domesticated other. The importation and eventual incorporation of elements of jiu-jitsu into Western martial arts paralleled a similar trend in the consumption and domestication of Asian culture and goods as an extension of Orientalism and American imperialism.[106] By selectively adopting elements of Japanese culture, in this case specific techniques from jiu-jitsu, Americans, in their minds, subdued and tamed the supposedly dangerous and degenerate Japanese martial art by transforming it into a safe and morally justified addition to American fighting systems. Even as advocates argued that every male should acquire some knowledge of jiu-jitsu to defend himself in case of an attack, they continued to assert the supremacy of Western martial arts. The *Arizona Republican* noted, "All American soldiers and sailors should have some knowledge of jiu-jitsu . . . and the average American citizen could well afford to give up some time to acquiring knowledge of this Japanese art." However, the author noted, individuals "should first learn the American accomplishments of boxing and wrestling, for in many ways either are of infinitely greater advantage as a means of self-protection than jiu-jitsu." Although the author recognized the merits of jiu-jitsu as a fighting system and advocated the appropriation of jiu-jitsu techniques, he still felt compelled to reaffirm the supremacy of Western fighting arts and insisted, "A hard-hitting boxer could with ease repel the attack of a jiu-jitsu professor."[107]

The emergence of Japan as a major world power in the early twentieth century generated anxiety over the United States' place in the world. Fears of race suicide combined with a fear of the feminizing effects of overcivilization exacerbated internal cultural tensions. Japanese jiu-jitsu was an important symbol in these debates. As a physical example of the Yellow Peril, Japanese martial arts posed a threat to Western martial arts of boxing and wrestling. Favorable, exoticized descriptions of jiu-jitsu simultaneously sparked interest in the study of the art while making it appear mysterious and foreign. At the same time, critics of the system used racialized anti-Japanese language to describe both jiu-jitsu and the Japanese in general. Through gendered language and descriptions of jiu-jitsu, some Americans emphasized the feminine aspects of the Japanese martial art, in direct contrast to more manly forms of Western boxing and wrestling. Others, including President Roosevelt, tentatively acknowledged the effectiveness of jiu-jitsu while insisting on the ultimate superiority of Western martial arts. Matches pitted jiu-jitsu experts against boxers and wrestlers in an attempt to determine once and for all the superiority of American manliness, but these contests failed to determine a clear winner. The adoption of certain techniques from jiu-jitsu seemed necessary to improve the effectiveness of American fighters and ensure their ability to compete against foreign threats. This was justified in part by Roosevelt and others who viewed the Japanese, and therefore their martial art, as more civilized then other races. However, critics still resented and feared the unmanly tricks of a foreign martial art. In the end, the Yellow Peril threat, as represented by jiu-jitsu, was subjugated by simultaneously exoticizing, vilifying, feminizing, and selectively appropriating aspects of it in order to reassert the dominance of Western martial arts, the white race, and American manliness. For women, however, their training in mixed martial arts represented much more than a simple expression of physical dominance. As we shall see in the next three chapters, women's self-defense training served as a means of physical and personal empowerment at the same time that it represented an expression of their new social and political freedoms. For other women, training in self-defense symbolized potential freedom from forms of domestic tyranny.

3

# Self-Defense and Claiming Public Space

On a spring evening in 1909, Wilma Berger decided to go for a short walk after work. Twenty-year-old Berger, an American-born white woman and the daughter of a prominent local doctor, was studying to be a nurse at the Henrotin Hospital in downtown Chicago. As she walked along Ontario Street and approached Lake Michigan, she suddenly felt a piercing pain from a blow to her head. In the next instant, a stranger's arm reached around her neck and pulled her to the ground. Just as she came to her senses and prepared to stand up, a man sat on top of her, pinning her firmly down. The attacker clenched her throat with a choking grip with one hand and used his other hand to cover her mouth to prevent her from screaming. At first Berger panicked, but then she decided to relax and wait for her opportunity. As soon as she saw her chance, she caught hold of the man's arm, pulled him toward her, and sent him flying through the air with a jiu-jitsu move. Berger immediately fled to safety, knowing that she had successfully fought back against a violent surprise attack.[1] The publicity surrounding the incident vaulted Berger to local celebrity status as newspapers praised her mental prowess and physical skill in fighting off the assailant.[2]

Shortly after this incident, reporters revealed that Berger had learned jiu-jitsu under Tomita Tsunejiro in New York City and later went on to teach her own female students in Colorado Springs before moving to Chicago. She used her moment in the spotlight after the attack to advocate that all women train in the art of self-defense, and she began teaching a class of Chicago society women. The necessity of being able to protect oneself in the city was on the minds of many women. Dr. Maude Glasgow, a New York physician, was also a firm believer in self-defense training for women. Glasgow argued that girls and women should be taught boxing so they would be able to protect themselves. As she explained, "Woman has the same weapons for defending herself that man has, and a little instruction in the manner of using them would enable her to beat off brutal assailants."[3] In response to Glasgow's advocacy of boxing, Berger countered that jiu-jitsu was more effective for women in that it allowed smaller individuals to defeat larger opponents. Both women agreed, however, on the importance of some kind of self-defense training for all women.

Women's self-defense training thus emerged in large part out of the practical concern of providing women with a means of protection as they stepped out of the sheltered domestic realm and into the very public space of the city. Rapid immigration, urbanization, and industrialization fueled anxieties about shifting social and gender norms. Increasingly women ventured out into urban centers to find employment, purchase goods and services, and engage in recreational activities. Although working-class women, immigrant women, and women of color had always operated within the public sphere, a growing number of native-born white women of the middle and upper classes were beginning to leave the security of the domestic sphere to pursue a range of activities outside the home. Envisioning themselves as the purveyors of the advances of white civilization, some middle- and upper-class Protestant women justified their movement into the public domain as a way of civilizing and uplifting people whom they believed represented the less advanced classes and races. These moral reformers feared that working-class women in the cities were especially at risk for exploitation and moral ruin, since their economic dependence made them more vulnerable to harassment and assault from white male coworkers and bosses. This and other issues related to their desire to advance and improve civilization motivated these women to take on a more public presence.

However, the existence of these women in public generated a great deal of cultural anxiety. The potential that men would view them in sexualized ways seemed to threaten the reputation of respectable women.[4] The inevitable clash of cultures on the city streets reflected nuanced cultural and class differences over existing gender norms. As these middle- and upper-class white women increasingly moved into traditionally male domains, they encountered a range of responses from men, varying from mild flirting to more extreme forms of sexual harassment and sexual assault. The influx of a highly mobile population of migrants into the nation's cities, freed from the social controls enforced in smaller rural communities, created a sense of anonymity that provided opportunities for some perpetrators. News media reports of attacks against white women coupled with literature and films focused on white slavery heightened anxieties about the dangers women faced on the city streets. A common cast of sinister characters, including the flirtatious masher, the foreign white slaver, the black rapist, and the shadowy stranger, played lead roles in the stories generated in the public imagination. Although the threat of sexual assault was very real, the extent of the stranger danger fell far short of the hype, and the suspects rarely lived up to the stereotype.

A movement for women's self-defense was born in this climate of inflated anxiety and fear that soon began to take on a more significant meaning in the advance of women's rights. The study of self-defense provided a means for women to physically lay claim to public space, negotiate new social norms of appropriate sexual behavior, and protect themselves from more serious threats that potentially awaited them on the street. On a deeper level, the fact that the practitioners and advocates of women's self-defense were predominantly middle- and upper-class, native-born white women and their attackers native-born white men revealed an undercurrent of discontent that suggested a fissure in white racial solidarity.

## What Separate Spheres?

In the mid-nineteenth century, the notion of separate spheres dictated that women's ideal place was in the home. In this role, a woman held important responsibilities as wife, mother, and guardian of the domestic sphere. She was expected to embody the traits of true womanhood through purity, piety, domesticity, and submissiveness while creating a model Christian household. The home provided a haven from the harsh realities of the outside world. Men, in contrast, occupied the public sphere, economically supporting the family while also navigating the dangers of the cities. The notion of separate spheres has been largely dismissed as an ideal rather than a strict reality. Nevertheless, it held great influence as the model of proper domesticity, especially among middle-class families. Working-class women rarely adhered to, or aspired to, this middle-class vision of ideal domesticity. These women worked out of

Figure 3.1 "New York Mashers, Their Insulting Tricks and the Different Brands of the Pests," *Evening World*, July 18, 1912, 8.

necessity to support their families, and physical labor was a normal part of their lives, both inside and outside the home.[5]

Predominantly white and middle-class, women's rights advocates resisted their confinement in the domestic sphere and insisted on the need to expand their role to fulfill their Christian duties in the public world. Ironically, just as they were casting aside the notion of separate spheres in their own lives, middle-class social reformers envisioned separate spheres as a model of civilized domesticity and sought to impose this ideal on nonwhite, immigrant, and poor families as a precondition to their cultural assimilation. Thus, nonwhite women were compelled to exhibit middle-class norms of femininity and domesticity to counter notions of inferiority and prove their worthiness among the civilized races. Historian Louise Michelle Newman has pointed out the irony in that at the very moment that white women were rejecting a patriarchal model of domesticity and gender norms, many of these reformers were imposing these same rigid notions on nonwhite women.[6] Thus, although the ideal of separate spheres was rarely a strict reality for most women, it remained the dominant image of home life in the public imagination and the ideal of the middle class through at least the mid-nineteenth century.

By the late nineteenth century, the boundaries between the public and private spheres had become even more salient. A number of factors combined to encourage more women to seek opportunities to work, shop, and play in urban environments. Working-class women found employment in the growing number of factories in the major industrial urban centers. Between 1870 and 1920, the number of women wage earners in the United States increased dramatically from 1.72 million to 8.28 million. By 1920, approximately 24 percent of women workers were employed as mill or factory workers. Job opportunities also emerged in offices, shops, and department stores. Around 26 percent of working women were clerks, saleswomen, or stenographers in 1920.[7] As more women began to earn their own wages, producers recognized the significance of the female consumer and sought to draw women in as new customers by creating a shopping experience catered specifically to them. Restaurants and grocery and department stores attempted to attract middle-class women by constructing safe, gendered spaces for them to eat, shop, and socialize. Increased recreation and leisure activities also combined to draw women into the city center.

White middle-class reformers used the argument of separate spheres to justify their own movement outside of the domestic sphere. Female reformers argued that women's natural maternal instincts authorized their work to protect the interests of women and children of the working class. In an effort to preserve the femininity and virtue of wageworkers, middle-class women encouraged working girls to pursue careers that allowed them to maintain their feminine traits and protect them from the coarse nature of labor. By focusing on uplifting the working-class woman, these white women of the upper classes justified their own public work. Evolutionist theories that emphasized the superiority of Anglo-Americans as the most evolved race further justified the role of white women in the public sphere as civilizers of the masses. By the late nineteenth century, the concept of separate spheres had lost its appeal and utility.[8]

Still, the presence of these women in the public space created tension and cultural anxiety. The long association of the city streets with

Figure 3.2 "Smash the Masher! Cry Gotham Women in Crusade," *Day Book*, September 8, 1916, 14.

working-class women and prostitutes led middle- and upper-class women to fear that appearing in public threatened to tarnish their reputations by subjecting them to men's gaze. Shifting cultural norms required compromises to ease the anxieties generated by this sudden change.[9] Women seeking to maintain their respectable reputations negotiated their new, more public role in a variety of ways to eliminate any suggestion of impropriety. Women were advised to avoid communication or eye contact with individuals on the street, to wear modest, unimposing clothing, and to avoid drawing attention in any way. The fear of being identified as a working-class woman or even as a prostitute remained foremost in their minds. By seeking to make themselves virtually invisible in every way, women ensured the protection of their physical selves as well as their reputations as they ventured out into public.[10]

Women who challenged these social conventions laid claim to the public sphere in a variety of ways. Some working-class women ignored the warnings and rejected middle-class standards of modesty, instead choosing ostentatious displays of clothing or flirting with friends and strangers on the street as a means of asserting their independence.[11] At the other extreme, women seeking to preserve their reputation and maintain their personal distance from strangers determined to arm themselves with a variety of self-defense techniques as protection from any threat to their physical safety and dignity as they learned to navigate the urban environment. This was especially important as stories of the looming menace of street mashers, workplace harassers, white slavers, rapists, and shadowy strangers abounded.

## The Street Masher

Beginning in the late nineteenth century, newspapers offered accounts of the perils that awaited unescorted women who ventured into the cities by themselves. From annoying mashers to devious white slavers, danger lurked in the shadows of the city streets. A "masher" was a slang term used to describe a man who made unwelcome sexual advances toward women. These advances ranged from seemingly innocent flirtations to solicitations for sex and, in some cases, threats of sexual violence. Mashers clearly violated social conventions by seeking to close the physical distance and pierce the aura of invisibility created by the proper woman on the street. Norms of appropriate behavior were beginning to shift, and the masher took advantage of this precarious situation.[12]

The typical masher was described in the newspapers as a white, native-born male who was impeccably and loudly dressed, with gloves, cane, and hat. He was often described as older (thirty-five or older) and married. He smoked incessantly while waiting on the street corner for his prey. Though appearing much less frequently in popular constructions of the masher, young and single mashers were often depicted as traveling in herds and as more bold and unruly in their insults toward women, except when separated from the pack. The masher, young or old, was described as arrogant and conceited, overconfident in his flirting abilities. The masher's ego was believed to be the cause of the behavior. Mashers were described as a distinct species with observable and predictable habits. They grinned, ogled, and made goo-goo eyes at women. They "accidentally" brushed their legs and arms against ladies on streetcars. They catcalled or offered unsolicited compliments to women as they passed. The boldest of mashers threw his arm around the shoulder or waist of a woman and offered to walk her home, take her to the theater, or buy her a drink. The suggestion of impropriety undergirded every stare, remark, or touch.[13]

The women who were subjected to these repeated insults described feeling annoyed, threatened, and even fearful. The constant harassment felt like a barrage of assaults, and many women expressed a sense of violation of their person. As women increasingly found themselves the objects of unwanted sexual attention in a variety of public places, they demanded protection against these insults. Mary Collins took offense when, while watching a movie at a museum in New York with her two small children, she was annoyed by a masher. Isaac Moses approached her from behind and whispered, "Hello Dear," and then added, "Let's sneak out while it is dark and go next door and get a drink."[14] Moses may have been seeking feminine companionship for a drink or perhaps hoping for a sexual encounter. Regardless of his intent, the violation of respectability in directly speaking in public to a woman he did not know was enough for the vast majority of polite middle-class society to condemn the man. Law enforcement officials sympathized with Collins and arrested Moses. Magistrate Pool also concurred with the general feeling of disapproval of the man's behavior and held him on $1,000 bail until his trial. Collins's determination to press charges revealed her knowledge of her right to protection against such insults.

While Isaac Moses was perhaps more subtle in his approach, other mashers clearly stepped out of the bounds of propriety by suggesting that the mere presence of a woman on the street implied that she was sexually available. One New York City woman described being approached by a man who asked if she would have a glass of wine with him. When she refused and demanded that he leave her alone, he continued to follow her. Next he asked, "What's your price?" This insulting inquiry led the woman to have him arrested. Judge John J. Freschi sentenced the man to serve jail time for speaking to the woman in that way.[15] The masher's suggestion that she could be bought implied that any woman on the street was a prostitute. By demanding that the man

Figure 3.3 "What Can Be Done to Rid the Palmer House of Mash," *Chicago Daily Tribune*, February 4, 1906, F2.

be arrested, this woman was claiming her right to walk about the streets free both from assault and from the suggestion that she was only there for men's sexual pleasure.

The masher presence was widespread enough to become a topic of discussion in the nation's newspapers. News stories offered frequent accounts of men pestering women on the city streets. Esther Andrews, reporting on the issue of mashers in New York, declared "an epidemic of ogling and nudging by men" in the city.[16] Judge Charles E. Foster in Omaha, Nebraska, became so fed up with the problem that he vowed to prosecute these men to the fullest extent. Foster went so far as to create a sliding scale of fines ranging from ten to twenty-five-dollars depending on the severity of the insult.[17] Law enforcement and the courts began to take this type of harassment very seriously.

The newspaper accounts from this era overwhelmingly implicate native-born white men as mashers and white women as their victims. In the vast majority of cases the race or ethnicity of the instigator and his nativity are not mentioned directly, suggesting that the masher usually was a native-born white male. In cases where the masher was nonwhite or an immigrant, the newspapers frequently emphasized this, highlighting his "otherness." Reporters and victims sometimes described the masher simply as a "dark man," deflecting blame onto a nonwhite or immigrant "other."[18] Journalist Nixola Greeley-Smith shrewdly pointed out this tactic in an article on mashers in the January 2, 1917, edition of the

*Evening World.* The daughter of Horace Greeley, Nixola Greeley-Smith had made a name for herself as a journalist, writing for the *Evening World* from 1901 to 1919 and focusing on a variety of topics of interest to female readers. In her article from January 2, 1917, she detailed the masher problem at prominent hotels in the city such as the Waldorf-Astoria and the efforts of officials to eliminate it. Greeley-Smith quoted hotel authorities as saying that "nearly all mashers are foreigners." However, she had found "one bold spirit who was willing to admit that he (the masher) may be native to the soil as well as imported." Thus the reporter challenged the construction of mashers as "other." Greeley-Smith took this a step further by quoting hotel managers who declared "that no patron of a hotel is ever a masher. 'It is only people from outside who use the hotel lobby as a meeting place who are guilty of mashing,' I was assured." By including the phrase "I was assured" and placing this quote after her previous revelation of the potential dishonesty of hotel managers in reporting the true identity of the masher threat, Greeley-Smith cast more doubt on the credibility of the statement that the mashers came from outside the hotel. She challenged, then, not only the construction of the masher threat as a nonwhite other but also the class bias of hotel officials. At times, Greeley-Smith also cast doubt on the extent of the problem, suggesting that the obsession with the masher threat had been greatly overinflated.[19] Yet the tendency to deflect blame onto lower-class nonwhite and nonnative men was clear to the reporter, and this trend had serious implications, since immigrant and black men were often portrayed as sexual deviants who preyed on white women. An encounter with a nonwhite and/or nonnative masher thus suggested a much more sinister danger than a simple encounter with a white, native-born flirt.[20]

Despite some attempts to redirect blame for the masher menace onto nonnative men of other races, newspaper accounts overwhelmingly suggested that the masher was primarily a native-born white male, and his target was typically a middle- or upper-class white female. A review of three newspapers from Chicago, New York, and San Francisco for the period of 1900 to 1919 helped to unravel some of the mystery surrounding the masher. A search for the term "masher" in the *Chicago Tribune,* the *Evening World,* and the *San Francisco Chronicle* revealed that the masher menace was reported on much more frequently in Chicago than

Figure 3.4 "To Drive the Mashers Out of Chicago," *Chicago Daily Tribune*, January 27, 1907, F3.

in the other two cities. A breakdown of the individual cases across the three cities, however, reveals some common trends. Only 7 to 8 percent of the mashers were identified as foreign-born or non-Anglo. In a majority of the cases the masher's race, ethnicity, or nativity was not mentioned, suggesting that the culprit most likely was a native-born white male. When their occupation was mentioned, the mashers were nearly equally divided between skilled working-class men and professional men, with professional men in the majority at 52 percent. This trend was consistent across the three cities. Physicians, lawyers, government officials, salesman, and clerks were just as likely to be caught mashing as were laborers, factory workers, butchers, or plumbers. In an overwhelming 99 percent of the cases, the race of the woman assailed by the masher was not mentioned, suggesting that she was most likely a native-born white woman. Upper-, middle-, and working-class women all filed charges against mashers, yet the occupation of the victim was mentioned in only 10 percent of the cases, possibly suggesting that most of the victims were middle- to upper-class nonworking women. Mashers were frequently charged with disturbing the peace or disorderly conduct, and the severity of the sentence varied depending on the severity of the mashing. Cases of simple flirting often resulted in a fine of between $5 and $10. A masher who put his hands on the victim or followed her home was more likely to receive a higher fine of $50 to $100 or thirty to ninety days in jail. In some especially grievous cases, such as where the masher may have assaulted the victim, bystanders, or police officers, judges imposed sentences of up to six months in jail.[21]

In an effort to write a more salacious story or perhaps to elicit more public outrage, reporters often emphasized the whiteness and sexual purity of the female victims of mashers. Mary Collins was described as pretty, with a "perfect figure" and "laughing blue eyes." When she greeted the judge in court during the masher's trial, the reporter described her extending her "soft, pink" hand to the magistrate, implying her status as a respectable member of the white, civilized class. The reporter also carefully alluded to the victim's sexual respectability by highlighting Collins's shock at the masher's inappropriate suggestion and her distaste for the public notoriety that the incident generated.[22] Another reporter emphasized a mashing victim's whiteness by titling an article "She Smashed Masher with Her White Fists." An accompanying portrait revealed the profile of Alta Hyde Gilbert, a "young matron" of the white upper class. Another newspaper emphasized that Gilbert was "prominent in society" and "noted for her beauty."[23] The focus on these women's middle- or upper-class status and especially their whiteness reinforced the severity of the masher threat, especially to white men who were concerned with protecting the sexual purity of white women.

Black women were rarely mentioned in the newspapers as victims of mashers, although they most certainly were subject to harassment and assault on the streets. Newspapers produced by white men and intended for a white audience were less likely to report instances of harassment and violence against black women. Editors of mainstream newspapers may have chosen not to print articles about assaults against black women, assuming a lack of interest among their predominantly white readership. However, even black newspapers reported very few incidents of mashers harassing black women during the Progressive Era. A search through black newspapers such as the *Chicago Defender*, *Philadelphia Tribune*, *New York Amsterdam News*, and *Pittsburgh Courier* revealed only a handful of articles about mashers in the 1910s and 1920s. Historian Estelle Freedman found similar results in her research and has suggested, "Most black women had experience in navigating public space, where white men posed the greater threat. In the South they had long endured sexual insults from white men as they traveled, but they had little recourse for complaints."[24] Enduring assaults from both black and white men in the North and the South, black women knew that police officers would not take their complaints seriously. Oftentimes, the police officers themselves were responsible for assaults against black women.[25]

Black women also may have been reluctant to report sexual harassment and sexual assaults in a conscious attempt to resist the depiction of themselves in the white press as hypersexualized and immoral. In what Darlene Clark Hine has described as a culture of dissemblance, black women actively worked to protect the privacy of their personal lives by creating an outward image of forthrightness while in actuality keeping their personal lives a mystery. This allowed them to safely exist within a hostile white patriarchal society. Middle-class black women, in focusing their philanthropic activities on racial uplift projects, especially recognized the importance of establishing their public identity as moral and sexually virtuous. This was essential to combating stereotypes and protecting black women from sexual harassment and abuse. The desire to counter negative depictions of black women's sexuality and/or the fear of public condemnation and insinuations about one's virtue may have led some black women to avoid reporting sexual assaults to law enforcement authorities or to the press.[26] White women, on the other hand, did not assume the same risk to their reputations by reporting sexual assaults. The bodies of native-born white women were generally held in higher regard than those of black women and therefore were deemed worthy of protection.[27] In the early twentieth century, the white press encouraged women to speak out against mashers and prosecute them in court. Thus it gradually became less damaging to the reputation of middle- and upper-class white women to appear in court or have their names printed in the paper in the crusade against the masher.[28] Black women, facing much more social stigma, still hesitated to report assaults.

Following World War I, however, the harassment of black women by white men on the public streets became a more frequent topic in the black press. Hine argued that black women who left the rural South during the Great Migration were inspired not only by economic motives but also by a desire to escape the sexual subjugation they faced there from white and black men.[29] The corresponding increase in newspaper reports in the 1920s detailing the harassment and sexual violence against black women may reflect the expanding sense of autonomy among female black migrants to urban areas, especially as they came to realize that sexual exploitation plagued urban life as well.[30] An article in the *Chicago Defender* from 1924 described the harassment of a black woman, Estelle Richardson, by a white masher, John Elliot. Emphasizing Richardson's respectable status, the article noted that she was a "musician and a young woman of culture." Despite this, Elliot approached her on a subway car and began making inappropriate and insulting remarks. When Richardson rejected his propositions, Elliot grew angry and threatened her, saying, "If you were in Georgia I would have you strung up." The threat of racial violence did not deter Richardson from insisting on her rights as she replied that "she was not in Georgia and that it would be advisable for him to return to Georgia where he could commit those acts and get away with them." Elliot's anger reached a boiling point, and he moved to strike Richardson. He missed, however, and instead struck a white woman, Mrs. Gamey. Reflecting her privileged status as a native-born white woman, Mrs. Gamey's complaint to the police was immediately acted upon, and Elliot was arrested. The two women later appeared side by side in court to testify against him. The judge commended them for their pluck in standing up to the masher.[31]

Emphasizing the sexual respectability of black women, the black press focused on stories such as Estelle Richardson's to highlight efforts of black women in successfully fighting off white mashers.[32] In addition, black newspapers focused primarily on cases involving white male mashers in an effort to emphasize the harassment and insults that black women faced on public streets from white men. In one case, Mrs. Clyde Howell and Grace Garth were driving in Los Angeles when two white men in a car began flirting with them and following them. The women ignored the men's attentions despite their persistence. Eventually the men became so bold as to force the women to the curb and begin insulting their respectability. The women stepped out of the car and gave the mashers "a sound thrashing." In printing these incidents, the editors insisted on the sexual respectability of black women and their right to move unmolested on the city streets.[33]

Black women were also subject to harassment by black men, although there were substantially fewer accounts of these incidents in the papers. Estelle Freedman concluded that this makes sense given the antilynching movement's efforts to "refute white stereotypes of uncontrollable black male sexuality." Black women may have felt less threatened by encounters with black mashers, may have been more reluctant to report such incidents to authorities, or "may have felt constrained from reporting insults lest they fail to express solidarity with men of their race."[34] The reluctance to report incidents of black mashing may have reflected a conscious effort to resist attacks against a woman's modesty and the perpetuation of stereotypes of black female sexuality. However, it should not in any way be misinterpreted as evidence of black women's complacency regarding black male harassment and violence. Black clubwomen openly criticized black men for their failure to protect black women from assault and demanded that black men treat women of their race with more respect. Black periodicals echoed this call for black men to stop perpetuating white stereotypes of black female sexuality, to stop taking advantage of black women, and to live up to their obligation to protect black women from sexual harassment and assault.[35] Thus, for black society women and their supporters, protecting black women from abuse became part of a larger campaign to uplift the race.

The masher problem, as it impacted all women, began to demand so much attention that police were eventually forced to take more decisive action. Some law enforcement agencies responded by assembling special teams of undercover officers to catch mashers in the act of making unwanted advances toward women on the street.[36] Major cities such as San Francisco, Los Angeles, Chicago, and New York even hired female police officers to provide additional protection for women. These policewomen trained in both armed and unarmed combat in preparation for their law enforcement duties.[37] Recognition that women of all classes, ethnicities, and races were harassed by mashers and the necessity of hiring women who understood the nuances of the community and could sympathize with female victims led to calls for a diversified police force. In 1919, the New York Police Department hired an Italian policewoman to patrol the Italian quarter and a black policewoman to patrol in Harlem.[38] Police departments in Chicago, Los Angeles, and Washington, DC, also hired black female police officers in the 1920s, most likely in response to the demands of prominent black clubwomen and the black press, which called for more protections for black women against white and black mashers.[39] By 1920, 146 cities had hired female police officers to protect the morality of young women in urban spaces.[40] Mary Hamilton, chief of the New York women's squad, asserted that the threat was indeed very real and very serious, and she insisted that daily complaints from victims warranted swift action. The female officers were charged with the task of working undercover to identify and arrest men who harassed women on the streets.[41] Police officers, judges, reporters, and officers of women's clubs all condemned the masher and launched campaigns to eliminate the pest. Strict enforcement of ordinances against disorderly conduct, harsher fines and jail sentences, and public shaming in the newspapers represented the best efforts to deter the masher.

## The White Slaver

Middle- and upper-class reformers feared that women's economic dependence on men both inside and outside the workplace would ultimately lead to the moral ruin of young women. Low wages reinforced this female dependency. The reality was that social norms of courting and dating were quickly changing, especially among the working class. Because women earned substantially less than men, treating was becoming a more common practice in this era, as women often relied on suitors or male friends to treat them to movies or dinner. However, as the masher discussion suggests, accepting offers from strangers often stepped outside the boundaries of acceptable social conventions. Still, some young women ignored decorum, endured popular condemnation, and did so anyway. Other women actively sought to attract the attention of men through their appearance and flirtatious behavior to accrue their favor and therefore free meals and entertainment. The implication of sexual favors in return often accompanied the practice of treating. The actual extent of sexuality varied from innocent flirtation to sexual encounters.[42]

Moral reformers took this issue very seriously. They recognized that sites of public leisure such as dance halls, movie theaters, and amusement parks offered opportunities for mixed-sex interactions that represented potential threats to women's respectability. Alice Stebbins Wells, a Los Angeles police officer, described how mashers stood outside of movie theaters and offered to buy poor young girls tickets to the show. In exchange, the men expected sexual favors. According to Wells, the morally ruined girl then could be further tempted or forced into prostitution.[43] One young woman expressed her frustration with dating men who were only trying to pursue her sexually. She was equally annoyed, however, at how reformers implied that she would sell her body for a night out: "Where is the logic in thinking that a girl is going to sell her soul for a dinner at Murray's or a trip to Coney Island? If a girl is good, nothing under the sun can buy her honor, and if she's bad, surely she can command a higher price than that!"[44] Still, the assurances of these good girls did little to assuage the fears of the older generation.

Anxiety about the moral dangers that young women encountered in the city were exacerbated by popular stories in the national press of white slavers preying on innocent girls. Newspapers, magazines, and books told tales of unscrupulous men luring naive young women into a false sense of security with promises of dinner and movies. Once baited, the woman might be drugged and kidnapped and, upon waking, would find herself forced into a life of prostitution. Undercover policewomen Marian Wightman and Marie Crot in Chicago described the dangers of the "professional flirt," whom they claimed was actually a white slaver who seduced women into the trade. Rose, a seventeen-year-old girl, met a handsome young stranger in St. Louis. The man had to return to his home in New York City but promised to write. He sent many friendly letters from New York and eventually promised to marry Rose if she would come to the city. When Rose arrived via train in Chicago, Officer Crot observed her step off the train and sensed that this unescorted and inexperienced young lady seemed out of place. Crot spoke to Rose and learned that she was traveling on to New York City to meet her fiancé. Suspicious, Crot asked to read Rose's letters and immediately recognized the modus operandi of a white slaver. The most incriminating evidence was the insistence by the fiancé that Rose *not* speak to any policemen. Officer Crot broke the news to the young woman that her soul mate was most likely an unscrupulous white slaver and sent her home accompanied by her brothers.[45] Stories like these were used to warn young women about the danger of accepting gifts, meals, or movies from strangers.

Movie theaters proved to be not just the site of potential moral dangers but also a site for generating fear about the white slave threat. Fictional accounts in films such as *Traffic in Souls* (1913) and *The Inside of the White Slave Traffic* (1913) alerted the general public to the dangers that awaited women in the city, including kidnapping, sexual assault, and being forced into the sex slave trade. These stories of the dangers of city life as told through horrific accounts of sex trafficking obscured larger concerns about shifting gender norms and women's entry into the urban world of work and recreation.[46]

Popular constructions of white slavery also played into xenophobic stereotypes. Through novels, films, muckraker accounts, and stories in the popular press, the white slaver was often racialized as an eth- nic "other." The classic white slavery story described a young girl lured and seduced by a foreign predator in a metaphoric tale that reflected nativist fears of the immigrant threat facing the nation. Victims were almost always depicted as sexually pure young, white, and frequently middle-class women. As symbolic representations of America, these young virgins risked sexual violation and moral ruin by an immigrant threat. White slavers were almost always depicted as sexually deviant, foreigners (usually of Asian or southern or eastern European descent) who stalked or preyed on white victims. Nativists insisted that these new immigrants had inherent criminal propensities and therefore posed a danger to Anglo-Americans.[47] Yet the evidence failed to support that conclusion. Historian Robert Zeidel has shown that the findings of the Dillingham Commission (1907–1911), a congressional commission charged with investigating immigration and its effects, found no correla- tion between immigration and an increase in crime. Instead, the com- mission's findings revealed that native-born men were more likely to commit crimes than immigrant men.[48]

Thus, despite the stereotypes of foreign men preying on white middle-class women, those charged with and convicted of human traf- ficking under the Mann Act (which was intended to eliminate sex traf- ficking by making it a crime to transport women across state lines for immoral purposes), at least in the American West, were most frequently American-born, working-class white men.[49] The Mann Act was in- tended to eliminate sex trafficking by making it a crime to transport women across state lines for immoral purposes. The popular stereotypes revealed more about nativist anxiety over the perceived influx of mor- ally inferior immigrant hordes and eugenicist fears about the potential of miscegenation and race degeneration than they did about the reali- ties of human trafficking and sexual slavery in the Progressive Era. The existence of white slavery cannot be denied. However, discussions about the extent of the trade, the racial and ethnic diversity of its perpetrators, and the physical and emotional devastation that it inflicted on its victims were obscured by the public need to fix blame on a foreign threat.[50]

## The Rapist and the Shadowy Stranger

Although the white slavery peril figured more prominently in fiction than in reality, nevertheless late nineteenth-century and early twentieth-century cities could be very dangerous places. Jeffrey Adler's study of violence in Chicago concluded that the city had one of the highest homicide rates in the nation.[51] The potential for sexual or physical violence against women was clear in the accounts of several women who described their encounters with aggressive men on the streets. Eighteen-year-old Bertha Lehmann was walking one afternoon in New York City when Louis Kora approached her and said, "To see her was to love her, and as he had seen her, he was her slave." Lehmann walked away, ignoring Kora's flirtation, but he persisted. Kora approached Lehmann again, this time offering to take her to the theater. She declined once again and walked away, with Kora continuing to follow her. At this point Lehmann was clearly feeling threatened and at risk of physical attack by her pursuer. She turned quickly and punched him three or four times in the face before fleeing for help. Policemen arrested Kora, and he appeared in court with a disfigured nose and one eye badly swollen shut.[52]

Although most perpetrators stalked or accosted women with verbal insults, physical assaults were not uncommon. The bold man might brush against a woman's arm or leg, put an arm around her shoulder or waist, or even try to hug her. Accounts of more violent physical attacks appeared in the newspapers as well. In June 1912, Dorothy Watson was leaving her job at the telephone office in Los Angeles when she was confronted by a stranger who attempted to flirt with her. She spurned his verbal advances, but this only made him angry, and he punched her in the face and the head. Watson reacted by hitting her attacker with her purse. When the purse broke, she switched to using her fists.[53] Goldie Haugh was walking down the street in Frederick, Maryland, in 1919 with friends when a car pulled up alongside them. The men in the car offered to give the women a ride. When they denied the request, John Cramer jumped out of the car and grabbed and struck Haugh. The women managed to escape, and Cramer was arrested for assault.[54]

In some cases, attackers employed weapons to intimidate women. In New York in 1913, Martha Goldstein was walking home from a friend's house when she noticed she was being followed. Eventually the man caught up with her, and he took her by the arm and offered to serve as her escort. Startled by the aggressive suggestion, Goldstein responded by striking the man. He drew a knife and cut her in the face.[55] Stalking, physical assault, attempted kidnapping, and the use of a weapon implied that the stranger's intentions extended well beyond flirting.

Rape and sexual assault remained ever-present threats even though the words were rarely openly spoken. Sometimes the press would report that a man had "violated a woman's honor" or "criminally assaulted" his victim. Sensational, high-profile cases tended to dominate the headlines. In 1899, Henry Slipka earned the nickname of the St. Anthony Hill Terror in St. Paul, Minnesota. Slipka stalked women, mostly domestics, on their way home from work. Early accounts of his attacks described his method of sneaking up behind a woman, grabbing her by the throat, throwing her down, and robbing her.[56] Police suspected that his ultimate motive was rape. Julia Keefe survived an attack by Slipka and successfully fought back, after which Slipka was shot and captured by police. The court, however, sentenced him to only ninety days in the workhouse for his transgression.[57] Three years later, Slipka was arrested again. This time he was found guilty of attacking and robbing a sixteen-year-old girl and sentenced to six years and six months in prison. The newspapers suggested that his motive was both robbery and "criminal assault."[58]

In the search for a culprit, race figured prominently in the discussions about the dangers awaiting women on the street. Just as the white slaver was often racialized as an immigrant "other," the street rapist was often depicted as a foreign or black man who preyed on white women. During the post-Reconstruction era, the fear of racial mixing contributed to the construction of a powerful myth about a dangerous black male rapist. Allegedly unable to control his lust, the black rapist viciously attacked white women, dominating them physically and sexually. White vigilantes used the threat of a ravenous black beast intent on defiling the purity of white women to justify the practice of lynching and as proof of their own moral and racial superiority. The black rapist was thus added to the imaginary cast of characters who purportedly stalked and preyed on white women in the urban jungle. The scapegoating of black men and other men from allegedly primitive and uncivilized cultures served to obscure the truth about white men's violence against both white women and women of color. This conspiracy of silence that covered up the sexual violence of white men and instead exalted them as civilized exemplars of moral superiority and sexual integrity did not go unchallenged. The black press and middle- and upper-class black clubwomen resisted the construction of a racialized black rapist and repeatedly implicated white men for sexual assaults on black women. Their efforts to deconstruct pervasive and racist stereotypes in part reflected not only a campaign against the lynching of African American men but also an attempt to draw attention to the sexual victimization of black women.[59]

Among the other dangerous characters who reputedly roamed the city streets, the shadowy stranger also posed a threat, often portrayed through sensationalized stories about serial killers. The idea that someone would target women with a murderous intent was indeed terrifying, and real-life cases of serial killers created a frenzy of anxiety. The murders committed by serial killer Dr. Henry H. Holmes (whose actual name was Herman Webster Mudgett) in the vicinity of the Chicago World's Fair in 1883 horrified the city and aroused fear in the minds of many women. Holmes operated a hotel and drew his victims from among his female employees and guests. He had designed and built the hotel with the purpose of murder on his mind, incorporating soundproof, airtight rooms fitted with gas lines that he used to silently asphyxiate his victims. Holmes carried out dissections and medical experiments on the corpses in a room designed for those purposes, and he disposed of the bodies by cremating them in furnaces or dissolving them in pits of acid. In the end, Holmes confessed to twenty-seven murders, although he may have had many more victims. Although such heinous crimes were exceedingly rare, this real-life horror story enacted on the city streets of Chicago heightened existing tensions about women in the public sphere.[60] High-profile cases such as these brought the issue of violence against women to the forefront but rarely resulted in realistic or concrete solutions. Instead, the tendency was to focus on pointing the finger and assigning blame to some mysterious psychopathic stranger. The construction of the white male perpetrator as a deviant sociopath functioned to separate him from "normal" men and therefore to disassociate the average man from sexualized violence and to depict normal men as incapable of perpetrating violence against women. These men then were able to retain their moral reputation and their status as defenders of women.[61]

Larger concerns about the impacts of rapid industrialization, urbanization, and immigration and the changing roles of women culminated in the idea that the modern world was a dangerous place for women. Foreign white slavers, black rapists, and shadowy strangers earned notoriety in the press and came to represent the dangers that faced women who ventured out of the safe confines of their home. Some used these horror stories to regulate the movement and behavior of women and keep them restricted to rigid gender roles. Others insisted on efforts to make the streets safe for women. Reformers focused primarily and almost obsessively on the flirts who stalked their prey on street corners, waiting to sexually harass women who walked by. The press conflated mashers with murderers, with descriptions such as the following: "They are one with the depraved creature that commits burglary, murder, or nameless crimes, differing only that the depravity of their natures takes a different turn . . . they are as regardless of the rights and feelings of others as the cutthroat and holdup man possibly could be."[62] The masher proved a more visible and manageable scapegoat for law enforcement, which immediately began a campaign to crack down on these public nuisances. Community leaders, reformers, and the press rarely engaged in more complex discussions about the origins of and solutions to the issue of violence against women.[63] The masher was easier to catch and to prosecute, and campaigns to smash the masher offered a tangible answer to a deeper-rooted problem of violence against women. Other threats were frequently alluded to in discussions about the dangers women faced on the street; however, this focus on the outward threat of a deviant, mentally deficient, mostly innocuous, and almost comically stereotypical masher, diverted attention from the threats against women posed by perpetrators they knew.

## The Workplace Harasser

Despite the public attention on stranger danger, the sexual harassment and assaults that women encountered were neither committed primarily by strangers nor confined to the public street. Women were much more likely to confront an assailant in their places of employment. Although public discussion about the masher menace drew some attention to the issue, sexual harassment in the workplace was a generally unnamed and rarely discussed problem. Yet, for many working-class women, sexual harassment and even sexual assault in the workplace were an ever-present reality. Subject to the sexual innuendos, insults, and physical attacks of male coworkers and bosses, women seeking a solution found little public acknowledgment of the problem and little recourse.

Newspaper discussions about the masher menace often hinted at the more serious issues women faced. Some women found solace in writing about their concerns to female journalists, such as a New York woman who wrote a letter to journalist Nixola Greeley-Smith to tell her story. The letter writer claimed to have encountered sexual harassment continuously while working as a waitress, assistant teacher, seamstress, and stenographer:

> Many times I changed [jobs] to better myself, but mostly on account of attentions of the boss was forced to leave. Truthfully, during my entire business experience, from fourteen to twenty-seven, every married man I came in contact with in business (except three) tried to make love to me—I call it "love" to be charitable—and in every case absolutely without provocation on my part, for I've always been called good, refined, reserved and haughty. Married men make business girls the receptacle for their domestic troubles, it's always their wife is narrow, slow, does not sympathize with nor understand him, and he needs a congenial, intellectual comrade and companion.[64]

This woman's candid account of her experience helped to illuminate the extent of the problem.

Other women also anonymously shared accounts of their encounters with sexual harassment in the workplace. A nineteen-year-old New York woman who worked in a store described being annoyed by her boss, who kept insisting she go out with him: "Because I don't do as he wishes he is making my work hateful to me by making me do everything and always finding fault." Anticipating comments from critics who would question why she continued to work there, the woman explained that she had to endure her boss's harassment because her parents had died when she was a child, and she relied on her aunt for financial support. As the woman viewed the situation, "To take his insults means lowering myself and to resist them means ruin to my aunt and to me."[65] She clearly felt the powerlessness that her economic dependency created in this situation. Sexual harassment on the job posed a different, and most likely more common, kind of threat than did an encounter with a strange man on the street.

This was especially true for lower-class women who depended on their wages to help support their families. The threat of losing one's job for reporting indiscretions by their bosses had dire consequences for these women. One young woman wrote to Laura Jean Libbey at the *Chicago Tribune* to ask advice. She explained that her father had been injured in an accident at work, and she had been working as a stenographer to supplement the family income. The increasing attentions of her boss, however, were causing her great distress. He would demand she stay late at work and attempt to touch her hand. She repeatedly declined his requests that she accompany him to dinner. He would complain that he was unhappy in his life with his wife at home. The young stenographer found the repeated inappropriate requests of her boss unsettling but saw few options for resolving the conflict other than leaving her job. The limited recourses that women had in such situations revealed the vulnerability of their positions. Female journalists, like Libbey, felt compelled to draw more attention to the issue by writing articles and printing letters such as these in an effort to demand a solution.[66]

Increasingly, the campaigns of moral reformers and government investigations into the conditions of women workers revealed the prevalence of sexual harassment in the workplace. An investigation conducted by the Senate Commission on Industrial Relations in 1914 disclosed numerous cases of men sexually harassing women who worked in department stores. Benjamin Gitlow of Brooklyn, New York, testified before the committee, explaining his observations as president of the Retail Clerks' Union. Gitlow described how young women, fearing job loss and dependent on their meager wages to pay the rent and sustain themselves and sometimes their families, endured repeated harassment from male coworkers, bosses, and clients. One twenty-three-year-old woman, who worked as the head of stock in a department store, described the repeated advances of a colleague. She explained that the high cost of living coupled with low earnings created a desperate situation for young women like her.[67] Workingwomen of color likewise faced a great deal of harassment in the workplace. A 1911 Senate report on women and children working in the glass industry included an account of black women in one factory who had repeatedly complained about their male coworkers carrying on obscene conversations. Sexual assaults were also a frequent problem in the factory.[68]

## Backlash and Blaming the Victim

The discussion of the dangers posed to women by male aggressors elicited some backlash from critics. Responses ranged from those who denied the problem entirely or recommended that women stay at home to those who blamed the victims for the attacks. Some went so far as to argue that the women were in essence "asking for it" through their manner of dress or behavior.[69] Behind the propaganda of the backlash, the reality of a culture that contributed to the physical and sexual subjugation of women was made abundantly clear.

The most common example of backlash was to insist that the problem was not real. Some people publicly challenged the popular conception of the masher threat and accused the newspapers and magazines of exaggerating the dangers of the city or altogether fabricating the threats for dramatic effect. One female doctor who frequented the streets at all hours in the course of her job duties posed the question to other female workers of whether or not "there is any such thing as a real masher." She told reporters from the *Washington Post*, "I've been a doctor for twenty years, out at all hours and in all parts of the town, and I've never met a masher."[70] By questioning the very existence of the masher, critics minimized the reality of sexual harassment and violence that women faced in their daily lives. Reporter Marguerite Mooers Marshall dismissed the masher threat, arguing that the streets were safe for women and that "only the hysterical woman talks of actual danger."[71]

Another common early reaction was to insist simply that women stay at home. Conservative thinkers generally advised women to avoid going out in public. However, Anna E. Blount, a Chicago doctor, pointed out the ridiculousness of this solution: "We were told at that time by the commissioner of police that it would be well for all the respectable women of the city to remain indoors after 8 o'clock in the evening unless they were escorted by a gentleman! Imagine when the telephone rings for a woman doctor to attend some critical case that she shall be required to either get a male escort or remain at home!" Blount argued that women physicians needed the right to vote to help create safer city streets and secure their right to move about freely to practice their profession.[72]

Recognizing the necessity of women's movement in public spaces, some concerned people suggested that if a woman must be out on the streets alone, she should try to render herself less visible. Advice manuals suggested that women should dress modestly and speak quietly. Women were also advised to walk quickly to their destination while avoiding making eye contact with strangers or asking for assistance.[73] In 1914, New York City judge John J. Freschi insisted that to avoid unwanted attention from mashers and potential attackers a woman "should dress quietly and strive to make her general appearance refined and inconspicuous."[74] This advice offered a rather passive approach that discouraged women from claiming public space.

Others argued that if women needed to venture out into the public sphere, they should rely on male relatives for guidance and protection. In 1885, the St. Paul Daily Globe suggested that to deal with possible harassers, a woman "take her husband, father or brother" and "turn the male protector loose on them." In the absence of a male relative, women were encouraged to seek the assistance of law enforcement: "If she has no proper male protector, or should be insulted while on the street alone, she should at once call a policeman to her defense and have the brute arrested."[75] However, some women complained that police officers, their supposed male protectors, ignored their requests for help. A thirty-seven-year-old woman insisted, "What's the use of having them arrested? They are allowed to go and called gallant for worrying a girl several blocks."[76] One New York woman reported to a police officer that a man had attempted to "detain and drag" her; rather than arresting the man, the officer insisted that the woman must have "made eyes at him."[77]

By blaming the victim, some skeptics suggested that women were responsible for the inappropriate behavior of men they met on the street.
A reporter for the *Los Angeles Herald* declared that it was "not always the
men" who were to blame. "She who 'looks neither to the right nor to the
left' is never accosted. It is only those who trip along in a semi-inviting
manner and look as if they had lost somebody that are accosted." The
author noted that crowds of boisterously chatting young girls attracted
attention, and the absence of chaperones also invited the advances of
the masher. The author further condemned the woman whose "eyes are
'here, there and everywhere,' and they glow upon a masher as they pass,
half inviting him to venture a remark."[78] The writer recommended that
women mind their own business and try to make themselves invisible in
public. The woman who failed to do so invited the attack of the masher.
This deflection of blame from the aggressor to the victim, however,
served only to downplay the real extent of the problem.

Other cynics went so far as to argue that women blackmailed men
by threatening to accuse them of being mashers. One male author suggested that New York women swindled unsuspecting men by engaging
them in conversation and then threatening to turn them in as mashers if
they did not pay the women to keep quiet.[79] In answer to the question of
what causes the masher to behave the way he does, a thirty-one-year-old
bachelor from Newton, New Jersey, concluded, "It is the overdressed or
'sporty' girl or woman." He argued that overly dressed women attracted
the flirtations of men with the intent to use them for their money.[80] In
1914, a New York City reporter asked Judge John J. Freschi if women
made false charges against innocent men for purposes of "blackmail or
for self-advertisement." Judge Freschi agreed that that was a possibility
and suggested, "A woman who by her dress or manner challenges attention ought not to be surprised if she gets it. I have no sympathy with the
woman who lures a man on and then is highly insulted because he rises
to her hook."[81]

Some doubters reacted by turning the tables and suggesting that
women were the actual aggressors. The *Washington Times* reported that
there was a general problem with girl mashers in the city who were in
the "heart-smashing business." Gaudily dressed with hat, veils, flowers,
and ribbons, the female mashers attracted the attention of their prey.
Such a woman's irresistible appearance was sure to "break the heart of

Figure 3.5 "How to Defend Yourself," *San Francisco Call*, August 21, 1904, 11.

the most foppish masher that ever smirked on a corner."[82] This sort of role reversal of the stereotypes not only served to playfully critique the idea of any real masher threat but also sought to criticize the stereotypes of men as sexual aggressors and women as passive victims.

Scholars have noted that in the popular narrative, especially in the early twentieth century, women were often depicted as either helpless victims or seductive temptresses. The image of an overly dressed female masher who manipulatively sought the attention of men through loud fashion and scandalous behavior was closely related to the seductive temptress stereotype. However, this behavior more likely reflected a subtle shift in fashion and sexual mores occurring in the early twentieth century among men and women of the working class.[83] Yet this shift should not be used to justify women's sexual exploitation or obscure the reality of sexual violence and assault for women. While in some ways they were rebelling against the sexual values of earlier generations and creating a style of their own, young working-class women remained in a state of economic and sexual dependency that revealed a potentially dangerous vulnerability.[84]

Women's rights advocates of the era recognized the danger in downplaying the threats against women and especially attacked the suggestion by critics that women were essentially "asking for it" through their manner of dress and behavior. Nixola Greeley-Smith struck back by stressing that women were not in any way inviting sexual harassment through their clothing and countering the argument of a man who believed that only women who wore makeup were targeted by mashers. The "New York masher cares not at all whether the woman he pursues is promisingly spectacular in her attire or make-up. He is just as likely to speak to a country school girl in a muslin dress as to a queen of burlesque."[85] Greeley-Smith insisted that a woman may be pestered by a masher

> whether she is attired soberly or indiscreetly—any day at the noon hour as she leaves her place of employment she is likely to hear an oily voice call over her shoulder, "Come to lunch, now, do!" If she is shopping and sees some garment in a window that may be what she is looking for, she dares not stop even for a moment, for she knows that if she does some elderly unknown satyr will remark with a leer: "out for a little stroll? May

Figure 3.6 "Iceland Girl Shows the American Girl How to Repel a Masher," *Omaha Daily Bee*, April 12, 1914, magazine section.

I join you?" If she lunches alone she cannot raise her eyes from her plate without encountering some ingratiating masculine ogle that would be laughable if it were not so insulting.[86]

In countering the argument that plain dress may be used as a method of deterrence, Greeley-Smith noted, "Nothing is further from the truth! Here you may look as modest as St. Agnes and some day, as you are walking about your business, an oily voice will say over your shoulder, 'Come to lunch,' or 'May I walk with you?' or even 'Aren't you feeling lonesome, little girl?'"[87] Modest or "proper" clothing thus failed to protect women from sexual harassment and, by implication, violent assault.

Frustrated by the general backlash, some writers suggested that women should take the problem into their own hands. Greeley-Smith stressed that women had the power and the right to resist unwanted advances: "I have no sympathy for the woman who cannot rid herself of a man's unwelcome attention or pursuit . . . one short, brutal sentence, one tiny shaft of ridicule, and the most persistent lady killer is rendered harmless."[88] At times, she downplayed the masher threat and seemed to criticize working-class women who encouraged the attentions of mashers.[89] At other times, she acted as their defender, countering sexist notions that women invited harassment. Ultimately, however, she insisted that women who experienced unwanted attention on the street had the power to fight back against sexual harassment and assault. Greeley-Smith wrote lengthy articles with accompanying illustrations to detail exactly how a woman could physically fight back against attacks on her physical safety.

Fighting Back

The idea that women had the ability to eliminate the masher threat and protect themselves from more violent attacks was radically empowering. Through self-defense training, women rejected the notion that they needed white men to serve as their protectors. Instead, women began to recognize their right and ability to protect themselves. Frances Howlett Write of the Purity Federation in New York insisted, "Women must help themselves." She urged women to resist sexual harassment by verbally standing up for themselves. Describing an incident on a streetcar with a man who kept trying to make physical contact with her by rubbing his knee against hers, Write explained how she turned to him and said, "You and I cannot ride in the same car and I am not going to leave." The man left, embarrassed. Write said that "women have it in their own hands to stop this indecent practice." Reporter Esther Andrews declared a "smash masher" crusade for the women of New York City and insisted on women's ability to resist the masher by verbally or physically striking back.[90] When, in 1909, a woman stenographer in New York turned the tables on a masher, punching him in the face, she told authorities, "The police can't be everywhere at once, I decided to take care of myself." She explained to a newspaper reporter that she had taught women boxing in Alabama, where she came from, and she would teach New York women boxing as well.[91]

The woman who engaged in boxing or jiu-jitsu as a form of self-defense training confronted her perceived unsafe world head-on, claiming her body and, indeed, the city, as her own.[92] In 1889, the Los Angeles Times announced the opening of an athletic club for women in the city. The reporter insisted that the training of women in self-defense was essential to protect them from mashers. One mother explained that she would feel more comfortable knowing that her three daughters were physically capable of defending themselves: "Our girls would not be insulted so often on the streets if the brainless puppies who make a business of annoying unprotected females know that our girls can strike out from the shoulder with telling effect." She further argued, "The average women of today, except in England and some of the Eastern States, are as helpless as infants when they are alone; but how different it would be if they were taught the science of self-defense."[93] She clearly saw self-defense training as a way of preparing her daughters to stand up for themselves against male aggressors and assert their right to walk down public streets safely.

Stories of women successfully protecting themselves and fending off violent assaults fueled the trend of female self-defense training. Sordid tales of women's victimization appeared in print media along with successful accounts of brave women fighting back through their own will and power. Newspapers reported that Blanche Bates fought off an attacker in the streets of New York in 1901. Bates, who credited her boxing training for her success in defending herself, stated, "I would not advocate any woman going through life leaving a trail of bruised masculinity in her wake, but if a man insults her, she ought to know where to use her fist on him where it will do the most good."[94] Bates insisted that all women should be able to protect themselves from such insults by training in the art of self-defense.

Law enforcement and the courts increasingly showed support for women who chose to act as their own protectors. Alexander Mullowney, a police court judge in Washington, DC, urged women to protect themselves on the streets and promised them impunity in his courtroom.[95] Mayor George W. Dilling and chief of police Claude Bannick of Seattle similarly insisted that if "a masher accosts a woman she is certainly justified in giving him a good, stiff punch on the point of the jaw."[96] This endorsement of women's self-defense contributed to a general change in attitude regarding the rights of women over their own bodies and the ability of women to defend themselves.

The organization of self-defense clubs suggested the formal ways that some women chose to empower their bodies and claim their right to freely occupy public spaces. In 1906, Virgie Drox determined to form a jiu-jitsu club for the women of Los Angeles after having seen similar clubs organized in New York. Her intent, she stated, was to allow women the security of defending themselves on the street: "The girls in New York who are members of the club never think of having an escort if they want to visit one another after dark and from examples of their prowess I would think it inadvisable for any masher to attempt to speak to them."[97] The idea that self-defense training eliminated the need for a male escort was especially empowering to women like Drox who were socially and politically active and frequently traveled throughout the city.

Figure 3.7 "Safe from Attack," *Cosmopolitan*, June–November 1910, advertising section.

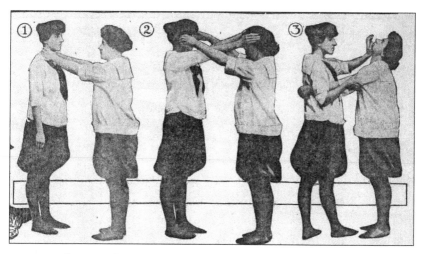

Figure 3.8 Edna Egan, "Every Woman Her Own Bodyguard," *Ogden Standard*, July 14, 1917, magazine section, 23.

The rising popularity of jiu-jitsu and boxing classes was a trend that was especially common among native-born white women of the upper classes. Young women may have learned some self-defense in high school or college. In 1914, fifty girls at Lewis and Clark High School in Spokane, Washington, enrolled in a self-defense class in which the instructor, Jack Carnahan, told them they would learn techniques to stop attackers: "A couple of short hooks to the jaw, a jab from a skillfully handled umbrella, or a forced back flip on a hard pavement will do much more than moral suasion to repulse unwelcome attentions."[98] Similar courses were offered in other high schools across the nation from New Jersey to Los Angeles.[99] Universities also provided opportunities for women to learn self-defense. Women at Nebraska State University were encouraged to enroll in boxing classes, and images from Temple University and Barnard College show female students practicing both boxing and jiu-jitsu.[100] After these elite women graduated from college, many joined athletic clubs for society women. In 1904, women in Boston started the New Hub Athletic Club, which offered classes in jiu-jitsu.[101] By 1920, more than 200 girls were reportedly studying boxing at the Albert Barnes Club in Philadelphia.[102] Older women found opportunities to learn self-defense through their churches and social clubs. The women of Wesley Methodist Church in Chicago formed their own jiu-jitsu classes. Motivated by a concern about arming themselves with techniques to prevent victimization, the church ladies advocated carrying cayenne pepper as a means of defending themselves against potential attackers.[103]

Working-class women also eagerly signed up for free self-defense courses when the opportunity presented itself. Responding to the demands of women who complained about harassment as they traveled to and from work, some companies offered self-defense classes for employees. A department store in Newark, New Jersey, hired a professional boxer to teach its female employees self-defense. This on-the-job training provided additional tools to safeguard women from threats that prevented them from freely pursuing public occupations.[104] Although middle- and upper-class women had more access to self-defense training, the fact that women of all social classes trained in self-defense when they could suggested a common sense of female solidarity in their efforts to resist gender-based violence.

Women who did not take formal self-defense courses could pursue a program of home training. The Yabe School of Jiu-Jitsu in Rochester, New York, offered free lessons through the mail. According to advertisements for this program, learning these simple techniques would enable "a little woman to overthrow a big, powerful man," affording "sure protection from attack by thieves and thugs."[105] Books offered in-depth tutorials on how women could privately prepare themselves for defensive combat. In 1904, Harry Hall Skinner insisted that the purpose of his book *Jiu-Jitsu* was to teach any man or *woman* how to defeat "a more powerful assailant."[106] Harrie Irving Hancock wrote three books in 1904 and 1905 designed to teach men, women, and children self-defense through jiu-jitsu.[107]

Films could also serve as primers on self-defense. A short film, starring the vaudeville actress and boxer Vera Roehm and produced by Paramount-Bray Pictograph, promised to teach "the Womanly Art of Self-Defense." In an article in the 1918 *Toronto World*, Roehm was quoted as saying, "Women would do well to learn boxing. . . . It would teach them to take care of themselves at all times. The vast majority are helpless at present if insulted or attacked as often happens in cities and country."[108] In the film, Roehm "gives a forceful illustration of how with such a knowledge a woman may maintain her right to sit on a park bench unmolested."[109]

Newspapers also published articles and illustrations that detailed step-by-step techniques to fend off a variety of potential attack situations. Articles targeting female readers offered illustrations so that women could teach themselves the techniques in the privacy of their own homes, learning everything from the manipulation of wrist, elbow, and shoulder joints to more deadly techniques such as gouging the eyes, strikes to the nose or throat, and the use of weapons. The fighting techniques described in the various articles and books were intended to cause bodily harm. The degree of force recommended to repel the masher suggested the seriousness of the threats that women faced. One writer described how a woman could place a man's arm in an elbow lock and with a "quick jerk with her shoulders" break his arm "as though it were a pipe stem." After throwing the man on the ground and kneeling on his ribs, "she braces the captured arm against her other knee and holds the man captive until the police arrive. Should the man struggle the girl is still the master and can break the bone with a light pressure on the tortured arm."[110] These techniques were designed to subdue the attacker, but the author noted that the woman also had the option to use force to break the assailant's bones.

Although articles on self-defense rarely mentioned the attacker's intent, the images alluded to a variety of serious situations. The aggressor was usually shown grabbing a woman's arm or waist, but the implication was that his true intent was physical or sexual assault. Pickpocketing or robbery was sometimes suggested as the motive of the attack. One article recommended using self-defense techniques to defend against "the ruffian who attempts to steal your brooch."[111] An ad for the Yabe School of Jiu-Jitsu in *Cosmopolitan* showed a woman twisting an assailant's wrist and elbow to gain control of his gun-wielding arm.[112] Some articles showed the attacker poised with his hands around the woman's throat, attempting to strangle his victim. Although rape was seldom mentioned as the motive for an attack, the aggressive nature of the attacks and the recommended techniques to defend against them hinted at the possibility of sexual violence.

The countertechniques detailed in the images and articles were often deadly and clearly intended to protect a woman against violent physical assault, rape, or murder. Edna Egan asked her readers what they would do if they ever "felt an assailant's hands on your throat." She went on to provide descriptions and illustrations demonstrating how to break a strangle-hold, culminating in a move that threw the assailant to the ground. Egan recommended kneeling on the attacker's back to hold him down until the police arrived.[113] Instructors insisted on using deadly force, if necessary, to stop an assault. An article in the *San Francisco Call* showed a woman repelling a stranglehold attack by jamming a hat pin into a man's face. The article also demonstrated how a woman could use the heel of her palm to strike a man in the nose or her thumbs to gouge an attacker's eyes.[114]

Ruth Helen Lang suggested that women should use whatever force was necessary to stop a violent assault. Lang directly contradicted the perception of the female as a passive victim and insisted that women use their self-defense skills to incapacitate an attacker. She advised: "To knock a man out, hit him with the fist just on the chin point. To drop him, hit him just beneath the ear. To put him out of commission, land him on the bridge of the nose between the eyes. If he comes up behind you, suddenly swing backward quickly with your elbow." Lang further advised: "Remember, sisters, don't lose your nerve. Hit and hit hard . . . cultivate your nerve and your punch, and soon the race of mashers will be but a bruised and battered memory."[115] Lang believed that letting go of hesitation and fear was essential to success in a self-defense situation. Photographs published in the newspaper graphically illustrated the techniques she described.

Learning self-defense techniques from a mail-order pamphlet, book, or newspaper article not only made self-defense training accessible to a wider range of women but also had lifesaving implications for some women. In October 1905, the *New York Times* reported an incident in which a woman used self-defense techniques she had read about to defend herself against a mugger. The assailant grabbed her pocketbook as she was walking through Central Park. Rather than scream or freeze in terror, she put him in a jiu-jitsu hold. The angered attacker pushed her against a fence and threatened to kill her if she did not give up her possessions. The woman refused to do so and instead held him in a jiu-jitsu lock until the arrival of the police, who were surprised by her cool demeanor. The woman explained that she would never "run from any man of that kind who lives."[116] Although she had no formal training in self-defense, she told officers that every woman should learn jiu-jitsu.

In a battle to protect their body and life, women were encouraged to employ any means possible to defend themselves. Everyday objects such as parasols, umbrellas, and hat pins were also advocated as means of self-defense. Some women apparently took this advice to heart. After getting off a train in Omaha, Nebraska, in 1913, a young woman was followed by a man who pinched her arm and called her "some cute chicken." She responded by stabbing him with a hat pin.[117] A woman walking home after seeing an ailing friend was approached by a man who said that "he would like her company." She responded to his request by hitting him several times over the head with her parasol until it broke.[118]

The idea of women studying and using self-defense to protect themselves engendered a great deal of anxiety and fear especially among white men, who, as we have seen in previous chapters, were already anxious about threats to white masculinity. A physically empowered female body represented a serious threat to a white man's position at the top of the sexual hierarchy and to his perceived identity as a protector of women. However, by promoting women's self-defense as a means for women to defend themselves in the absence of their white male protectors, some self-defense advocates managed to rationalize women's boxing and jiu-jitsu as a way of reinforcing the existing hierarchy and seemingly reaffirming white men's status as the primary protectors of white womanhood. Furthermore, recasting the perpetrator as a nonwhite and/or nonnative male obscured the sexual offenses committed by white men and positioned them as polar opposites of primitive and bestial men of "other" races. Women's self-defense posed little threat when it was suggested as a means of protecting white women against attacks from nonwhite men and therefore helping to preserve their bodies for white men.

Despite the rhetoric, however, the irony was that most of the perpetrators of violence against women on the street were native-born white men. Women's self-defense therefore represented an unstated but powerful challenge to the sexual domination of women by white men. The fact that most of the women who advocated and trained in self-defense were middle- and upper-class, native-born whites suggests a gendered breakdown in the solidarity of whiteness as they physically disputed the rights claimed by the men of their own race and social class.

## Class Matters

White upper- and middle-class reformers also recognized in self-defense training a means of protecting and potentially preventing the moral downfall of working-class women. Concern about the predominance of sexual predators on the street and in the workplace led reformers to consider how they could help protect the sexual purity of workingwomen. Applying the doctrine of protection to their social welfare work, these women took on the role of protector of working-class women—ironically, at the same time that they were rejecting their own confinement in the role of the protected. In the process, they found a means of exerting political power without upsetting their predefined gender roles.[119]

Progressive reformers had already made the argument that athletics was a means of protecting young working-class women from immoral influences. Gertrude Dudley, the director of the Women's Department of Physical Education at the University of Chicago, and Frances A. Kellor wrote a book titled *Athletic Games in the Education of Women* (1909). Dudley, a pioneer in women's athletics, created the Women's Athletic Association in 1904 at the University of Chicago, which sponsored a variety of sports clubs for female students. Prior to writing the book, Kellor, one of the first female graduates of the sociology program at the University of Chicago who later worked on behalf of working-class immigrant women, was also an advocate of equality between men's and women's physical education programs.[120] In their book, Dudley and Kellor stressed that athletic play, in addition to being necessary for women's physical well-being, was important for solving "city problems," especially those associated with dance halls. They insisted that play was "a great safeguard against immorality, since it provides a normal, wholesome outlet for physical energy."[121] Progressive ideals about the influence of the environment thus figured prominently into their analysis of the value of athletics training for women.

Other progressives recognized the value of athletics in helping women counteract the negative effects of urbanization and industrialization, and elements of the desire for social control are evident in their discussions as well. In his book *The Woman Citizen: A Problem in Education* (1918), Horace A. Hollister, a professor of education at the

University of Illinois, wrote that athletic training was especially important for keeping working-class women away from the negative influence
of unhealthy and morally degenerate forms of recreation such as dance
halls, cabarets, theaters, moving picture shows, and amusement parks.
Hollister insisted, "Too often the only escape from the racking grind,
or even brief respite from their sordid existence, is to be found through
a doorway that leads to degradation and shame. Long hours and a low
wage bar them from effective membership in any organized movement
for wholesome recreation and social enjoyment."[122] Hollister supported
efforts to expand healthful leisure and recreational programs for workingwomen. The purpose, he insisted, was to "rescue and uplift the vast
crowds of young womanhood from this mad and hopeless struggle in
this 'dead sea' of modern civilization."[123] Proponents of boxing and jiu-
jitsu training relied on similar arguments in pointing out the benefits
of self-defense in uplifting and protecting working-class women. Self-
defense as a form of athletic training served the dual purpose of providing a healthy outlet for excess physical energy and also protecting
women's bodies from violation and therefore moral ruin.

Working women, however, often resented the attitude of moral superiority of the reformers and their implication that working-class women
were in need of rescue and uplift. They also resented the suggestion
that they required moral policing. Nevertheless, workingwomen did
recognize the benefits of self-defense training in fighting back against
harassment and assault. Some elite white women, such as Anne Morgan, managed to walk a fine line, balancing her interests as a reformer
with the concerns of workingwomen who expressed annoyance at the
continual harassment they faced on the street and on the job. Morgan
desired to empower working girls to act as their own protectors through
self-defense training. The daughter of the financier John Pierpont Morgan, Anne Morgan used her wealth to support philanthropic efforts on
behalf of working-women. Morgan was a union activist and suffragist
who worked to bring attention to the plight of immigrant workers. In
1912, she arranged for four men and four women jiu-jitsu instructors
with the Barnum and Bailey Circus to come teach self-defense to more
than 500 working girls in New York City. Her explicit goal in forming
the jiu-jitsu class was to prepare the working girls to protect themselves
from attackers on the street.[124]

Yet even Morgan's organization was not completely altruistic as it reflected many of the social control goals of Progressives and the ideals of purity reformers. Morgan's self-defense class was organized under the auspices of the Working Girls Vacation Club. The vacation club movement was an attempt to provide opportunities for working-class girls to take a break from the demands of city life through healthful recreation. One component of this movement advocated a Vacation Savings program for working-women to help them save for occasional retreats to the country to rest, renew their health, and get away from the immoral temptations of city life.[125] The vacation clubs also hosted athletic activities, such as jiu-jitsu. Writing in *Munsey's Magazine* in 1913, Hugh Thompson explained that the larger goal behind these efforts was to teach women to use "all those public utilities which are theirs by virtue of their citizenship. With this knowledge comes the equipment which makes them better and more healthful mothers, sisters, and citizens generally."[126] The author further argued that the vacation movement helped to make women more efficient employees, a key concern of some Progressive reformers.

Regardless of the intent of reformers, workingwomen pursued self-defense training for their own purposes. The daily reality of sexual harassment and violence prompted them to take advantages of opportunities such as those offered by Morgan to learn how to protect themselves. When telephone operator Nellie Griffin was ogled and pestered by a masher on her way home from work in Oakland, California, she repeatedly rebuked his advances, but he continued to follow her and at one point grabbed onto her arm. Frustrated and offended, Griffin clenched her fist and punched the man square in the face. She later explained to a male reporter, "If you could be forced to stand everlasting insults that a woman is, you could understand why I acted as I did tonight. I have waited too long for some bystander to take up the fight for me, but as no one ever volunteered, I was compelled to assert my rights. No man has a right to seize my arm and attempt to detain me on the street." Griffin clearly articulated her right to serve as her own protector, rejecting the notion that she needed someone to save her, someone to act on her behalf and take up the fight. Instead, Griffin recognized that she had the right to defend herself.[127]

Despite all the talk about protecting workingwomen from moral threats and the sense of empowerment that self-defense training offered workingwomen, some critics recognized the limitations of physical expressions of power and the shortcomings of reformers who attempted to "protect" women in this way. For example, a Socialist Labor Party newspaper criticized Anne Morgan for her narrow-mindedness, insisting that the stated intent of teaching jiu-jitsu to shopgirls to protect them from mashers and dangerous men on the street missed the mark. Instead, Morgan "forgot to explain how the shop girls' acquisition of jiu jitsu expertness would protect them against those worst of 'mashers and rowdies'—the employers, together with the pets of these, inside the shops." The consequence would be that the employers would "put in operation against the girls the Capitalist Class jiu jitsu of 'firing' the girls and throwing them breadless, sprawling upon the street."[128] The limitations of jiu-jitsu as a means of self-defense are thus made readily apparent in considering the limited power and protections of women in the workplace. More radical reformers recognized the inherent inequalities in the existing hegemonic structure and demanded change, especially with regard to women's economic dependence on men.

## Conclusion

The rapid industrialization and urbanization of the nation in the late nineteenth century provided new opportunities and redefined gender norms, especially for middle- and upper-class white women. As these women increasingly moved into the public sphere, differing class-based views of acceptable behaviors sometimes led to conflict. The clash of cultures on the city streets required a renegotiation of social norms. Middle- and upper-class white women unaccustomed to strange men addressing them on the street had to redefine the limits of acceptable behavior for themselves and for the men they encountered. Learning to identify and assess danger from the solicitations of the innocuous flirt to the more perilous threat of a potential sexual assailant required skills of self-defense that many women lacked. The idea of physical empowerment, although radical in its time, was part of a larger Progressive Era conversation about enabling women to navigate the new, potentially dangerous urban environment. The trend of women's self-defense training was spurred on by fears of the dangers that women faced as they increasingly moved into the public realm. As middle-class women began to more freely walk the streets, ride streetcars, shop, and visit dining or entertainment establishments in the early twentieth century, they increasingly claimed their right to public space. At a time when middle- and upper-class white women considered it socially unacceptable for men to speak to them in public, the specter of physical assault and especially rape engendered so much fear that it made the radical idea of white female physical empowerment seem less threatening. Society women justified their movement into the public sphere with evolutionist rhetoric and utilized self-defense training as another tool in their campaign to uplift the masses of nonnative and working-class women into the status of civilized citizens.

White men, who had long envisioned themselves as the protectors of white women's sexual purity, acquiesced to the idea of women's self-defense if only as a means of providing white women with the ability to protect their bodies from attacks by racialized others when white men were unavailable. Framed in this way, then, self-defense training was seen as preserving white women's bodies for white men. However, a close look at the data reveals the frailty of the stereotype of the black rapist and the foreign white slaver. In pulling back the curtain, the truth about violence against women begins to emerge, revealing the perpetrator most frequently as a native-born white man. Self-defense training, then, was even more radical than simply a form of physical empowerment for women. Instead, women's self-defense became a rejection of the doctrine of protectionism and a means for white women to empower themselves against attacks from their alleged natural protectors—white men.

For many women the larger solution to protecting women from violence lay in the acquisition of political power in the form of the vote. Women's expansion into previously male-dominated public spaces such as boxing halls and gyms coincided with the movement of the suffrage campaign out of the parlors and into the public space of city streets.[129] Suffragists took a bold stand on the streets, canvassing and making speeches to gain support in their campaign for women's rights. Similarly, women practitioners of self-defense seized public space to assert their independence and political power. The New Woman, educated in physical techniques to defend herself, was ready to confront the challenges that awaited her in her new public role. Some women dared to dream even beyond the narrow goal of suffrage, peering into a future in which all women's bodies would be free of the sexual subjugation imposed by white men. These women recognized the radical political implications of women's self-defense training. The connections between the physical empowerment and the political empowerment of women will be explored in more depth in the next chapter.

# 4

## Self-Defense in the Era of Suffrage and the New Woman

Boxing and jiu-jitsu had benefits extending beyond protecting women on the streets from violent attack. Women's self-defense training had potential broad cultural and political implications as well, especially as it threatened to upset the balance of binary notions of gender and disrupt the notion of the male natural protector. Irene Gammel, in her study of the history of female boxing, has written: "By engaging with boxing as practitioners and spectators, some used their own bodies as legible scripts for new identities—indeed scripting strength, agency and subversion into their musculature as a gendered narrative of modernity. By exhibiting muscular corporeality, the modern woman unscripted the traditional female body, which was codified in rigid opposition to the male body and inescapably tethered to her reproductive and domestic functions." Gammel argues that the New Woman used her body to renegotiate "boundaries of self and others."[1] Women's self-defense training thus questioned the idea that strength, aggression, and violence were traits inherent in males or that females were weak, passive, and peaceful. This in itself was a radical challenge to existing gender norms, but the idea that women were capable of and willing to use violence to protect themselves contested deeply entrenched beliefs about the roles of men and women. Self-defense training thus had the potential to subvert traditional gender norms, challenge the doctrine of male protection, and redefine women as strong and powerful individuals capable of serving as their own protectors and worthy of their full rights as citizens.

The radical suggestion that women were capable of serving as their own protectors both emerged from and was influenced by larger campaigns for women's rights. By the early twentieth century, some women who were pushing the boundaries of their new political freedoms discovered the advantages of self-defense training in empowering their minds and their bodies for the fight that lay ahead. Their training in boxing and jiu-jitsu therefore took on political meaning. They sought to subvert the status quo by challenging traditional assumptions that only men had the right to train in combative arts. American suffragists took lessons, both figuratively and literally, from radical English suffragettes who transformed their bodies into vehicles for expressing their discontent with existing structural inequalities. However, even women with no affiliation with suffrage organizations enacted a physical transformation imbued with political connotations through their self-defense training. By rejecting the notion of the necessity of male protection, these women discovered the intimate link between their physical liberation and their political emancipation. Yet this liberating concept would ultimately lead to additional revelations about the limitations of their newfound freedoms in protecting women from the most personal forms of violence.

## The Doctrine of Male Protection

The notion of man as woman's natural protector was a powerful idea in the Victorian mind. Just as the ideology of separate spheres had prescribed very narrow gender roles for women that emphasized their docility and frailty, the cult of domesticity confined men to gender roles that required not only that they serve as the primary wage earners for their families but also that they exhibit strength, courage, and physical aggression when necessary. The expectation that a man must be a loving father and husband coexisted with the requirement that he be physically able to protect and defend his family and his nation. Women were contrasted with men and designated as the weaker sex, dependent on men to guard their presumably weaker bodies from attack.[2]

As we saw in the last chapter, the movement of women into public space created anxiety about the potential violence they faced away from the security of the home and in the absence of their natural protectors. Commentators recommended that husbands, brothers, and fathers continue to escort women and guide them through the dangers of the urban environment. In the absence of male friends or relatives, women were advised to seek assistance from other males in positions of authority such as train conductors, watchmen, and police officers. Men who defended the honor of a woman on the street by attacking other men who preyed on defenseless women earned the praise and admiration of society. The message was clear. Men's aggression was powerful and dangerous, something that must be controlled and used for good. When this violence was directed toward women, it was unacceptable. It was therefore the duty of *good* men to use their natural physical strength and innate tendency toward aggression only against other men who threatened women.

Nineteenth-century women's rights advocates appealed to this idea of the male protector to elicit sympathy for their cause. They urged women and *good* men to acknowledge that not all men protected women and pointed out instances in which men victimized women. Lucy Stone, a vocal women's rights advocate, used her *Woman's Journal* not only as a medium for expressing support for women's suffrage but also as a means of highlighting the extent of women's oppression. Stone's magazine included a column that featured stories of men's violence against women to emphasize the idea that men often failed to protect women. Cases of child abuse, rape, incest, and wife-beating served as graphic evidence to prove her point. Stone and other women's rights activists used these incidents of male-on-female violence as evidence for their argument that women needed the power to protect themselves.

Susan B. Anthony was an influential advocate of the idea that women should serve as their own protectors. In a speech at Platt's Hall in San Francisco in 1871, Anthony countered the idea that all men always protected women. Instead, she provided examples to the contrary and at the end of her speech proclaimed: "I declare to you that woman must not depend on the protection of man, but must be taught to protect herself, and there I take my stand."[3] In this context, Anthony was referring to the necessity of women's suffrage as the key to ensuring the right of women to protect themselves, but other activists would apply this thinking to argue for the necessity of women's self-defense.

The idea that women did not have to depend on a male defender was a radical notion that encouraged some women to advocate for and enthusiastically pursue training in self-defense. Still, women's self-defense was tolerated by society only as a last resort to ensure the protection of white women's bodies from the threats posed by dangerous and racialized strangers. In the absence of their male protectors, then, women were allowed the right to protect their own bodies from attack, if only to protect their reputations from insult by impertinent mashers and their bodies from violation by foreign white slavers and black rapists.

Harrie Irving Hancock broached this issue in his book *Jiu-Jitsu Combat Tricks* (1904). Although Hancock argued that women who train in jiu-jitsu are "capable of holding their own in combat with men," he revealed his gender bias in insisting that self-defense by women was intended for use only when their "natural protector" was away.[4] Ironically, however, the women who learned these techniques were challenging the very notion of the "natural protector." By empowering their bodies in this way, female jiu-jitsu practitioners were stretching the boundaries of mainstream ideals of white femininity. The suggestion that middle- and upper-class white women were capable of fighting to protect themselves disrupted racialized gender norms. Hancock offered a caveat that eased tensions and justified women's temporary use of violence by recommending their use of jiu-jitsu only when a male protector was unavailable, and by implication only against attacks by nonwhite strangers. Like Hancock, most men and women still insisted that women should rely primarily on male friends and relatives as their primary defense.

Women's rights activists embraced the right of women to physically defend themselves while also challenging the notion of the male protector. This was consistent with the goals of the campaign for women's suffrage and the broader goal of ending the subjugation of women. Elizabeth Cady Stanton openly promoted the idea that women should empower themselves to fight off assaults, arguing that all men did not necessarily protect all women. In the suffrage newspaper the *Revolution*, Stanton defended a woman's right to kill any man who attempted to sexually assault her: "We would suggest that every young girl should be taught the use of firearms, and always carry a small pistol for her defense. Moreover, that she should be accompanied by an immense Newfoundland dog whenever she is in danger of meeting her *natural protector*."[5] Stanton thus rejected the idea that man was woman's natural protector and, even more radically, asserted that man (even the allegedly *good* man) represented the primary threat to woman's safety and security.

Similarly, Alice Stone Blackwell, daughter of Lucy Stone and Henry Blackwell, writing in the *Woman's Journal* in 1887, advocated women's self-defense as a means of self-protection. Blackwell insisted, "It would be a good thing if all women would take such lessons [in boxing]," especially since "assaults upon women are so common." She also stressed that women of all classes and ages could benefit from the knowledge of self-protection, including society women, shopgirls, and mothers. Blackwell referenced the female heroine in novels by George Borrow who fought back against "rough characters." Blackwell quoted from Borrow's novel *The Romany Rye*, advising "any woman who is struck by a ruffian to strike him again; or if she cannot clinch her fists—and he advises all women in these singular times to learn to clinch their fists—to go at him with tooth and nail, and not be afraid of the result."[6] The mere acknowledgment of a woman's capacity for violence and indeed her right to use such violence when necessary to protect herself from assault was a significant step forward. Although Blackwell acknowledged the importance of "turning the other cheek," she noted that sometimes "patience ceases to be a virtue."[7] Thus, when confronted with violence, women retained the right to step outside the strictures of respectable femininity and cast off the submissiveness prized by the notion of true womanhood. Men's violence against women was a violation of their role as defender of women and therefore, according to Stanton and Blackwell, a justification for women's use of physical force in return.

The actual women who embraced self-defense training also rejected the notion of the natural male protector, favoring instead a view of themselves as their own hero. Jennie Heade of Philadelphia endured constant unwanted attention from a man who persisted in following her to and from church. Despite her repeated requests that he leave her alone, the man continued to stalk her. When Heade's brother offered to accompany her and protect her if the man bothered her again, Heade declined the offer and determined instead to learn how to box. When she once again encountered her stalker, who this time had followed her home, she turned and hit him hard on the jaw. He fled the scene, never to be a bother again. Heade told her brother, "I can take care of myself."[8]

Many women who determined to take up self-defense training recognized the links between their physical empowerment and their political empowerment. They asserted that bodies could serve as a site of political and cultural resistance. By training their muscles through boxing and jiu-jitsu, they resisted popular conceptions of the female body as weak and rejected the imposition and inscription of patriarchal cultural beliefs onto their bodies. Scholars of women's self-defense in the modern era have repeatedly reflected on the significance of this embodiment.

Building off the groundbreaking and influential work of Judith Butler, scholars have argued that through the performance of gender, male and female bodies are inscribed with cultural values and norms. In this manner men's bodies perform violence and aggression, and women's bodies perform passiveness and victimization. Women's self-defense therefore has the power to disrupt these notions and empower women's bodies as sites of resistance against violence and aggression.[9] Similarly, women in the Progressive Era used self-defense to rescript their bodies. Through their self-defense training, these female practitioners challenged social norms and subverted binary categories of gender. They attempted, with limited success, to create new social norms that recognized women as powerful and capable of defending themselves.

## Subverting the Status Quo

Women who trained in self-defense made powerful political statements, whether or not this was their stated intention. This is perhaps best illustrated by returning to the story of Theodore Roosevelt and examining how some women responded to his ideas about manliness and the fighting arts. Roosevelt advocated physical culture not only as a means of fighting emasculation and strengthening the bodies and characters of American men but also as a way of strengthening the virility of the nation as a whole. It is well known that Roosevelt sought to emulate these attributes in his own life by aggressively pursuing a variety of athletics, including the "manly art" of self-defense through his training in boxing and jiu-jitsu.[10] What is perhaps less well known is that several elite Washington women determined to best the president at his own game. They resolved to make a political statement and challenge preconceived notions of feminine weakness by publicly training in the art of jiu-jitsu at the same time that the president did. Their example demonstrated the ways in which some women politically used self-defense and their own bodies to challenge the status quo.

Martha Blow Wadsworth, a wealthy Washington heiress, was upset by Roosevelt's blatant political maneuverings and use of jiu-jitsu to elicit public attention. According to martial art historian Joseph Svinth, Wadsworth despised Roosevelt "so much that she insisted on duplicating virtually every physical feat he claimed, once riding a relay of fast horses several hundred miles in 24 hours just to spite him."[11] In 1904, when Roosevelt invited Yoshiaki Yamashita to Washington to offer him private instruction, Wadsworth determined to organize a class for women and girls under the direction of Yamashita's wife, Fude. Among the students in the class were the wives and daughters of prominent Washington businessmen and politicians, including Maria Louise "Hallie" Davis Elkins (wife of Senator Stephen Elkins) and her daughter Katherine Elkins, Grace Davis Lee (Hallie's sister), Jessie Ames (daughter of a former Civil War general and politician), and Re Lewis Smith Wilmer (wife of prominent Washington surgeon William Holland Wilmer). The class for young girls included Katherine Brown, Frances Moore, Ogden Jones, and Margaret Perrin.[12] Newspapers highlighted not only the social status of these women but also their athleticism as a sign of the changing roles of women.

These elite women and the women who followed in their footsteps embraced Japanese martial arts not simply for physical exercise or to protect themselves on the streets but as a political statement about their physical capabilities and their rights as women. Their training symbolized a means of broader empowerment for themselves and their daughters.[13] These upper-class women took issue with the notion that women were inherently weak or incapable of the same physicality as men, choosing instead to engage in the same rigorous sports pursued by men in their social class. They used their power to challenge the very definition of the "manly arts" by seizing for themselves the sense of liberation offered through self-defense training and converting it in a sense into a "womanly art."

The elite women who publicly practiced jiu-jitsu on the lawn of the White House clearly recognized the symbolic significance of their appropriation of the manly arts as signaling women's new role in the political arena. As upper-class white women, they enjoyed the privileges of operating within a world ruled by men of their race and class. Their wealth enabled them to hire private jiu-jitsu instructors, an option unavailable to most working-class women at the time. Their class status also provided them with the leisure time and sense of obligation to participate in social reform movements. Some led suffrage organizations or fought in other arenas on behalf of women's rights. Their athletic pur-

Figure 4.1 Children's class: Margaret Perrin—Miss A. Lee, ca. 1904. Yoshiaki Yamashita Photograph Album (PH 006), Department of Special Collections and University Archives, W. E. B. Du Bois Library, University of Massachusetts Amherst.

suits coupled with their political work exposed the tangible connections between physical and political empowerment in the Progressive Era.

The life and work of Jessie Ames, one of the female jiu-jitsu practitioners at the White House in 1904, illustrate the connections between the physical and the political. Ames came from a politically connected family and was a noted political activist in her own right. Ames's father had been a Reconstruction era governor and senator from Mississippi but then moved back to New England, where the family earned a fortune in flour milling. Jessie's brother Butler Ames was a member of the U.S. House of Representative from 1903 to 1913. The children of this politically prominent family all established themselves as reform-minded professionals. Jessie graduated from Smith College in Massachusetts and would have been considered a "modern woman" for her time. She actively participated in many of the extracurricular activities Smith had to offer, which included a wide array of sports. She was the captain of the basketball team and a member of the Gymnasium and Field Association.[14] Ames continued her athletic endeavors beyond college. She was twenty-two years old when her family visited her brother Butler in Washington, DC, in 1904. On March 18, Jessie's mother mentioned in a letter to her daughter Blanche that Butler and Jessie were enjoying practicing jiu-jitsu with the Japanese instructors.[15] Jessie's expanding physical pursuits coincided with her growing political activism on behalf of women's rights, including her involvement in the fight for women's rights through the birth control movement and the women's suffrage campaign. Her sister Blanche Ames, a class of 1899 Smith graduate, led the Birth Control League and Woman Suffrage League of Massachusetts in the 1910s.[16] The Ames sisters' advocacy of political and physical empowerment reveals the connections that some women saw between the benefits of political and personal independence.

The example of the Washington women paralleled a growing trend of viewing women's self-defense training as a symbol of their expanding political empowerment. As women's self-defense courses became increasingly popular for preparing women to protect themselves from dangers on the street, more women began to articulate the sense of empowerment they felt in remaking their bodies in this way. Some clearly recognized the political implications of their body projects. Louise Le Noir Thomas, writing in 1917, associated women's self-defense training with what she described as a "feminist rebellion," or the vast political, economic and social changes that had been occurring in women's lives as a result of the suffrage fight. Thomas came from a well-connected family. Her mother, M. Louise Thomas, was president of Lenox Hall, a college preparatory school for girls in St. Louis, Missouri, and an advocate of equal rights for women at least as far back as 1888, when she served as a founding member and officer of the National and International Council for Women alongside Susan B. Anthony. Louise Le Noir Thomas followed in her mother's footsteps as an advocate of women's suffrage and a member of the Equal Suffrage League in her hometown of St. Louis. Le Noir Thomas was a former Smith College student who engaged in a variety of athletic pursuits in addition to her work on behalf of women's rights. After college, she pursued a career in writing and advertising and advocated for women's self-defense as an extension of the quest for political equality.[17]

In her 1917 article, Le Noir Thomas insisted that the idea that a woman was the "protected sex" who must busy herself with the gentle arts of singing, cooking, and sewing had long since disappeared. As she explained, "Women have been drawn more and more into the business world. . . . They have formed clubs that they attend at night sessions and they have innumerable activities and interests that take them out of the snug seclusion of the home and make them subject to the dangers that exist on every highway." Thomas argued that women "have refused to be called the 'weaker sex,' and the 'pampered sex,' and have shown such aversion to the 'protection of the male,' so-called that men have almost begun to take them at their word and treat them as equals in not only intellectuality, but in physical strength." She further insisted, "It is not unwomanly to protect herself—rather it is unwomanly to be overpowered by the assailant."[18] Le Noir Thomas reasoned that through self-defense training a woman embodied the new feminism.

Although not all women so articulately identified the link between their new physical empowerment and women's emerging political freedoms, they may have intuitively recognized the connection. In 1912, Ethel Intropodi explained that she had decided to study boxing in Chicago for personal rather than specific political reasons: "I am not a suffragette nor even a suffragist; but I do believe that a woman should be able to protect herself from that breed of brutes commonly known as mashers." Intropodi insisted that women did not need to be weak, running away and screaming to a policeman. Instead, she stated that a "girl of spunk and independence is able to take care of herself. If she can land a stinging blow behind the ear on one of these mashers, she is safe. If she can deliver a strong upper cut, or lead a 'solar plexus' blow, she can walk the streets unmolested and unafraid." She went on to explain that boxing not only is healthy but also "gives a woman a feeling of power that is exhilarating."[19] Although Intropodi refused to identify herself as a suffragist, she clearly recognized the potential for physical empowerment of women through self-defense training. Women who took self-defense classes may not have always consciously realized the symbolic implications of their actions, but by training in self-defense and resisting patriarchal notions of feminine passivity and weakness, they in essence embodied feminist politics. Through the assertion that women have the right to physically fight back against mashers and to safely walk the public streets, the practice of self-defense in itself became an unconscious form of political activism. Thus, although some Progressive Era women insisted that their intention in studying self-defense was primarily for personal empowerment, the entrance of women into the previously male-dominated field of self-defense had political implications that in effect both emerged from the new attitudes by and toward women and influenced new attitudes by and toward women.

## Inspiration from British Suffragettes

The militant suffragettes of Britain who were already using their bodies as sites of resistance made the link between self-defense for physical empowerment and the political empowerment of women most explicit. Their use of their bodies as sites of political activism inspired American suffragists. British women seeking the vote confronted antisuffragists by using direct action techniques to challenge their second-rate status. They were often met with violent assaults from bystanders and police alike. At an event on November 18, 1910, later referred to by suffragists as Black Friday, 135 women reported being assaulted by police. The demonstration began after Prime Minister Herbert Asquith refused to meet with suffrage leaders to discuss the passage of the Conciliation Bill that would grant women a limited right to vote. Hundreds of women marched to the House of Commons in protest. The police began assaulting demonstrators—punching, throwing, kicking, and shoving the suffragettes.[20] Sylvia Pankhurst described the brutality with which the police struck at the women: "If they carried flags or banners the police at once snatched those from them too and tore them into shreds, struck and cuffed the women and knocked them down and struck them with their knees—some even kicked them."[21] Pankhurst later wrote that the women "were torn apart, felled to the ground, struck again and again, bruised and battered, and tossed hither and thither with a violence that perhaps excelled anything that had gone before."[22] Witnesses and victims testified to the brutality of the day, and this experience converted many to the suffrage cause and further solidified the convictions of many more.

Violence from the police was as common as attacks from the general public. Through the course of their daily business, suffragettes could be heckled, pushed, shoved, kicked, and pelted with rotten fruit and vegetables by bystanders. Gertrude Harding described marching in a protest parade in London in 1912: "From fruit and vegetable vendors they would select the most luscious of overripe plums, tomatoes and apples to hurl at us as we plodded along in the rain trying to be oblivious to all that went on around us. Being the last in line, I was a prime target and received a perfect barrage of these unsavory objects."[23] Garbage, dead fish, and newspapers soaked in urine were also sometimes hurled at the women. Women fighting for the right of suffrage also endured verbal attacks, sexual harassment, and sexual assaults.[24] Many suffragists and female observers became even more politicized and radicalized through such direct experience with harassment and violence.

The range of suffragist responses to this violence varied widely. Some proposed nonviolent passive means of resistance such as petitions, marches, and deputations to the prime minister and king. Others, known as militant suffragettes, proposed more radical and visible demonstrations of active resistance, ranging from interrupting meetings and heckling politicians to breaking windows or destroying public property. The members of the Women's Social and Political Union (WSPU) determined to take militant action by chaining themselves to public buildings, hurling objects or setting fire to structures, and using their bodies as sites of protest to demonstrate for political rights.[25] Speaking on behalf of the WSPU, Christabel Pankhurst justified this use of militant tactics, arguing, "It is by acts of revolt, if history has anything to teach us, that the limits of freedom are extended . . . each extension of the franchise to men has been the outcome of violent agitation or the fear of it."[26] Thus, in establishing the historical precedent of men's use of militant methods to achieve the right to vote, Pankhurst extended the logic to women's suffrage. These militant suffragettes then justified their use of violence by insisting that they had no constitutional means to express their discontent.[27] In response to detractors who suggested that such behavior was "unbecoming" of women, Pankhurst asserted that milder methods of protest had failed, that their actions were moderate compared with those of male reformers, and that militant methods helped bring the issue of women's suffrage to the government's attention.

Figure 4.2 Political cartoons reflected views of critics of the tactics of the militant suffragettes by mocking the women who studied jiu-jitsu. "A Stiff Job at Attercliffe Election: Suffragettes Are to Learn the Art of Ju-Jitsu," *Daily Mail*, April 28, 1909, 3. British Library Board, London.

THE SUFFRAGETTE THAT KNEW JIU-JITSU.

Figure 4.3 Cartoons such as this one reflect a broader uncertainty and anxiety about how to make sense of militant suffragettes who powerfully stretched the boundaries of acceptable feminine behavior. "The Suffragette That Knew Jiu-Jitsu," *Punch* 139 (July 6, 1910): 9.

Pankhurst clarified that suffragettes were at war not with men but with the government.

Suffragettes adopted militant methods that utilized their bodies as a means of protest even after their imprisonment. Following their arrest and placement in prison as common criminals, some suffragettes resorted to hunger strikes to protest the government's refusal to recognize their status as political prisoners. These demonstrations were useful in garnering publicity, inspiring other suffragists, and sometimes eliciting public sympathy. More important, however, the hunger strike symbolized a powerful bodily protest against the oppression of women.[28] The government, fearing bad press if a hunger striker died under its care, began the policy of force-feeding by shoving tubes down the woman's nose and throat. Some women endured this process up to three times a day, and many experienced dangerous side effects from the procedure. Lilian Lenton became gravely ill from pneumonia when a poorly performed force-feeding caused food to enter her lungs. Cases such as this aroused even more public sympathy for the jailed suffragettes. Eventually the government responded to public pressure to end the force-feedings. The Prisoners (Temporary Discharge for Ill-Health) Act of 1913 allowed officials to release hunger-striking prisoners who became too weak to remain in prison. Once a sufficient amount of time had passed for the woman's recovery, she was ordered rearrested to carry out her prison sentence. Suffrage leaders nicknamed this law the "Cat and Mouse Act," as the cat (the police) seemed to taunt its prey (the suffragettes) with an endless game of arrest and release.[29]

In this more militant context, self-defense training took on explicit political meaning as suffragettes sought to invert the violence directed at them. In response to such violent outbursts from antisuffragists and blatant abuses of authority by the police, members of the WSPU determined to physically defend themselves from attack. Gertrude Harding helped to organize a bodyguard for the WSPU in England, explaining that the purpose was to protect the Pankhursts from assault by the police.[30] By 1909, Edith Garrud, who had studied under Raku Uyenshi in England, was asked to teach jiu-jitsu to the bodyguard of the WSPU. Garrud welcomed all women who sought self-defense training; she advertised her class in suffrage newspapers as "ju-jutsu for suffragettes" and promised to teach "special methods for suffragette self-defence."[31] The estimated twenty-five to thirty female recruits of the bodyguard practiced self-defense in secret, hid from the police, and changed their meeting locations frequently after discovering that detectives were spying on and following them.[32]

These women explicitly pursued the study of jiu-jitsu to protect themselves and the WSPU leaders from assaults not by criminals but by aggressive antisuffragists and the police. Other suffragettes also began advocating for women's self-defense training. Frances Weste started advertising her services as a jiu-jitsu instructor in suffrage newspapers in 1913 and offered "reduced fees to Suffragettes."[33] In 1911, Elsie Chapin formed the Women's Development Society in London to encourage militant British suffragettes to pursue a physically active lifestyle. This new organization offered classes in jiu-jitsu and boxing to help prepare women to defend themselves. In addition, Chapin insisted that they would play rugby, hockey, and football. When an incredulous reporter expressed surprise at Chapin's advocacy of such rigorous sports, she

Figure 4.4 Through a reversal of traditional gender roles that position women as the assailants, postcards such as this one depicted the police and antisuffragists as the innocent victims of suffragette violence. This postcard suggests a chaotic world turned upside down where hysterical women have forcibly taken the law into their own hands and seized masculine aggression as their own. "Suffragists on the War Path," Miller and Lang Ltd., ca. 1909, TWL.2004.1011.35, Women's Library Suffrage Collection, London School of Economics and Political Science Library.

replied, "Why not?"[34] To the reporter, Chapin's insistence on women's right to train in sports typically deemed too strenuous was surprising indeed and perhaps very radical. The idea of using their boxing and jiu-jitsu training in the fight for suffrage was even more radical. An exploration of the route that Chapin traveled to reach this state of radicalization suggests some of the motives that may have induced other suffragettes to pursue self-defense training.

Elsie Chapin and her mother, Alice Chapin, were members of the Women's Freedom League (WFL), a branch of militant suffragists who had broken away from the WSPU in 1907. Alice Chapin wrote and starred in a number of suffrage plays alongside her children. In October 1909, she was arrested for pouring ink into ballot boxes at the Bermondsey by-election as a means of highlighting women's political oppression, and the ink accidentally splashed into the eye of an election official. This incident elicited outrage from antisuffragists and some suffragists who disagreed with the militant tactics. Elsie watched as her mother was tried and sentenced to four months' imprisonment. Alison Neilans, Alice's accomplice in the act, was sentenced to three months in prison. Neilans went on a hunger strike in Holloway Prison to protest the government's failure to recognize suffragettes as political prisoners. Neilans endured force-feeding about twenty times while in Holloway and upon her release gave a stirring speech in which she told her audience: "I went in militant, but I am coming out a raging fire." Elsie Chapin, upon hearing these words and awaiting the release of her mother, no doubt also felt the fire raging inside. She had sneaked past court officials in October to witness her mother's trial, visited her in prison a few days before Christmas, gave speeches at rallies protesting the treatment of her mother and other suffragettes in prison, and celebrated along with the WFL when the prisoners were released from Holloway. After she witnessed firsthand the brutal treatment of the suffragettes, it is no wonder that a year later Elsie Chapin began training in jiu-jitsu and boxing and insisted that all suffragettes train in self-defense.[35]

Besides fighting for women's suffrage and advocating women's self-defense, the WFL also demanded full economic and social equality for women. Its focus on broader issues, including domestic violence and sexual assault, foreshadowed many of the issues that would arise in the women's movement of the late twentieth century.[36] Even more radical, however, was the idea of training their bodies in boxing and jiu-jitsu and employing corporeal acts of protest that transformed their bodies from sites of oppression into sites of liberation. Militant suffragettes in the WSPU and the WFL advocated picketing, hunger strikes, and the destruction of public property to make their presence known to a government that refused to listen to their words. Through corporeal acts of protest such as chaining themselves to public buildings or starving themselves, these activists refined the practice of using their physical bodies as a means of and sites of protest. Boxing and jiu-jitsu provided another method of remonstrating against the physical and political oppression of women and in effect liberating themselves from subjugation while recasting their bodies as sites of empowerment.

Edith Garrud embodied this form of physical feminism by teaching suffragettes techniques that allowed them to take control of situations they felt were out of their control. Suffrage newspapers that promoted self-defense training for women empowered their members to reconceptualize their own perceptions of their bodies. One anonymous young reader of *Votes for Women* wrote a letter to the editor in 1909 expressing a strong belief in her physical abilities: "I am sure I could fight as well as many of my boy or men friends if I had to—at any rate, I am quicker and have more presence of mind."[37] A member of the WSPU bodyguard expressed similar confidence after completing her jiu-jitsu training with Garrud: "I believe we will teach male rowdies who try to bother us a lesson. I have already ejected one or two disturbers of our meetings with a speed and dispatch that has surprised their lumbering masculine minds."[38] By 1913, the WPSU leaders were advising all women in the movement to be trained in self-defense. Sylvia Pankhurst, addressing a suffragist meeting at Bromley on August 19, 1913, said, "We have not yet made ourselves a match for the police, and we have got to do it. The police know jiu-jitsu. I advise you to learn jiu-jitsu. Women should practice it as well as men." She also advised women to go armed with their sticks to meetings in case they encountered hostility from outsiders.[39] The idea of armed suffragists seemed extreme to many critics, who insisted that the new tactic in no way furthered the cause of women's suffrage.

In response to critics who portrayed the jiu-jitsu suffragettes as masculinized Amazons preying on innocent policemen, Edith Garrud insisted that training in jiu-jitsu and boxing was intended only as self-defense against those who attacked the women first. As Garrud explained in an interview, "We are not going to teach Suffragettes how to look after themselves in order that they might make a regular practice of scrimmaging with the police." She added: "I only hope there will never be any need for me to be really cross with any policeman, because most of them are very decent fellows. But in this world there are a lot of very unpleasant young men who would be all the better for an occasional dressing down from a woman." Garrud demonstrated her skills on two police volunteers, who were incredulous at her strength and abilities.[40]

Jiu-jitsu and boxing training proved useful to the suffragettes in several encounters with police. Emmeline Pankhurst, risking rearrest under the "Cat and Mouse Act," made a public appearance at Campden Hill Square on February 10, 1914, and, using boxing imagery, gave a stirring speech exhorting the crowd of women to fight for their rights: "Would it not be well, when we leave this life, as leave it we must, to leave it having struck a blow for what is truer life; having struck a blow for the freedom of our sex; having struck a blow against the subjugation of our sex." Pankhurst further insisted on the power of women: "I have reached London in spite of the armies of police. I am here to-night, and not a man is going to protect me, because this is a woman's fight and we shall protect ourselves."[41] She boldly asserted that women cannot and, more important, should not rely on men for their protection, stressing that women should instead serve as their own protectors. Furthermore, Pankhurst's followers had empowered themselves with the ability to do so.

Gertrude Harding described what happened next as Pankhurst stepped off the stage. When the police moved in to arrest her, "the bodyguard drew their clubs and attacked the police who were swarming about the door from which Mrs. Pankhurst would emerge." Harding described how the police fell unwittingly into a suffragette trap by arresting a decoy Pankhurst while Harding and the bodyguard escorted the real Pankhurst into a taxi. Unfortunately, the decoy Pankhurst, who had donned the attire of Mrs. Pankhurst to fool authorities, was subject to a blow to the back of the head and cracked ribs through rough treatment by the police. By the time police had returned to the station with the suspect and realized their mistake, it was too late to capture the real Pankhurst, who was long gone.[42]

The bodyguard fought similar battles with law enforcement in the following months. In an incident referred to as "The Battle of Glasgow," the women used their clubs to fight off the police who tried to arrest Emmeline Pankhurst when she was scheduled to speak at Saint Andrew's Hall in Scotland on March 9, 1914. The police knocked Pankhurst down and then kicked and shoved women as they climbed up onto the platform to defend her. The officers dragged Pankhurst down the stairs by her feet, bumping her head against the steps.[43] Swinging their truncheons, the police freely struck at any woman in their path. Gertrude Harding described a scene of violence, with the audience shouting "disapproval against the police. The elderly ladies (who had no use for Suffragettes) rose up in their boxes, and using umbrellas as weapons, began hammering on the heads of two policemen trying to climb on the platform."[44] Women dumped water on the heads of the policemen and then began throwing flowerpots and chairs. The policemen were slowed down by barbed wire hidden under a garland of flowers that the body-guard had used to booby-trap the stage for the occasion. Female doctors who attended the suffragette victims after the incident described how the women were badly bruised by the police batons, several with their scalps cut down to the bone.[45] Eunice G. Murray described the violence they encountered as a transformative experience: "When I watched a policeman fell a girl to the ground and kick her across the platform, my only regret was that I had no weapon with which to strike him an effective blow." Murray insisted, "Militancy provokes militancy. Women did not invent it, they have learnt it from men; they have been forced to use it, because it is the only argument the average man understands."[46] Thus Murray became a convert to militant methods and a believer that "deeds, not words" were necessary to achieve the justice the suffragettes demanded.

Reporters described these confrontations between the militant suffragettes and the police as skirmishes or battles. One account from May 1914 explained what happened when a delegation of WSPU women under the leadership of Emmeline Pankhurst marched to Buckingham Palace to present a petition to the king. When police attempted to disperse the crowd, the women, armed with sticks, "fought with vigor, using their sticks with such force that the police charged."[47] Torn garments on the ground reflected the intensity of the fighting. Forty arrests were made that day. The battles were not without casualties either, as both police officers and suffragettes reported injuries. Several women were carried away in ambulances.[48] Through military analogies and use of phrases such as "hand-to-hand fighting" and "casualties," the popular press illustrated the physical intensity of this sex war that literally pitted female bodies against male bodies in a battle to dismantle gender roles and end the oppression of women.

Suffragettes also increasingly described their struggle as a war. Emmeline Pankhurst frequently referred to her followers as soldiers in a suffrage army, writing, "We who remain as soldiers in the women's army, must continue the good fight until the victory is won."[49] She insisted they were "waging a war" in a fight for human liberty.[50] Her daughter Sylvia Pankhurst went so far as to organize an "army" of suffrage supporters—men and women from the working-class neighborhood of the East End who were encouraged to train in jiu-jitsu, arm themselves with clubs, and prepare to defend the suffragettes against unjust attacks. Inspired by Sylvia Pankhurst's socialist beliefs in the power of the people to resist their oppressors, the "army" made a clear show of force by drilling with clubs and marching in formation every week in the East End. At one point, up to 700 women were members of this "People's Army." Pankhurst was, however, a pacifist and advocated the use of force only as a means of self-defense against a system that denied them any other legal recourse.[51] She concurred with her mother, Emmeline, who had earlier insisted that "the only justification for violence, the only justification for damage to property, the only justification for risk to the comfort of other human beings is the fact that you have tried all other available means and have failed to secure justice." Emmeline explained, "Men got the vote because they were and would be violent. The women did not get it because they were constitutional and law-abiding."[52] Thus the advocacy of jiu-jitsu, the creation of a bodyguard, and the training of an army of women were intended as means of protection against a government that failed to protect them. The suffragettes sought to dismantle preconceived notions of female passivity and weakness and reconstruct their bodies as strong, powerful weapons in the war for the equality of women.

## American Suffragists

Some American suffragists drew inspiration from British suffragettes who had consciously trained to use their bodies as physical sites of political struggles. There was a clear exchange of ideas and tactics as prominent suffrage leaders crisscrossed the Atlantic. Sylvia Pankhurst met Zelie Emerson while speaking in Chicago. Emerson—an upper-class reformer from Michigan who worked at Chicago's Hull House—was inspired by Pankhurst's words and traveled with her back to London. While in England, Emerson had multiple violent confrontations with the police. Her skull was fractured by police truncheons on two separate occasions in 1914, and she was arrested multiple times for breaking windows. Imprisoned at Holloway, Emerson protested through hunger, thirst, and sleep strikes. She testified at one of her trials that after having had her skull fractured by the police, she decided to carry a "Saturday night club," a rope dipped in tar and weighted with lead, to defend herself. When fellow American suffragette Lillian Scott Troy was imprisoned in 1913, Emerson organized a march of more than 1,000 people to Holloway to show support for her.[53] That same year, Emerson helped establish Sylvia Pankhurst's East End People's Army, whose purpose, Emerson told the *Chicago Examiner*, was "to protect militants from the brutality of the police, who during the last month were ordered by the authorities to make no arrests, but to inflict as many bodily injuries as possible." Emerson reported that all members of the People's Army would be drilled "in the use of clubs, fists, and jiu-jitsu."[54] American women such as Emerson and Scott Troy directly experienced police brutality and antisuffragist violence in England and through these experiences became believers in militant tactics and self-defense training.

The vast majority of American suffrage organizations, however, sought to distance themselves from the militant tactics of the English suffragettes. Yet American women turned out in large numbers to hear the Pankhursts speak on their multiple visits to the United States and drew inspiration from both their deeds and their words. The leaders of national American suffrage organizations did not go so far as to emulate the militant zeal of their English sisters by organizing a bodyguard of trained jiu-jitsu experts. Still, some individuals and a few organizations advocated self-defense training for suffragists. Other suffrage leaders and women's rights advocates voiced their support for the concept of training suffragists in self-defense if only to prepare them physically and empower them psychologically for the battle ahead. For example, Sofia Loebinger, a leader of a militant suffragist group in New York, expressed admiration for the actions of the English suffragettes who practiced jiu-jitsu: "Strong situations need strong women, and I am heartily in favor of the movement." She admitted that although it might not assist them directly in achieving the right to vote, "boxing would be a good thing for women if only to teach them to concentrate their minds on one thing at a time. The ballot, for instance."[55] She hoped that self-defense courses modeled after the English Women's Development Society would emerge in the United States. Loebinger explained: "Women have courage and endurance and all they need is lessons in the scientific way to develop their muscles. Boxing and wrestling lessons will give them these qualifications."[56] Loebinger recognized the transformative potential of physical training in strengthening women for their political fight. Moreover, for activists who used confrontational mass resistance techniques to demonstrate for the vote, empowering themselves with these skills could serve them well on multiple fronts.

American suffragist and feminist writer Charlotte Perkins Gilman similarly expressed her support of the English suffragettes and their use of self-defense. Gilman recognized that women's use of violence was sometimes necessary and considered women's athleticism as essential to their health and well-being. In her own life and in the lives of other women, Gilman associated physical fitness with emancipation from restrictive gender roles and the confinement of the domestic sphere. In her youth she pursued a training regimen that included weight lifting, running, and gymnastics. After marrying and giving birth to a child, however, she found herself suffering from severe postpartum depression. Gilman sought the assistance of Dr. Silas Weir Mitchell, who prescribed an intensive rest cure that confined her to a long period of complete isolation and bed rest devoid of intellectual or physical exercise. Although she willingly accepted the assistance at the time, Gilman later blamed Mitchell's methods for the further weakening of her physical and mental strength, leading her even deeper into a downward spiral. This trying period of her life inspired her to write *The Yellow Wallpaper* (1892), a fictional account in which a woman describes how her confinement and rest cure led to mental breakdown, hallucinations, and insanity. Ultimately, Gilman argued that physical culture was essential to strengthening women's bodies and minds.[57]

Gilman also recognized the link between the physical and the political, insisting that women's use of violence was necessary not only for self-defense but also for securing their political freedoms. In her article "Should Women Use Violence?" (1912), Gilman confronted head-on the debate over the British suffragettes' use of violence and considered the question of whether violence by women is ever justified. She argued that women were often depicted as naturally passive and weak and in need of men as their natural protectors. In the process, women were subjected to violence at the hands of their so-called protectors and were "restrained, coerced, condemned and executed" by "law, religion, education, public opinion." By taking aim at the myth of the male protector, Gilman carried on the fight of women's rights activists of the late nineteenth century, arguing that the public condemnations of the actions of the British suffragettes in their efforts to fight back reflected male fear of the potential for violence within women. Gilman insisted that objections to the radical tactics used by suffragettes in Britain were based primarily on the deep-seated fear that women might use violence to rebel against their male oppressors. She acknowledged the necessity of women's self-defense and expressed a firm belief in the ability of women to protect themselves with violence if necessary, stressing that demonstrations, protests, and violence were necessary tactics for any independence movement and in fact had noteworthy historical precedents. She further insisted that gendered objections to the behavior of the militant suffragettes, which suggested that their use of violence was unladylike and unfeminine, were ridiculous, explaining, "If their cause is a just one and their course wisely chosen, there is no reason whatever why they should be 'feminine or 'ladylike' in this field of conduct." She rejected the arguments of some critics who insisted that suffrage militancy invited further retaliation in the form of assault and harassment from male antisuffragists and police. Gilman concluded that "whether the special bit of heroism which has set the gallant band of English women to breaking windows and trying to shake the Premier is wholly mistaken, no present-day observer can say. But we can give them credit for immeasurable courage."[58] In defining the suffragettes and their tactics as heroic, Gilman clearly identified physical empowerment as a key element in the political liberation of women.

As the battle for women's suffrage grew in the early twentieth century, suffrage leaders expanded their views on violence against women and women's use of violence. Encounters with violence challenged American suffragists to reconceptualize their worldview. By staging a very public suffrage parade in Washington, DC, in 1913, women simultaneously claimed their right to safely walk down the public streets and the right to exercise their political freedoms. The violence they encountered in response from antisuffragists was intense and shocking as participants were subjected to jeers, spitting, demeaning comments, name-calling, shoving, pinching, and grabbing.[59] Parade participants and organizers were incensed by the mistreatment. The day after the parade, a Senate committee was appointed to investigate the conduct of the police. Cordelia Powell Odenheimer from Jessup, Maryland, who had been an observer at the parade, appeared before the committee and testified to the insulting remarks and physical assaults she suffered that day: "They tore a woman's suffrage badge from off of my coat and nearly knocked me down. When I managed to get up the crowd was very dense. A woman cried out—she was crying—that they had torn two children away from her."[60] Witness after witness testified that the police showed indifference and in some cases joined in, laughing and taunting the marchers as well. Some women struck back at their attackers. Vernat Hetfield, a female student who rode on a float in the parade, described being touched and grabbed by the crowd of men as the float passed them. When one man grabbed her foot and tried to pull her off the float, she kicked him. Frustrated by the inactivity of the police, the female parade marshals began using their canes to force the crowd back and strike back at men who grabbed them.[61] Historian Kimberly Jensen has noted, "As women took to the streets to claim the rights of citizenship, they saw and experienced violence in new ways. And they increasingly constructed their citizenship claims as including freedom from this new vision of violence."[62] This experience allowed women to reconfigure their views of violence against women in World War I and fight against sexual harassment and violence against women in the workplace on the war front and beyond.

Through their experiences in the 1913 parade, many American suffragists realized that policemen and male bystanders did not and would not protect them. Thus, the exhortations of a previous generation of women's rights advocates that women must be empowered to protect themselves came into sharp focus. As Stanton, Blackwell, and more recently Gilman had pointed out, women would indeed need to learn to be their own defenders. Their English sisters had already concluded that they could not depend on the police for protection, and in many cases their so-called protectors represented the real threat, since policemen often instigated the violence against women. British suffragettes' experience with violence and their own self-defense training politicized and empowered them to fight back against the attacks they faced on a variety of fronts. American women also were radicalized by their experience with violence, although on a much smaller scale than the British suffragettes. Some of the American women who organized and marched in the 1913 parade in Washington, DC, including Alice Paul and Lucy Burns, had already been radicalized by their experiences working with the WSPU in England. Many other American suffragists, though, were facing this hostility for the first time, and the assaults they encountered in Washington helped awaken them to the realities of violence against women. These experiences radicalized more suffragists and legitimized their own potential use of their bodies as a means of protest through picketing, hunger strikes, and, for a few women, self-defense training to achieve their goals. In this context, women's use of aggression took on an association with physically winning their freedom.

Individuals experienced these transformations on a very personal level, and their stories often led them to advocate on a societal level for women's rights and women's self-defense. Perhaps inspired by the British suffragettes and in reaction to the violence of the 1913 parade in Washington, DC, some suffragist women began to recognize the necessity of self-defense for women. In March 1913, two weeks after the parade, a group of suffragists from St. Louis, Missouri, determined to study boxing to better protect themselves in their fight for women's rights. Whether or not they were directly inspired by events in Washington remains unknown. The sixteen women chose to keep their identities anonymous, but their actions did not go unnoticed by the local press. Significantly, and perhaps symbolically, they trained at a local gymnasium owned and operated by a woman.[63] Louise Bodecker was a single, immigrant woman from Germany. In her home country, women's athletics and especially training in boxing and jiu-jitsu had become quite popular.[64] Bodecker, a strong advocate of physical culture for women who committed her life and career to that pursuit, established her gym in St. Louis after immigrating to the United States in 1900 (in the 1913 city directory, it was listed as a "women's and children's gymnasium").[65] Bodecker's advocacy of physical culture for women and her support of the suffragists to some degree symbolized a larger transnational alliance among women committed to advancing the rights of women around the globe. Clearly, the violence encountered by women in Washington, DC, earlier in the month fostered a mutual sense of empathy with suffragists experiencing similar situations in Britain and in other parts of the world.

Like those in St. Louis, suffragists in Badger, Washington, were likewise motivated by recent incidents to study boxing. Three months after the parade in Washington, DC, suffragists in Badger started their own boxing club. A visitor to the club noted the ferocity of the women's abilities, commenting, "The suffragettes take as kindly and naturally to the art of self-defense as a duck does to water."[66] The use of the term "suffragettes" in referring to these American women suggests that the author clearly associated them with the radical suffragettes of Britain. Whether some of these women had directly participated in the Washington parade remains unknown, but given the timing of their decision to train in boxing, it is likely that they were motivated to action by the experiences of the women who were subjected to the violence there. For the St. Louis and Badger women, this motivation led to their determination to learn boxing to better prepare themselves for the fight for suffrage.

Although the violence American suffragists faced was much less severe than that experienced by the English suffragettes, they increasingly came to realize that they could not and should not rely on men to protect them. For some women's rights advocates, the connection between their personal empowerment and their political liberation seemed obvious. Alta Hyde Gilbert of Cleveland, Ohio, recognized the links between the physical and the political even before the battle for the vote took a militant turn in England. Alta Hyde married Frank J. Gilbert, a salesman and later vice president of a music publishing company, in 1902. Alta was described as an active society woman in Cleveland. As a child, she had learned boxing from her father, and after she married Frank Gilbert, she continued to pursue her athletic conditioning by running and hitting a punching bag daily for health.[67] She gained some public attention in 1904 when she used her boxing skills to deter an assailant on the street. In reaction to the assault and the notoriety she attracted from the incident, Gilbert proposed organizing a woman-only society to train in self-defense so that women could empower themselves to act as their own defenders and prepare to protect themselves in any situation.[68] She recognized that women needed to be both physically prepared to protect themselves and politically empowered.

Although Gilbert was extremely active in the Cuyahoga County Woman's Suffrage Party, over time she grew dissatisfied with the elitism of the upper-class women in the organization. Inspired by the Pankhursts in England, she decided to form a more radical organization of her own, known as the Home Protection Equal Suffrage Club. This split in the Cuyahoga party occurred simultaneously with Emmeline Pankhurst's visit to Cleveland in October 1913. Some members of the

Cuyahoga County Woman's Suffrage Party refused to attend Pankhurst's lecture, expressing a desire to distance themselves from her militant tactics. No doubt Gilbert was among the many women who did attend the lecture, and within a few months she announced the formation of a new organization with more than 600 members in alignment with the Pankhursts' cause. This new organization, which reflected Gilbert's socialist philosophy and expressed sympathy and support for the efforts of organized labor, was intended to mobilize and empower working-class women in the suffrage movement.[69] Gilbert admired the militant suffragettes in England, adopting a similar philosophy and approach in her own political life, even as she insisted that the situation in the United States did not require militant protest tactics. She did, however, advocate that women should serve as their own protectors, training their bodies for defense, and she carried out that philosophy in her own political activism.

Professor Emily Putnam of Barnard College recognized the correlation between women's self-defense and the broader campaigns for women's political and social freedoms. Speaking to a group of Vassar College women in 1915, Putnam articulated the connections between the personal and political empowerment of women. Putnam (who had previously served as the first dean of Barnard College and at the time of her Vassar address was a professor of history at Barnard), offered an in-depth feminist analysis of the status of women by highlighting the broader dangers of gender stereotyping. She not only decried women's subordinate political status in society but also suggested that items of clothing such as skirts reinforced the objectification. Putnam explained how women's fear and lack of knowledge about how to defend themselves kept them in a state of subjugation:

> If I might have my way, all girls would be trained to be manly. They would be stripped of their hampering dress, which is in itself a badge of physical incompetence. They would be practiced in dangerous sports, where life and limb depend on nervous control; public opinion would require of them the same standard of physical courage as it requires of boys; they would not be allowed to cry when they are hurt; the schools would have courses in not being afraid of things, beginning with mice and progress through men-under-the-bed to fire-arms; they would learn the ordinary

arts of self-defense, and, in view of their special liability to attack, would supplement these with the open carriage of weapons when circumstances rendered it advisable.[70]

Putnam's radical suggestion (as one reporter labeled it) that women be trained to be manly through self-defense clearly reflected her belief in the potential of physical training to help women embody the political and liberate them from their subservient status.

American women who followed Putnam's advice and chose to study self-defense endured attacks on their femininity and accusations that their physical training had grotesquely masculinized them. When the University of Illinois announced the introduction of boxing classes for women, a reporter declared it a "good thing" and then added sarcastically, "A man naturally wants a wife who is able to protect him from insult."[71] The juxtaposition of gender roles in this statement was intended not only as humorous commentary regarding women's entry into the world of athletics but also as commentary about women's advances in the political realm. It also exposed the anxiety that these changes in gender roles inevitably created. A writer in the *Evening Star*, a Washington, DC, newspaper, took a similarly humorous approach to the issue of women's boxing and athletic training by predicting a complete reversal of gender norms. He insisted that sooner or later the newspapers would be printing stories such as the following:

> Willie Clarency, a delicate and beautiful young man with dreamy eyes, creamy complexion and graceful and petite form, was rescued from a gang of rowdy girls last night. The female thugs were cruelly disarranging his appearance when his shrill screams for help attracted Gladys Strong, right tackle, stroke oar, hammer thrower, shortstop and heavyweight pugiliste of the young ladies' seminary of this place. Rushing to Willie's aid she tackled the bunch, tossing one of the footpads forty feet in the air, punching four of them into the middle of week after next, swinging one in each hand and trampling the others to death. She clutched Mr. Clarency in her arms, bore him to a place of safety and revived him with aromatic salts. As a result of this romance Gladys has asked Willie's mother for his hand, and the wedding bells will ring. Mrs. Gladys Strong and husband (nee Clarency) have our best wishes.[72]

This excerpt ironically highlights the sexual objectification of women, their inferior status in a patriarchal culture, and the gender-based violence that women faced at the same time it expresses anxiety over the potential reversal of the status of men and women. The entry of women into the field of self-defense signaled the advances of the new socially and politically empowered modern woman. Yet some men feared that women, in their new role, would reduce men to the same objectified and inferior status that they had imposed on women. Women's self-defense represented not just women's empowerment but women's potential to subjugate men.

Other detractors offered less amusing critiques, choosing instead more insulting tones. An American newspaper writer described Charlotte Perkins Gilman's theory about the necessity of exercise and physical strength in helping women secure their rights and linked it to the Women's Development Society and the study of jiu-jitsu and boxing among British suffragettes. The author also pointed to Katie Sandwina, a weight lifter and performer in a New York circus. As part of her act, Sandwina "tosses her 155-pound husband around in the air as if he were a child." In comparing the suffragettes who pursued athletic training to a circus performer, the author attempted to marginalize suffragettes as masculinized "others" akin to sideshow "freaks." The author, who explained that Sandwina had developed her strength by using a washboard and carpet sweeper, concluded that "there is no exercise more beneficial than housework," and then queried: "Will the suffragettes, eager to excel in athletics, take a hint?"[73] This last comment implies that the British suffragettes had stepped outside their natural bounds in the private sphere and that their true place was in the home. Thus the author believed that women's political empowerment, and more specifically their physical empowerment, threatened to undermine American manliness.

Chauncy Thomas, writing for the magazine *Outdoor Life*, insisted that American men must take up boxing to counteract the ill effects of feminization. Thomas wrote that the breed of effeminate men, "Mamma's darling, the six-foot suckling with a lisp and a vision, is about done—or the American is done," arguing that this "sissy, Mamma's boy" is "the product of the chinless husband and the iron-jawed suffragette, hermaphrodite hybrid of a sheep and a wasp—a neuter from two neuters."[74] The new politically empowered, masculinized woman posed a looming threat to American manhood, according to men like Thomas.

In response to cynics who insisted that women's pursuit of male privilege reflected their masculinization or, worse, their desire to be men, journalist Nixola Greeley-Smith wrote, "So long as the great desire of one's soul is for freedom, independence, the advantages of being a boy are obvious."[75] Upon hearing about the jiu-jitsu practiced by English suffragettes, Greeley-Smith asserted, "Woman is no longer the weaker sex," explaining that the suffragettes' self-defense training would "place woman upon the same physical plane as man."[76] She had long advocated that American women should follow the English example and recommended the introduction of a required course in jiu-jitsu in schools and women's colleges.[77] While Greeley-Smith waited for such sweeping changes, she also authored a series of articles that featured tutorials in jiu-jitsu so that women could empower and teach themselves self-defense in their own homes.[78] Greeley-Smith recognized women's self-defense as essential to their evolution into empowered New Women.

## The New Woman

The politically and physically empowered woman came to represent the quintessential New Woman. The origin of the term "New Woman" remains a matter of disagreement, but by the 1890s it was clearly in use in mainstream periodicals, usually to describe a modern woman who seemed significantly different from the women of earlier generations. The phrase signaled a change in the roles of women. The New Woman was typically depicted as dedicated to women's suffrage and Progressive Era reforms. Carroll Smith-Rosenberg identified successive waves of New Women. The first wave emerged in the 1880s and 1890s women, "rejecting conventional female roles and asserting their right to a career, to a public voice, to visible power, laid claim to the rights and privileges customarily accorded bourgeois men."[79] Many of these women were college educated and career oriented. Whereas in 1890 women constituted only 35 percent of university students, by 1920 women made up 47 percent of the college population. This was an elite group of women, however, since only 8 percent of college-aged women were attending college in 1920. These graduates became prominent leaders in medicine, education, art, literature, and social reform movements. Non-college-educated women were also moving into the workforce in greater numbers. By 1900, 5 million women were working in a range of careers in factories, farms, and offices.[80] The second wave, according to Smith-Rosenberg, emerged in the years around World War I and differed from the previous generation of New Women primarily in their rejection of dominant gender and sexual norms.[81] This created a conflict with the older generation of outward-focused and social-reform minded women. The new New Woman was associated with the flapper generation and her quest for personal freedom and self-expression. According to historian Martha Patterson, the image of the New Woman as constructed in the early twentieth century was much broader than that and varied substantially as it took on a range of race, class, ethnic, regional, and political influences. Patterson noted that the New Woman's sometimes contradictory forms included taking on the role of "suffragist, prohibitionist, clubwoman, college girl, American girl, socialist, capitalist, anarchist, pickpocket, bicyclist, barren spinster, mannish woman, outdoor girl, birth-control advocate, modern girl, eugenicist, flapper, blues woman, lesbian and vamp." Nevertheless, contemporary writers conceived of the New Woman as "a crucial modern social development."[82]

In the early twentieth century, self-defense training clearly came to symbolize the emerging status of both generations of the New Woman through the pursuit of personal and political independence. In 1913, an article in the *San Francisco Chronicle* highlighting the numerous female boxers in the country quoted a well-known athlete as saying that "the modern girl athlete is getting better every year. She is a very different creature from the old piano-playing, fancywork type who was half the time afraid of being alive. This new type of woman is alive all over, all the time."[83] Contemporaries also made more explicit links between political and physical empowerment, seeing women's entrance into a variety of athletic fields as a clear signal of their advancement in society. An article in the *Ogden Standard-Examiner* in 1922 noted the significance of women's participation in sport and self-defense: "Through the centuries she has been advancing from the lowly state when she was held as a slave and a chattel but it had been slow work until lately, when her victories began to come with a rush. She won the vote. She came to stand by the side of man in the business world. . . . And now it is being granted that she has successfully invaded a field that always has been considered peculiarly man's, the field of the display of his greater strength—the field of athletics."[84] The article continued by describing the accomplishments of a number of female athletes, including Gertrude Eggert, a wrestler and jiu-jitsu practitioner.

Self-defense training for the New Woman sounded the death knell for outmoded notions of male protection. An article in the *Milwaukee Sentinel* in 1911 highlighted the political connotations of women's self-defense training through a rebellion against confining gender roles: "It is the tradition that a woman must be timid. It is the tradition that she is helpless in the grasp of [a] strong, brutal man. It is the tradition that she is defenseless for the preservation of herself or her possessions against any attack made by a resolute and pitiless assailant. It is also false." By describing women like Blanche Whitney, who had mastered the art of self-defense, the article clearly countered gender stereotypes that positioned women as weaker than men and incapable of fighting. Self-defense training, then, took on a clear political meaning as women embodied feminism. Inspired by the suffragettes in England who had "bowled over cops with it [jiu-jitsu] most beautifully," the author insisted on women's physical and political capabilities as typifying the emergence of a New Woman.[85]

The *New York Tribune* insisted in 1918 that the entrance of women into the sport of boxing was a sure sign that suffrage was "here to stay."[86] In a similar article published in the *San Francisco Chronicle* in 1922, the author noted the power of the New Woman and offered a warning to potential burglars: "Life is not what it used to be even for burglars since women forgot how to scream. In the old days a marauder who encountered a stray female could be fairly certain that she would either cower beneath the sheets or yell for assistance. He acted accordingly. But now—what with higher education, bobbed hair, jiu-jitsu, knickerbockers and the like—she has ceased to function according to the best traditions of her sex. She neither cowers nor yells. And she may do almost anything."[87] Thus in this and similar stories, modern women had empowered themselves intellectually, politically, and physically. These multiple elements amounted to an independent identity for women, who could not only vote, cut their hair and hemlines, and drink and smoke in public but also venture into the urban environment equipped with the skills to defend themselves. An important characteristic of the New Woman was her ability to physically fight back and act as her own defender. Training in boxing and jiu-jitsu was a sign of her ability to exercise her new political and social freedoms.

## Conclusion

By the 1920s, the association between physically strong women and politically empowered women was clear. The entry of women into the world of the "manly arts" symbolized women's success in entering the political arena and casting aside the myth of the male protector. Just as the female body had long been subjected to violence and abuse, these women used their bodies as tools to resist assault and secure for themselves a sense of personal and political empowerment. Although not all women who pursued boxing and jiu-jitsu during this era recognized the revolutionary implications of their actions, most women noted the sense of personal empowerment that inevitably resulted from their physical activity. They embraced it as liberation from the oppressive gender stereotypes that had heretofore limited their activities and movement. Others clearly recognized the political link and used self-defense as a visible and physical sign of their new political empowerment.[88] To radical suffragists, self-defense training represented a tangible means of bringing about a revolution as they battled generations of constricting gender stereotypes in the gym and fought police and antisuffragists on the picket line.

The New Woman who emerged from the fray embodied many of the characteristics that feminists had fought so hard to achieve. She had overcome self-imposed limitations, as well as those dictated to her by society's rigidly defined gender roles. She had cracked open the door of every athletic institution previously restricted to men. By 1919, she had achieved the vote and secured a sense of political liberation. Suffragists recognized the vote as essential to their quest for female liberation, but they also increasingly recognized that women's political oppression was directly linked to their physical and sexual subjugation.[89] Ultimately, women would discover the limits of their new freedoms, since liberation in the political arena did not always translate to liberation at home. The most deeply personal and difficult battle was saved for last. As we will see in the next chapter, freedom from domestic tyranny required a mustering of a diverse set of personal and societal resources that not everyone was willing or able to commit. Self-defense training took on an immensely personal meaning as women battled for liberation in their own homes.

5

## Self-Defense in the Domestic Sphere

Beyond the political connotations of self-defense training, many individuals believed that the public discussion about women's self-defense could help draw attention to the very personal issue of intimate partner violence. This was an issue that plagued American families. The popular media focused on violent attacks by mashers, white slavers, black rapists, or shadowy strangers as the main dangers facing American women. However, the real threats of violence were often closer to home. This fact further shattered the illusion of the natural protector. Nowhere were the myth of stranger danger and the myth of the male protector more obviously disproved than in the homes of women who were subjected to violence perpetrated by the men they loved.

The discourse surrounding women's self-defense helped dispel powerful myths about the sources of violence against women. Self-defense instructors and women's rights leaders at first subtly and then more directly recommended that self-defense might be used to protect women from assaults by violent partners. Through the active deconstruction of the concept of the male protector, self-defense advocates called public attention to the issue of intimate partner violence, demanded a more realistic discussion of the sources of violence against women, and challenged woman to reenvision herself as her own protector, capable of defending her own physical safety and that of her children if necessary from violence perpetrated by male partners or relatives. Even though most of the women who were victims of intimate partner violence never trained in self-defense, the public discussion of women's self-defense helped bring the issue of violence against women to the forefront and in the process helped dispel myths about the sinister stranger. For self-defense practitioners, the mere recognition that women were physically capable of more than they previously thought possible rendered their own physical and psychological resistance to domestic violence within the realm of possibility.

## Debunking the Myths

The image of a racialized, mysterious, shadowy stranger figured largely into popular myths about the origins of violence against women. Newspapers, literature, and films helped contribute to the construction of a stereotyped representation of the assailant and victim. Morally pure middle- or upper-class white women were frequently depicted as the easy victims of black, Asian, or southern European sexually deviant predators. In these imaginary tales, black rapists stalked women on the streets, Chinese men lured women into opium dens and then brothels, and southern European white slavers drugged and kidnapped women and forced them into prostitution. The resulting racial and ethnic stereotypes were then used to justify discrimination and harsher sentences for black and immigrant men in the court system.[1] Kimberly Jensen has pointed out that emphasis on the "icons of popular representations of rape" in the form of "the mysterious stranger, the white slaver, or the black rapist" deflected blame from the real aggressors in the form of "boyfriends, neighbors, fathers, and male relatives." Furthermore, this focus on the dangers facing white women ignored the fact that "women of color faced sexual harm from white men in the community, workplace, and home and from men of color as well."[2] Thus these stereotyped depictions of the sexual assailant as a mysterious stranger or racialized "other" served to oversimplify the complexity of the issue of violence against women and deflected attention from the real dangers that women faced.[3]

The implication that the streets were dangerous for women because of the presence of a menacing stranger by default suggested that women were safest in their own homes under the watchful eye of their natural protectors. But as we have seen in the previous chapter, increasingly women's rights activists were deconstructing this myth. Radical feminists suggested that in reality the so-called natural protector posed the greatest threat. The perpetuation of the concept of the protector and the protected and the sinister stranger placed women in a dangerous position. Mary Odem has argued that rape narratives further served to discourage young women's pursuit of social autonomy and strengthen the patriarchal authority of fathers in the home, in effect rendering "women and girls more vulnerable to sexual abuse within the home."[4] By promoting an attitude of fear about the outside world and the "other," men encouraged women to seek security in the home and look to them for protection. Patriarchal authority was thus reinforced as men took on the role of protectors and women as the protected. By buying into this notion, women capitulated to their insecurities and may have even believed stereotypes about feminine weakness and their inability to defend themselves, thus making them more vulnerable to assault.[5]

A crime spree of violence against women in Chicago in 1905 and 1906 illustrates this tendency to sidestep the real issue. A series of murders of women in the city generated a media frenzy, followed by a great deal of public hysteria. The media blamed the crime spree on sinister strangers who stalked and preyed on innocent white women. Headlines across the nation proclaimed, "Chicago Enduring a Reign of Terror from Criminals." One newspaper reported that "criminals infest the city in every quarter, robbing, slugging and murdering as they will, not only in dark and isolated places, but on the highways and even in broad daylight." The media's emphasis on the criminal threat led to a fear that the streets were unsafe for women.[6] The *Chicago Tribune* insisted, "The record of the wave of reckless disregard for law shows how unsafe it is for a woman to go upon Chicago's streets unescorted."[7] The media and law enforcement supported the contention that the streets were not safe for women and encouraged them to stay home or to go out only when accompanied by a spouse or other male relative. Chief of police Collins both warned women to have escorts when walking the streets after dark and insisted on the need for more police patrols. A local lawyer, Quinn O'Brien, and the Marquette and North Shore Clubs called a mass meeting to discuss ways to defend Chicago's women. This "movement for the protection of helpless women" implied that women needed male relatives and male friends to safeguard them from threats to their physical well-being by dangerous outsiders.[8] A closer look at the evidence, however, reveals a more complex truth.

In January 1906, the *New York Tribune* listed seventeen women who had been murdered during this crime spree against women in Chicago during the prior twelve months. An analysis of the cases suggests that the primary threat against women was not from strangers. Of the seventeen women listed as victims, thirteen (76 percent) were killed by someone they knew well (intimate partner or male boarders). Furthermore, the threat was not really on the street. Twelve of the women (71 percent) were killed in the alleged safety and sanctity of their own home, room, or place of employment.[9] Thus, the evidence suggests that the real threat to women was not from random strangers on the street. Furthermore, this trend was not limited to this single year in Chicago's history. When one pulls back and looks at the larger pattern, the evidence tells a similar story. In the five years prior to the allegedly bloody year of 1905, a total of ninety-nine women were murdered in Chicago. Of those ninety-nine women, ninety-two were killed by men. The majority of those women (85 percent) were killed by men they knew (husbands, suitors, neighbors, friends, male relatives), and 66 percent were killed by husbands or lovers. In 67 percent of the cases, women were killed at home or in their place of employment.[10] The evidence from Chicago reveals, then, that in reality the most dangerous place for women was not on the streets but in their homes; the greatest threat was not a sinister stranger but their intimate partners, male relatives, and male friends.[11]

Mary Odem's research based on court records in Alameda County and Los Angeles County, California, during the Progressive Era further validates this claim about the true nature of the threats against women. According to Odem, the data suggest that women were less at risk in public spaces than they were in the private space of the home, where they faced assaults by male relatives. In fact, Odem found that 70 percent of female victims of sexual assault were attacked by a family member or acquaintance (43 percent by family members and 27 percent by friends or neighbors). An additional 17 percent were assaulted in the workplace.[12] Women's economic and psychological dependence on their male relatives coupled with threats of harm made it particularly difficult and dangerous to resist or fight back against abuse. The police occasionally intervened in exceptional cases of assault. Most women, however, found themselves trapped in a cycle of dependence and violence.

## A History of Violence

Family violence has not been limited to specific periods of time or places but has been a persistent problem throughout American history.[13] Nineteenth-century newspapers frequently published accounts of domestic quarrels. Even a cursory review of police records, divorce proceedings, and periodicals reveals the extent of violence in American family life. In an all too typical article in the *New York Daily Tribune* in 1870, a man was arrested for attacking his wife after returning home drunk. In this case, the assailant, John McGreery, pursued his wife with a razor. Accusing her of infidelity and threatening to murder her, McGreery eventually succeeded in slicing her arm and throat. Only her efforts to resist the attacks and flee the scene prevented her death. Police officers held McGreery for trial.[14] Domestic violence did not abate with the dawning of a new century either. Some forty years later, Eva Chester suffered abuse at the hands of her husband, Frank Chester, in Washington State. She filed for divorce in 1910, detailing years of physical and emotional abuse. Eva complained that on various occasions Frank called her "vile names," accused her of being a prostitute, and threatened to kill her, their children, and himself. Frank had even kidnapped the children and refused to tell her their location.[15] These cases and others that can be found in the historical record reveal that women who were the victims of violence most often experienced emotional, physical, and sexual assault by their intimate partners or male relatives.

Although the factors precipitating violent encounters in the home were numerous and complex, some themes emerge again and again in the record. For example, jealousy was common among abusers, often sparking violence. Alcohol was also frequently associated with domestic violence, triggering or exacerbating already tense situations. The husband's sense of sexual entitlement or sexual demands and the woman's refusal sometimes led to physical altercations. Infidelity, impending separation, or the suggestion of divorce by a woman contributed to outbursts of violence. Arguments over finances and/or a husband's failure to provide economically for the family also often led to quarrels that escalated to violence.[16]

Beyond these immediate triggers for domestic violence, larger societal factors contributed to a culture that condoned violence against women. Women's second-class citizenship status and limited political and economic power narrowed their options for escaping oppressive or violent relationships. Especially during the early nineteenth century, notions of masculinity, patriarchal authority, and male privilege contributed to a male sense of entitlement and justification of the right to use physical force to exert power and control over an intimate partner.

Abusers frequently defended their actions by insisting that they were simply responding to challenges to their status as head of the family and suppressing threats to their authority. Differing models of gender socialization further reinforced a culture that celebrated male violence and encouraged aggressiveness and assertion of dominance as essential traits of masculinity. At the same time, these traits were considered unbecoming in females. Women were rarely encouraged to assert themselves, express aggression, or defend against violence, thus creating socially constructed gender norms that demanded female submissiveness and passivity.

As ideas about companionate marriage emerged among the middle class, and women's rights activists fought for more egalitarian relationships between men and women, definitions of masculinity began to shift in the late nineteenth and early twentieth centuries. Men were increasingly expected to be loving husbands and fathers who ruled their households with less domineering authority and more gentle guidance. A man was expected to care for his wife and his children. Wife-beating was increasingly condemned as brutal and the antithesis of the ideal husband. Tensions over this new model of masculinity are evident in early twentieth-century divorce records, as women increasingly filed for divorce when their husbands failed to live up to the new ideal. Men who attempted to rule in the old style of patriarchal authority and physical domination faced allegations of physical or mental cruelty. Judges frequently granted divorce on such grounds, enforcing a new model of masculinity.[17] On the flip side, however, as men developed stronger bonds with their wives and relied on them more for emotional support, male violence may have emerged out of the husband's desire to avoid abandonment, prevent the dissolution of the marriage, and keep the family together. Women's growing sense of political and physical power coalesced with new expectations for egalitarian marriages based on love and free from oppression and violence. These newly empowered women who were determined to leave unhappy relationships met with resistance from men who were unwilling to give them up.[18]

Women who felt compelled to stay with violent partners sometimes risked their lives in the process. Domestic violence often intensified through the course of the relationship, with attacks increasing in severity. In 1916, Gertrude Waddell filed for divorce against her husband, Charles, on grounds of cruelty. She claimed that his attacks were becoming more violent and that he had recently threatened to shoot and kill her. Recognizing the severity of the violence, the court allowed for a temporary restraining order while the case was pending.[19] For Katherine Hlavaty, outside assistance came too late. Katherine and her husband, Thomas, had been married for more than twenty-three years, and Thomas was the well-known proprietor of a tailor shop in Chicago. Throughout their marriage, Thomas was frequently jealous of other men and abusive toward his wife. On October 4, 1905, following an argument in which Thomas accused Katherine of flirting with another man, he shot her twice in the head. Their four-year-old son, Miles, witnessed the entire event and was so traumatized that he clung to his mother and refused to leave her side even after the police and ambulance arrived. Katherine, the mother of nine children, passed away shortly thereafter.[20]

Without intervention, then, domestic violence frequently escalated, sometimes ending in murder. Historian Jeffrey Adler's research has revealed that domestic violence was the number one cause of homicide in early twentieth-century Chicago. Women were much more frequently the victims of male violence than the perpetrators of violence. Wives accounted for nearly 80 percent of the spousal homicide deaths between 1875 and 1920. Wives sometimes killed husbands as well, but the women who did kill men were likely to do so in self-defense after a long history of abuse.[21] Cynthia Grant Bowman and Ben Altman conducted a study of wife murder in Chicago and found that between 1910 and 1930 a minimum of 391 women were murdered by their husbands. The actual number of women killed as a result of family violence was no doubt even higher, since Bowman and Altman acknowledged that their sample did not include women who were murdered by suitors, jilted lovers, or other male family members. Nor did they count ambiguous cases in which the relationship between the man and woman was unclear but the perpetrator's subsequent suicide suggested intimate partner violence. While these murders accounted for only about 5 percent of the total murders in Chicago during this time, they "represent only a fraction of the violence directed at wives during this period."[22] Murder-suicides were common in intimate partner violence; studies estimate that around 50 percent of all husbands who killed their wives also killed themselves. This pattern most frequently occurred in cases where men felt helpless and despondent over their marital or financial situation and chose to end their suffering by murdering their partner and then killing themselves.[23]

Domestic violence also frequently involved more than one member of the family. In 1899, Margie Miller petitioned for a divorce in Washington, DC. Her husband, Frank, threatened to take her child away from her, saying that he would die or kill someone in the process. Justice Cox signed a restraining order to prevent Frank from "interfering" with his wife or children, and Margie retained full custody.[24] Thus, children and other family members were often drawn into arguments and violent conflicts between husbands and wives. In 1902, John Miller of Chicago was experiencing marital difficulties arising from his financial situation. John's drinking problem was making matters worse for his family. When his wife, Annie, confronted him about his problem after he stumbled home drunk one evening, he responded by shooting her to death. John then ran into the next room, where his two infant children were sleeping, and shot them to death as well. To ensure that the deed was completed, he cut their throats with a razor before unsuccessfully attempting the same on himself.[25]

Children who survived family violence often experienced extensive trauma. In 1910, a six-year-old Philadelphia boy, Leonard Donaldson, watched as his father, August Donaldson, held a gun up to his mother's head and threatened to shoot her. His mother started to cry and pleaded with her husband not to do it. The boy panicked and attempted to push his father away from his mother, but to no avail. He watched as his father fired five shots into his mother's body. After his father fled, Leonard ran to his mother's side. Leonard later detailed what had happened to the police: "I told mamma not to die." The boy sobbed as he explained, "I kissed her and put my hands over her face where the blood was." August Donaldson later walked into the police station and turned himself in. When questioned by detectives, he nonchalantly explained away his behavior, attributing his decision to murder his wife to "family troubles; that's all."[26]

Husbands were not the only danger that women faced; male suitors and male friends also posed potential threats. Nineteen-year-old Maria Luberto of Harlem, New York, was repeatedly stalked by an acquaintance, Sarraffino Franco, who eventually threatened to kill her if she would not agree to marry him. Luberto worked in a cigar factory, and after work Franco would wait for her at the factory door, then frequently followed her home, nagging her to marry him. One day, he became so frustrated that he drew a gun on Luberto and threatened, "You will marry me or I will kill you." One of Luberto's female friends attempted to intervene, but Franco threatened her as well. After Luberto reported the incident to the police, Detective Illich waited outside the factory and arrested Franco when he attempted to threaten her again. Judge Crane confiscated Franco's weapon and fined him fifteen dollars for disorderly conduct and carrying a weapon.[27] It remains unknown if the fine deterred Franco from future assaults against women, but in this case Luberto took the only legal course of action available to her at the time to protect herself.

Women also experienced assault by male relatives, neighbors, and friends of the family. Mrs. C. J. Bullacksen was killed by an angry brother-in-law, Nels Johnson, in Chicago in 1902. Johnson's wife had left him the week before because he refused to work and support the family. She sought refuge from her husband in her sister's house. Johnson, blaming his sister-in-law for the separation, sought revenge by shooting her.[28] Women such as Bullacksen thus became the target of misdirected anger and suffered the consequence of male violence. Male relatives or friends of the family also sometimes took advantage of their trusted position in the family, specifically choosing as their victims young women who looked to them for protection. A thirteen-year-old girl living on her family farm in El Reno, Kansas, was raped by a family friend and neighbor in 1902. Hiram Wheeler was gathering tomatoes in the garden when he attacked the girl and forced her into the house to assault her. Wheeler threatened to kill the girl if she told what had happened. She disregarded his threats, however, and immediately reported the assault to her parents, who pushed for Wheeler's prosecution in the courts. The mother was so upset and enraged that upon seeing Wheeler at the attorney's office, she lunged forward and hit him. Wheeler fled but was eventually arrested and charged.[29]

Although violence in the home extended across socioeconomic, racial, and ethnic lines, instances of domestic violence that came to the attention of social welfare agencies frequently centered on immigrant and poor families. This was partially because these families, lacking financial resources or an extended familial support network, often relied on private charities or public agencies for help. In Boston, Linda Gordon found that Irish, Italian, and Canadian immigrants predominated among the families reporting incidents of violence. Cultural factors, in addition to poverty, may account for some of the patterns of family violence. For example, Gordon argued that patriarchal Italian husbands tended to use physical force to assert control over their wives and children, and that drinking and fighting were common in Irish immigrant families.[30] Accounts of family violence detailed in the public record seem to validate Gordon's findings.

Cultural and historical factors also influenced patterns of violence among black families. In black communities, a culture of harsh discipline characterized family life as parents taught their children an essential attitude of deference that would help them survive in a white-dominated, racist world. Just as white society exercised rigid control over black fathers and husbands, these men sought to assert strict authority over their own families, often through violence and brutality.[31] Poverty and overcrowded living conditions exacerbated the situation. In their study of wife murder in Chicago, Cynthia Grant Bowman and Ben Altman found that African American and immigrant families experienced higher rates of wife murder than did native, white families. Bowman and Altman concluded that the abuse inflicted on African Americans during slavery and Jim Crow may have contributed to a cycle of violence and elevated rates of domestic violence within the African American community. However, their research revealed that black women were more likely to fight back against domestic abuse and that there were higher rates of husband killings by black women than white women. The authors argued that this reflected a greater sense of independence among black women, higher rates of employment than among white women, and a greater sense of equality with their husbands.[32] Black women's desire to escape sexual abuse and domestic violence from both white and black men was a major motive for the Great Migration in the early twentieth century. In uprooting themselves and their children, black women found a way to assert some control over their own bodies.[33]

In addition to these cultural and ethnic factors, research has suggested that poverty, high rates of unemployment, poor housing, crowded conditions, immigrant status, discrimination, and open racism are additional stress factors that may correlate with, although not directly cause, family violence.[34] Asian immigrant communities in the West, for example, also experienced cases of family violence related to a number of these factors. Limited economic opportunities combined with racial discrimination contributed to especially difficult conditions for immigrant farm families. Incidents of sexual harassment, assault, and violence were reported among Japanese American agricultural couples living in California in the early twentieth century. Some of these incidents culminated in homicide. In one case, a Japanese immigrant woman named Rei Handa fended off a violent attempted rape by shooting her attacker in self-defense. The perpetrator in this case was her husband's business partner and a friend of the family.[35]

Although these stress factors contributed to higher levels of violence in poor or immigrant families, it is inaccurate to assume that immigrant, racial, cultural, or socioeconomic factors alone cause violence against women, especially since domestic violence transcended racial and class boundaries. Furthermore, prosecution of wife beaters tended to be disproportionately directed at the poor and especially at African American and immigrant men, suggesting bias in the enforcement of criminal assault law.[36] As feminists of the era pointed out, centuries of male privilege and oppression of women—extending across racial and class lines—contributed to a culture that directly and indirectly condoned men's violence against women.

Women from middle- or upper-class families may have been more reluctant to report such incidents to the police in an effort to protect their status and reputation. At the time, many middle- and upper-class Anglo women embraced social evolutionary theory, which suggested that their status as members of the most civilized race freed them from the violence known to women of other races and classes. Violence and brutality were characteristics relegated to primitive nonwhite, immigrant, and poor men. This powerful cultural belief, suggesting that these individuals were more prone to violence, may have silenced many middle- and upper-class white women who were victims of their husbands' brutality and discouraged them from reporting incidents in their own homes. Although this failure to press charges alone does not account for the higher rates of violence reported among working-class families, it may account somewhat for the lower rates of reported cases of violence among middle- and upper-class families. In addition, the popular press and moral reformers tended to focus mostly on domestic violence among nonwhites, immigrants, and the working class, thus rendering cases of violence within those families more visible.[37]

Women from lower socioeconomic classes and nonwhite or immigrant women seeking assistance from law enforcement, the courts, or private charities found evolutionist and racialized views of violence so prevalent that they had to appeal to dominant Anglo-Protestant, middle-class views of femininity to even be considered worthy of help. Especially for women of color, who had been depicted in the mainstream press as hypersexualized and immoral, demonstrating respectable ladylike behavior was essential to gaining the sympathy and support of white reformers and officials. The doctrine of male protection extended typically only to middle- and upper-class women of the Anglo race. In appealing, then, to male police officers, judges, and juries, nonwhite, immigrant, and poor women had to exhibit the appropriate feminine qualities to gain sympathy and protection as victims of sexual assault and domestic violence.[38]

Although reformers, the press, and the courts tended to focus on violence in nonwhite or immigrant working-class families, middle- and upper-class white women were not immune from violence. In 1909, Harry S. Lott, a prominent local preacher and superintendent of "a home for fallen women" in Oklahoma City, was fined $100 and sentenced to thirty days in the county jail for assaulting his wife. Mrs. Lott petitioned for divorce on the grounds of cruelty, having earlier applied for and received a restraining order against her husband to prevent him from harassing her or their children.[39] In a similar case in 1913, Mrs. Margaret A. Novak of Omaha, Nebraska, filed for divorce against her husband, James W. Novak, a prominent and wealthy dentist, on grounds of cruelty. Margaret Novak obtained a restraining order forbidding Mr. Novak from returning to the house.[40] The behavior of these affluent local men challenged preconceived notions about the more civilized men of the Anglo upper class and proved instead that violence transcended boundaries of race and class.

## Efforts to Eliminate Domestic Violence

Historian Elizabeth Pleck has identified three major periods of reform efforts to end family violence in the history of the United States. Puritans in colonial Massachusetts, who were concerned with preserving the sanctity of their religious community, initiated the first wave of reform (1640–1680). The second wave began in the mid-nineteenth century and continued until around 1890 (although there is some evidence, as discussed later, that this period may be extended by at least two more decades). Pleck argues that the third wave of reform went hand in hand with the women's liberation movement of the 1960s and 1970s.[41] Similarly, Linda Gordon has noted that "concern with family violence usually grew when feminism was strong and ebbed when feminism was weak."[42]

For our purposes here, we are concerned with the second period of reform against family violence that coincided with the women's rights movement of the mid-nineteenth century. Reformers initiated a wide range of efforts in an attempt to solve the problem. From the liberalization of divorce laws to the formation of protective societies for female and child victims of abuse, concerned citizens sought to eliminate family violence indirectly. Leaders of the temperance campaign broached the subject of family violence as early as the 1830s and 1840s. Temperance reformers placed the blame for family violence primarily on alcohol. Later temperance advocates would link the issue of domestic violence to women's political subordination. The Women's Christian Temperance Union recognized physical security against abusive husbands as a major goal in the women's rights agenda. Frances Willard argued that the vote would protect women against family violence resulting from alcohol consumption. Still, Willard promoted public shaming and moral suasion as the primary means of ending intemperance and spousal abuse.[43]

The formation of the Society for the Prevention of Cruelty to Children (SPCC) in 1874 brought a great deal of attention to the issue of family violence by highlighting extreme cases of child abuse. Anticruelty organizations justified public intervention in the private domain of the family for the purpose of protecting the innocent. Although the SPCC focused primarily on rescuing children from abusive homes, agents of the anticruelty societies dedicated to investigating issues of child cruelty frequently also uncovered instances of wife-beating. Attempts to rescue children from dangerous family situations often led to attempts to assist women seeking to flee from violent homes. The work of the SPCC thus inadvertently helped to bring the issue of violence against women to the forefront of public discussions.[44]

Churches, missions, and settlement houses also played a significant role during this era in helping to raise awareness about and address the issue of family violence. Women seeking refuge and protection often turned to private charities organized by their churches or other Progressive Era reform organizations, which offered assistance and shelter to women. Although not originally created as domestic violence shelters, many settlement houses and mission homes intended to alleviate issues of urban poverty or rescue "fallen" women informally served as safe havens for women escaping a violent home environment. Victims became their own advocates by seeking out these organizations and requesting help. A few private organizations emerged during this decade specifically to support female victims of family violence. The Protective Agency for Women and Children, for example, was formed in 1885 in Chicago to provide legal aid, shelter, and support for women and children who were victims of abuse.[45] Through charitable settlement house work, reform-minded middle- and upper-class women discovered the significant issues facing many women.

Reformers frequently saw themselves as a civilizing force among poor, immigrant, and nonwhite people. Middle- and upper-class white Protestants applied their social evolutionist thinking to the issue of domestic violence by arguing that brutality against women was an attribute of primitive people (poor, immigrant, nonwhite) and that men of civilized races did not beat their wives. However, agitation against domestic violence emerged from poor, immigrant, and nonwhite families. These women increasingly advocated for themselves by pressing charges of criminal assault in the courts, filing for divorce on grounds of cruelty, and seeking aid from private charities. Reformers, then, were responding to the demands of women who clearly recognized their own right to live free from violence. Increasingly, though, reformers and the courts used their authority to expand their power over the lives of these families.[46]

Another nineteenth-century campaign to deal with violence against women is worth mentioning here, although it proved relatively unsuccessful. This movement, known as the whipping post crusade, advocated the physical punishment of wife beaters through flogging. This suggested solution emerged in the 1880s and received a great deal of newspaper coverage over the next three decades. Some commentators reacted negatively to the idea of the whipping post, doubting its ability to solve the problem of family violence. Justice Catherine Waugh Mc-Culloch expressed her opinion on the subject in 1912 when she said "a wife-beater is one of the lowest type of humanity the law has to deal with. But would whipping posts be the right remedy? I hardly think so." McCulloch was concerned about the safety of the women and children, explaining, "If a wife-beater was publicly whipped I think in the majority of cases he would return to his home and take vengeance upon his wife and children. That method is too much like the way they dealt with people during the stone age." Instead, McCulloch believed that wife beaters should be sentenced to the workhouse and their wages given back to the families.[47] Although some high-profile women's rights leaders and politicians, including Lucy Stone and Theodore Roosevelt, advocated the whipping post approach, ultimately only three states passed laws allowing it.[48]

Women's rights advocates were most vocal about exposing the issue of violence against women and seeking realistic, long-term solutions to family violence by recognizing that women's political subordination in the public sphere went hand in hand with their subordination in the domestic sphere. However, antebellum reformers approached the problem rather indirectly and rarely argued specifically for criminal prosecution of abusers or larger reforms to eliminate wife-beating. Instead, early activists focused on the issue of divorce. For example, in the mid-nineteenth century, Elizabeth Cady Stanton and Lucretia Mott openly condemned violence against women while using examples of domestic violence to support their argument for a woman's right to divorce. In the 1850s, Stanton and Susan B. Anthony went so far as to attempt to secure the passage of legislation in New York State allowing wives the right to divorce husbands who abused them. Stanton and Anthony continued to speak out against women's physical and sexual subjugation by broaching controversial topics such as marital rape. After the Civil War, a renewed interest in the issue of violence against women emerged as women's rights activists began to challenge male dominance and the sexual double standard. In 1876, Lucy Stone called public attention to the issue of family violence and challenged the notion of the natural protector by chronicling instances of physical assault against women in her *Woman's Journal*. Stone also (unsuccessfully) lobbied for the passage of laws to grant female victims of domestic violence legal separation, child support, and child custody.[49]

However, the leaders of national suffrage organizations were cautious in their approach to domestic violence issues for fear of alienating potential supporters in their efforts to win the right to vote. Calculated political moves sometimes forced these issues to take a backseat to larger issues of political equality. Backlash against those who advocated divorce as a solution to domestic violence emerged even from members of the temperance societies. Enduring intense criticism for promoting liberalized divorce laws and accused of attempting to destroy the stability of American family life, by the 1890s suffrage leaders chose to censor their own speech and focus more narrowly on women's suffrage. The suffrage movement experienced a sort of rebirth in the 1890s as leaders of the National American Woman Suffrage Association tapped into changing popular sentiment supporting woman suffrage and created an efficient political machine focused on the passage of the Nineteenth Amendment. Suffrage leaders hoped that once women had achieved the right to vote, they would be empowered to tackle other issues again such as violence against women.[50]

The efforts of nineteenth-century women's rights advocates did, however, succeed in educating the public about violence against women and providing options for women escaping violent home lives. By the early twentieth century, women more frequently turned to the courts for assistance in ending volatile relationships. According to the records of the U.S. Census Bureau, the number of divorces granted to wives on the grounds of cruelty increased from more than 6,000 in the years 1867–1871 to more than 64,000 in the years 1902–1906. This was due in part to the fact that many states added cruelty as grounds for divorce during this period. Whereas in earlier decades women were more likely to claim their husband's intemperance as the issue precipitating marital separation, increasingly wives filed for divorce citing instances of emotional, physical, and sexual abuse. Approximately 12 percent of the divorces requested by women in the 1860s were initiated on the basis of cruelty ver-

sus 24 percent by the first decade of the twentieth century.[51] In addition
to divorce, many women pursued criminal prosecution of their abusers,
and judges often sided with the victim, meting out punishments to wife
beaters. A search of digitized newspapers revealed thousands of articles
detailing the arrest and prosecution of wife beaters. The number of articles on the topic began increasing in the 1880s, peaking in 1905 before
declining again around 1918.[52] Interestingly, the number of articles on
the subject would not reach these Progressive Era numbers again until
the mid-1970s, during the second wave of feminism.

A new generation of female journalists also helped to keep the issue
of violence against women in the public eye. Many of the sensationalist
stories they wrote had widespread appeal in this era of yellow journalism, although more for their dramatic value than for the actual issues
they addressed. However, some of the women writers helped to frame
the stories within a feminist context and advocated against violence in
the home. Nixola Greeley-Smith, writing for the *Evening World*, published extensively on issues for and about women, and her writings reflected her personal beliefs as an active suffragist with the New York
State Women's Suffrage Party.[53] As we saw in previous chapters, Greeley-
Smith wrote many articles on the masher issue and the dangers that
women faced on the streets. She also helped to shed light on the issue
of sexual harassment as experienced by women in the workplace. Similarly, she wrote about the prevalence of domestic violence and published
articles on the whipping post debate. In one interview with a judge who
was a firm advocate of this approach, Greeley-Smith revealed her thinking when she posed the question, "But do you think a husband and wife
could resume living together after the man had been whipped at the post
on his wife's complaint?"[54] This reflected the concerns of other women's
rights advocates who argued that this punishment did little to ensure the
future physical safety or economic security of the women and children
of abusive husbands. Greeley-Smith was, however, a vocal advocate of
women's self-defense, publishing numerous how-to articles encouraging
women to teach themselves the necessary skills to defend themselves.[55]

Prominent scholars have suggested that anticruelty organizations,
women's rights advocates, and protective agencies appeared to be losing
popular support for their movements against family violence around
the late nineteenth century and that this shift resulted from increasing

concern about maintaining the privacy and stability of the family. According to Elizabeth Pleck's periodization scheme, family violence reform was undergoing a period of neglect during the time covered by the present study (1890–1920). In fact, Pleck argues that "lack of concern about the issue has been the normal state of affairs" in American history.[56] However, newspaper coverage and court case evidence seem to suggest a continued public discussion and legal concern with prosecuting wife beaters at least until around 1918. More recent research by legal scholars supports the need for revising Pleck's time frame. Carolyn B. Ramsey has argued that the stern punishment for wife murderers during the Progressive Era counters the arguments of scholars who may have overstated the level of public apathy toward violence against women. Elizabeth Katz has similarly noted that the historical sources that scholars have focused on in their research may have limited their view of domestic violence reform. Katz suggests instead that a review of legal cases clearly shows that judges in the early twentieth century vigorously punished wife beaters and sought to protect women from domestic violence in both criminal and divorce cases. Thus a variety of factors, including the very public discussion of wife-beating in the popular press, the continued debate over use of the whipping post for wife beaters, the increase in divorces filed on the grounds of cruelty, and the criminal prosecution of abusers, seem to justify an extension of the time frame that Pleck has defined as the second wave of reform from the 1890s to the turn of the century and possibly as late as 1918.[57] Future studies into the subject of intimate partner violence during this era may be able to further refine the nuances and chronology of antiviolence reform efforts.

Scholars do agree, however, that beginning in the early twentieth century and definitely by the 1920s, issues of family violence had gradually shifted away from criminal courts and toward the newly created juvenile and family courts. At this point, public discussion of the issue of family violence and efforts to pass legislation or prosecute abusers in the criminal courts waned. This new era of reform focused less on punishing the abuser and more on reforming the family. Whereas the courts had clearly rejected the idea that a man had the right to chastise his wife in favor of new ideas about companionate marriage, judges and jurists increasingly invoked concepts of familial privacy to justify their failure to seriously prosecute cases of intimate partner violence. Optimistic reformers recognized and sought to remedy a variety of issues that contributed to family stress, including poverty, unemployment, and poor housing. Social workers and psychiatrists played key roles in counseling families through troubled times. Ultimately, however, the primary goal in dealing with cases of domestic violence was the preservation of the family unit. Judges and caseworkers delved deeply into the personal lives of their clients by interviewing family and friends, visiting the family home, and offering advice on child rearing, housekeeping, and marital relations. Reformers preferred to focus on altering the behaviors of family members and eliminating the problems that led to the abuse rather than on granting divorces and child support. Social workers sought to recast working-class and immigrant families into idealized models of middle-class domesticity. This emphasis on reconciliation had the effect of decriminalizing and minimizing the issue of family violence, blaming the victim, and focusing on reforming the behaviors of the victim in order to avoid initiating the abuse. This approach rarely resolved the problem. In the end, the courts mostly failed in their goal of preserving the family and often acquiesced to the request of clients by granting battered women divorces and spousal support and in some cases removing abused or neglected children from the home.[58]

## Self-Defense in the Home

Women frequently resisted assault in a number of ways, including running away, seeking assistance from neighbors, calling the police, or asking private and public agencies for help. Yet advocates of self-defense training promoted a much more radical approach to addressing family violence by encouraging women to pursue training in boxing and jiu-jitsu in order to gain the confidence to resist aggressors. Discussions of the variety of uses of women's self-defense included a common theme in the potential of self-defense to provide women with an element of protection against the threat of violence in the home. These comments were initially subtly stated or insinuated in a playful or humorous way designed not to offend the reader but still posed as a potential solution to the problem of domestic violence. For example, in discussing the popular fad of women training in boxing, an 1892 article in the *St. Paul Daily Globe* offered an amusing though significant warning to men:

"Prospective husbands had better beware, not only of concealed claws, but of well-trained fists."[59] An article in the *St. Louis Republic* noted that "President Roosevelt's desire to punish wife beaters at the whipping-post and State Representative Marten's plan to send them to the rock-pile hardly meet modern ideas. Why not enact a law requiring brides elect to take a course in jiu-jitsu?"[60] Similar jokes continued along this vein. In 1911, Blanche Whitney, a jiu-jitsu practitioner, boxer, and wrestler, quipped: "If a husband is cross and disagreeable . . . just put him on his back as fast as he can get up. It will make a gentleman out of him in no time."[61] The discussion of women's self-defense on the street helped broach the largely taboo topic of violence against women in the home.

Commentary suggesting self-defense training as a remedy for domestic violence continued to increase over the next decade. In 1912, an article in the *Hawaiian Star* suggested somewhat tongue in cheek that through the study of jiu-jitsu a wife "could preserve the sanctity of the home by a light twist of the wrist . . . It seems to be wholly practicable to undo man in one inning even if he has had the forethought to bring home an axe. Usually bosship ends right there and instead of being the slave-driver of an unhappy household a man can soon be fed out of the hand or set to peel the sweet potatoes or pass the poi to the children or even to his mother-in-law."[62] DeWitt Van Court, a boxing instructor in Los Angeles, similarly insisted on the domestic advantages of self-defense and, only half-jokingly, suggested, "Such a course, girls, enables you to master the art of self-defense and that mastery might come in handy someday if you happen to marry a man who is inclined to become rambunctious."[63] Van Court clearly believed in the power of self-defense training, as he continued to teach boxing courses for women.

Some writers took the issue a bit more seriously, noting the prevalence of domestic violence. A female journalist writing for the *St. Paul Globe* began by acknowledging the reality of violence in the home. She then insisted on the right of women to fight back and sincerely noted the utility of jiu-jitsu and boxing lessons for women in the early years of marriage: "A man who is a wife beater at heart, no matter how gracious his exterior may be, will think twice before he lays his hand and heart at the feet of an expert boxer."[64] The author praised the enlightened decision of a judge who supported a woman's right to defend herself against a wife beater, perceiving it as a step forward in women's rights.

Jiu-jitsu instructors likewise advocated self-defense for women and suggested women use their knowledge of self-defense if necessary to protect themselves from intimate partner violence. The author of a 1913 article in the *Ogden Standard* noted that jiu-jitsu training had many advantages for women: "Masters of the art [of jiu-jitsu] advise wives whose husbands beat them to turn around and beat their husbands—as soon as they learn jiu jitsu."[65] This blatant advocacy of jiu-jitsu as self-defense against domestic violence no doubt reflects the opinions of other practitioners of the art who were well aware of its potential advantages for women.

Some advocates of self-defense for women used the idea of women's physical empowerment to contest existing constructions of gender and power. In 1909, Dr. Maude Glasgow, a New York physician, sought to counter stereotypes of the weak and helpless woman and further insisted on women's right to defend themselves against violence on the street and in the home. Glasgow, who said that "girls should be taught that the masculine defender is not always to be trusted. Who is to defend her against him? Only her own muscle and science," challenged the myth of the male protector by arguing instead that man *is* the threat to woman's safety. She further advanced the radical notion that a woman could be her own defender, insisting that a girl should learn boxing to feel as secure as "her father or brother or husband does." Glasgow explained her intent more explicitly, arguing that "if women knew a little more about the art of self-defense our police courts would not be disgraced by the appearance of so many wife-beaters."[66] The contestation of the notion of the male protector, the assertion that women have the right to live a life free from violence, and the contention that women are capable of defending themselves represented a radically empowering idea and the culmination, to some extent, of the ideals espoused by more radical women's rights advocates.

As discussed in the previous chapter, radical English suffragettes openly advocated the study of self-defense not only as a means for women to secure and express their political empowerment but also as a way to protect themselves in their own homes. Edith Garrud, the well-known jiu-jitsu instructor who trained English suffragettes, offered several public demonstrations of her skills through the performance of suffragette skits. A condensed version of one of her plays, illustrated

# Ju-Jutsu as a Husband-Tamer.
## A SUFFRAGETTE PLAY WITH A MORAL.

Figure 5.1 "Ju-Jutsu as a Husband-Tamer," *Health and Strength*, April 8, 1911. British Library Board, London.

with images of Garrud performing the techniques, was published in 1911 in *Health and Strength*, a British magazine that focused on physical culture. The play, tellingly titled "Ju-Jutsu as a Husband-Tamer," told the story of a produce seller's wife who, after being taught jiu-jitsu, "tames her drunken husband into subjection." Although the husband in the play made several attempts to strike his wife, each attack was thwarted by the woman's mastery of self-defense. His violent energy was redirected through jiu-jitsu, and eventually he was forced to surrender and agree to live in domestic harmony. When the wife warned her husband,

Figure 5.2 "Get Out, Get Under." Catherine H. Palczewski Postcard Archive, University of Northern Iowa, Cedar Falls, Iowa.

"When you're drunk I'll always be a match for you," he conceded, "Then I'll never get drunk again." The play ended with husband and wife embracing and the suggestion of future domestic bliss.[67] Diana Looser has argued that Garrud's "message was clear: the physical practice of jujutsu had revolutionary potential for women, opening up unprecedented freedoms through new bodily acts."[68] The idea that such training could empower women to defend themselves against domestic violence, the most personal and most common form of violence and oppression of women, represented women's hope in dismantling the patriarchal power structure.

Yet the suffragettes' advocacy of jiu-jitsu as self-defense in the home met with a powerful backlash. Popular British postcards depicting antisuffrage themes are revealing also for their reconfiguration of depictions of violence in the home. These images reversed the dichotomy of woman as the victim and man as the perpetrator, favoring instead a view of woman as the aggressor. In "Get Out, Get Under," a wife pins her husband on the ground, beating him with a rolling pin. The caption reads: "If you love your wife, and much less your life." Pennants hanging on the wall within this image advocate: "Votes for Women."[69] The sugges-

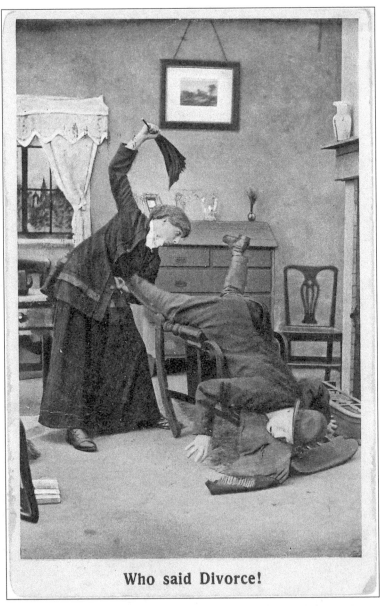

Who said Divorce!

Figure 5.3 "Who Said Divorce?," New York: Bamforth and Co. Publishers. Catherine H. Palczewski Postcard Archive, University of Northern Iowa, Cedar Falls, Iowa.

Figure 5.4 "Is Marriage a Failure?" Glasgow and London: Millar and Lang, Ltd., Art Publishers, ca. 1910. Personal collection.

tion was that a suffragist's home was a dangerous and potentially deadly place for a man, since as his wife gained political power, she also gained physical power over him. Similarly, in "Who Said Divorce?," a wife has her husband bent over a chair and whips him, presumably for suggesting divorce as a way out of his oppressive marriage.[70] "Is Marriage a Failure" shows a disheveled and abused husband hesitantly retreating from his wife, his left eye blackened from previous abuse. She has her fist cocked and ready to strike him again, threatening, "If you dare to say your'e [sic] not deliriously happy I'll black your other eye."[71] In these images, women adopted the traits of aggression and violence typically associated with men, and this female violence was redirected toward men. In this new world order, as imagined by the antisuffragists, women verbally assaulted, threatened, whipped, punched, and kicked their husbands into submission. Reflecting a larger fear of women's expanding political power and shifting gender roles, these images also suggested a concern that previously oppressed women would direct their newfound physical power and use it not in self-defense but offensively, to take vengeance on their former oppressor.

These fears about the politically and physically empowered New Woman and her capacity for violence were evidenced on both sides of the Atlantic. A series of three cartoons in the October 6, 1911, issue of the *Chicago Tribune* similarly depicted themes of domestic violence and the reversal of gender roles. The artist noted, "Boxing as a branch of domestic science would lead to interesting surprises." In the first image an angry wife stands, hands on hips, glaring at her cowering husband. A tipped-over chair and his torn clothing suggest that he has been the victim of his wife's violent outburst. The husband insists, "But my dear, you never told me you knew how to box." In a second cartoon, husband and wife sit in chairs on opposite sides of the room wearing boxing gloves and resting before the next round of fighting. A daughter coaches her exhausted mother, "He can't last ten rounds Ma. Believe me, you got him bluffed." Meanwhile, a son encourages his father, "Brace up Pa. Sidestep that left wallop of hers and you're all right." The artist notes, "Difficulties in the home may be settled without outside help under Queensberry rules." The final cartoon shows a number of female "co'eds in the study of 'The Manly Art of Self-Defense.'" The young women practice bag work and sparring at a "training camp for fiancées."[72] The implication of these cartoons was that women's self-defense training had the potential to disrupt the "natural order" of the household and raise women up to the same physical plane as men. The result would be a literal sex war where critics feared that the new physically empowered woman might attack and conquer her male partner.

Despite the mocking of women's self-defense as expressed in cartoons, advocates continued to take the issue seriously and made their case through a variety of media. Fictional accounts seemed to be one safe way that women could address the issue of violence against women without arousing too much criticism. A story written by Kathleen Fox and published in several papers by the McClure Newspaper Syndicate ran over a series of months in 1919. The title, "Taming My Husband," alluded to the efforts of a woman named Bess to tame the wild beast in her husband, Crittenden. Bess begins her story by explaining, "I realized that it would be utterly impossible for me to live with the lion that made his lair in my house unless he sheathed forever his claws. For I was afraid of the claws and dreaded them."[73] The couple struggled to find

Figure 5.5 "Boxing—The Newest Womanly Art, Difficulties in the Home May Be Settled without Outside Help under Queensberry Rules," *Chicago Daily Tribune*, October 6, 1911, 5.

happiness in their early years of marriage because of Crittenden's controlling ways and violent outbursts. Bess described numerous instances in which her husband's quick temper escalated to physical assaults. She referred to him as a beast and a primitive man, and she insisted that in the interest of protecting all that she held dear, she too harked back to the primitive age, "bared my teeth and flung wild my hair to battle for what was mine."[74]

Throughout the story, Bess gradually grew in her emotional and physical confidence. She began by refusing to capitulate to her husband's unreasonable demands and increasingly insisted on a relationship of mutual respect. One day, while walking with her friend Betty, Bess was shocked to witness Betty fend off a mugger with jiu-jitsu. As part of her personal awakening, Bess begged Betty to teach her the martial art.

Figure 5.6 "Boxing—The Newest Womanly Art, Coeds in the Study of the Manly Art of Self-Defense," *Chicago Daily Tribune*, October 6, 1911, 5.

Crittenden approved of the lessons, agreeing that it was a good thing for women to learn self-defense to protect themselves on the street. However, Crittenden soon learned the variety of applications of Bess's new knowledge. One evening he became extremely angry and lunged at Bess. As he reached for her throat, Bess grabbed his arm and twisted it, abruptly sending him crashing into a nearby dresser. In a "raging fury" and with his "face purpled with hate," he attacked her again. She again used a jiu-jitsu move to throw him to the ground.[75]

After this incident, Crittenden was contrite and promised to never attempt such behavior again. Bess remarked on her new freedom and personal power, noting how both she and Crittenden had acquired a new sense of independence.[76] As the story drew to a close, Bess reflected on their past domestic troubles and their present domestic bliss, insisting that Crittenden had kept his promise of good behavior. Crittenden asked her: "'Why in the name of time didn't you brain me, Bess?'" Bess explained: "He was referring to the time he had clutched and bruised my arms and then criticized me for wearing a sleeved gown at dinner. 'Why I couldn't,' I replied. 'I didn't know jiu-jitsu then.'" Bess noted that Crittenden was now repentant, and how "all of it lies in the past and we know it will not come again," while also noting that "jiu-jitsu is not in every woman's hands, nor is every man a Crittenden." This story reflects themes similar to Edith Garrud's story in that jiu-jitsu training proved the salvation for an abused and subjugated wife. Once the wife discovered her own physical power, she was able to subdue and tame her beast of a husband, just as the title of the story suggests.[77] It is also interesting to point out that Crittenden did not initially oppose Bess's self-defense training, justifying it as a means of protecting his wife's body from the

Figure 5.7 "Boxing—The Newest Womanly Art, Boxing as a Branch of Domestic Science," *Chicago Daily Tribune*, October 6, 1911, 5.

attacks of others. The fear of the dangerous stranger thus provided an excuse that allowed Bess to begin training. Bess no doubt also used this fear to validate her own desire to learn self-defense even as she innately knew that the most dangerous threat came her violent husband. This fictional story suggests some of the internal motivations of women who studied self-defense.

Charlotte Perkins Gilman also used fiction as a means of discussing issues related to sexual assault and domestic violence. In her short story "Joan's Defender," a young girl was rescued from an abusive home life where she was physically bullied by her brother, Gerald, and verbally abused by her parents. When her sympathetic uncle visited, he convinced Joan's parents that they should allow her to move with his family to his ranch out west. Joan reluctantly left her home and slowly warmed up both to her uncle and to the idea of freedom. When Joan declared her desire to be a tomboy, her kindly uncle allowed her to cut her hair as a symbolic act of freeing herself from her restrictive family and their confining gender roles. At the ranch, Joan learned the liberating lifestyle of her cousins, who all wore short hair and pants. Joan developed her body through active play and expanded her mind through her studies. As Gilman wrote: "Every one of those children was taught what we used to grandiloquently call 'the noble art of self-defense'; not only the skilled management of their hands, with swift 'foot-work,' but the subtler methods of jiu-jitsu."[78] Thus self-defense training helped complete Joan's transformation into a strong and capable woman.

When Joan was reunited with her family two years later, they were surprised at how confident and strong she had become. Eventually, Gerald resumed his old ways. Mocked and attacked by her brother, Joan warned him, "If you hurt me again, I shall have to do something to you." Gerald responded with jeers and punched Joan forcefully on the arm. Joan did not whine but instead knocked him down. Gerald stood up and "rushed at her, furious, meaning to reduce this rebellious sister to her proper place, Joan set her teeth and gave him a clean thrashing."[79] The story ended with Gerald promising to never harm her again. Joan, in return, promised to never tell anybody that she had beat him. Gerald, feeling emasculated by the fact that he was beaten by his sister, accepted the terms of the peace agreement. The title "Joan's Defender" may be interpreted as implying that Joan's uncle defended her against a life of abuse. More likely it was intended to convey a double meaning, since the story ended with Joan triumphantly serving as her own defender and using her new confidence and self-defense skills to free herself from domestic abuse and oppression. Thus Joan emerged as her own hero.

Although fiction proved a powerful medium for scripting stories of female physical agency, some writers did not limit their discussions of domestic violence and self-defense to fiction. Charlotte Perkins Gilman, for example, also clearly advocated for women's right to protect themselves against violence in her nonfiction writings. Michael Kimmel and Amy Aronson have argued that Gilman was quite progressive in her views on violence against women, with her suggestion that "the origins of such abuses were to be found not in demented, perverse, or evil individuals, or in 'demon rum,' but in the structure of the arrangements between women and men, and especially in women's economic dependence on men."[80] In her article "Should Women Use Violence?" (1912), Gilman pointed to a "popular masculine myth" that "assumes that man is woman's natural protector, though, as a matter of fact, he is often the worst danger she can hope to meet." Gilman argued that "our natural protector has used what violence he pleased throughout our gloomy history, toward the woman he assumed to have been 'given him,' for may not a man do what he will with his own? Not only by using his own physical force against hers to compel her to his will, but with the help of the accumulating forces of civilization—law, religion, education, public opinion—he has restrained, coerced, condemned and executed women in private and in public."[81] Thus Gilman linked women's physical subjugation in the home to their political and economic subjugation in larger society, all while dismantling the myth of the natural protector.

Gilman also asserted that women who studied jiu-jitsu and boxing directly challenged the false conception of men as the protectors and women as the protected.[82] She was an advocate of women's use of boxing and jiu-jitsu to defend against sexual assault and domestic violence. Gilman suggested that men possessed an underlying fear that "sometime, somewhere, somehow, women might 'hit back'" and rebel against their oppressor. She argued against the stereotypes that gendered women as weaker and less violent than men, stressing that "there is no reason whatever why the female . . . should not use violence whenever it is necessary." In fact, she wrote, "Girls of to-day taught ju-jutsu or even a little plain skill in wrestling and boxing, are far safer from the attacks of casual 'protectors' than they once were."[83] Gilman described a case in which a twelve-year-old girl successfully used her knowledge of self-defense to fight off an attacker. Gilman thus recognized self-defense training as one step in a larger process of freeing women from oppression both within and outside the home.

Like Gilman, other highly vocal advocates of women's self-defense training linked women's expanding political rights to their right to freedom in both the public and the private sphere. When the Evanston, Illinois, Mothers' Club voted in February 1909 in favor of a proposition to instruct girls in boxing for self-defense, the club members did not just focus on how such training would prepare them to resist mashers. Another one of their main arguments was that such instruction could be useful in preparing women to handle "their refractory husbands."[84] This is significant in that the woman who put forth the proposition, Catherine Waugh McCulloch, was a lawyer, the first female justice of the peace for Evanston, Illinois, and an active suffragist. As a lawyer and an advocate for women's rights, McCulloch fearlessly sought to empower women through her work.

Understanding the motivation behind McCulloch's proposal to the Mothers' Club requires looking at her professional background in more depth. In 1901, she drafted and pushed for the passage of a law guaranteeing mothers the same guardianship rights as fathers over their children. In 1905, she lobbied to raise the age of consent for girls (from fourteen to sixteen years) and thereby to protect them from sexual assault. She was elected as justice of the peace for Evanston, Illinois, in 1907. At the same time, she also served as both legal adviser (1904–1911) and vice president (1910–1911) of the National American Woman Suffrage Association. McCulloch had long advocated that the government do more to prevent and prosecute crimes against women.[85] As an active member of her local community, she suggested that the Mothers' Club support self-defense training for girls. This proposition did not sit well with all members, however. Some proposed to amend the language of the resolution by suggesting that women be taught to box in a "ladylike manner," but this amendment was rejected, and the original resolution was passed.[86] Ultimately, McCulloch believed that women's suffrage was the best means of protection for women by giving them a voice and enabling them to protect themselves from violence.[87] Her proposition before the Mother's Club that girls be taught to box was an additional measure intended to better prepare girls to defend themselves from violence in the streets and in the home.

McCulloch explained that through her work as a justice of the peace and a lawyer she knew of many instances of family violence: "I encounter much of the darker side of domestic life which is unknown to the average person. The average person would be astounded if he knew of the brutality that exists in many presumably respectable households." McCulloch, who argued that "the woman of today is afraid of her husband," blamed "religious influences and custom" for encouraging women to submit rather than rebel against domestic violence.[88] Her direct experiences assisting women who were the victims of such violence encouraged McCulloch to advocate for women's self-defense training at the same time she lobbied for political and economic reforms for women at the state and national level. McCulloch believed that physical training was necessary to empower women with the tools to resist their oppressor.

Some women chose to embody this new form of physical empowerment and transformed their words into actions. Exhibition boxer Minnie Rosenblatt Besser, for example, had spent years training in the manly art of boxing. She promised to meet any willing opponent, male or female, in the ring. Besser specifically called out several famous male boxers but insisted that she was most anxious to meet Brooklyn boxer Eddie Avery, who had been arrested for wife-beating. Besser explained, "Any man who will strike a helpless woman I believe to be a coward. Should Avery pluck up enough courage to meet me I think I will prove the truth of this proposition to the world at large. I am not helpless, like most women, and I am confident that I can whip Mr. Avery."[89] Besser determined to stand up against domestic violence by directly challenging a wife beater to meet her in the ring, at the same time wanting to prove that properly trained women were just as physically capable as men. Besser advocated the advantages of boxing training for all women in strengthening their bodies and fighting off sexual assault.

Middle- and upper-class Anglo women, envisioning themselves as stewards of the poor and dedicated to uplifting the lower classes, saw self-defense as yet another tool for their reform efforts. The belief that only lower-class men beat their wives proliferated among the upper classes. A female journalist writing in the St. Paul Globe in 1905 noted, "It is in the slum districts that wife beaters are found in large numbers, and it is their wives who must be taught to box." The author empathized with working-class women who were unable to pay for private lessons in boxing and jiu-jitsu. Instead she encouraged a "good and rich" woman to provide the money to teach the "worthy poor" jiu-jitsu. Uplifting the poor included training women in self-defense to help protect them from the violence of their husbands.[90]

Some advocates of self-defense training as a means of combating domestic violence resurrected the looming specter of the black male rapist and the shadowy stranger to support their argument for women's self-defense. For example, Besser stressed that boxing training was needed to physically strengthen white women against potential sexual assaults by black men: "Were the women of my time as lusty as those of the Greek and Roman eras there would be less of negro outrages in the south and of similar crimes, by brutal white ruffians in some of the barbaric states of the west. A woman even more than a man should be a trained athlete."[91] In her article justifying women's use of violence to defend against violence, Charlotte Perkins Gilman similarly used an example of the southern Negro rapist to make her point about the necessity of self-defense and the use of firearms for white women: "If the dangerous negroes of the black belt knew that every white woman carried a revolver and used it with skill and effect there would be less lynching needed." Yet, in the next sentence Gilman suggested her opposition to lynching, stating that "it would be better that one woman should shoot than that a hundred men should burn and otherwise suffer torture."[92] She mentioned the fear of the black rapist to make her point, fully aware that potential "negro outrages" elicited a great deal of fear in the minds of white men and women. Gilman thus linked the black rapist to the uncivilized primal rapist in all men, blaming both for the subjugation of women. Although she was aware that women were most likely to be victimized by men in their own families, she still relied on these stereotyped and racialized representations of the rapist to buttress her argument.

Many of these women clearly did believe in a racial hierarchy, and their writings reflect nativist and racial fears. Besser appealed to the eugenicist arguments prevalent at the time to justify women's use of self-defense: "Let the boxing glove take the place of the tight-fitting kid, the Kehoe club that of the needle, and we will breed a healthy, womanly race of men whom neither the Grecian or Roman matrons could surpass."[93] Gilman relied on similar views of civilization and race. Besser's and Gilman's references to the black male rapist as the greatest sexual threat facing white women, and therefore their rationalizations of women's training in self-defense, were clear extensions of their racial thinking.[94]

The southern European or Asian "other" posed a similar threat in the minds of middle-and upper-class white women. Dr. Maude Glasgow, in insisting that all girls should learn to box so they could defend themselves on the street and in the home, also played into racialized fears of the menacing "other." Glasgow referenced the recent murder of Elsie Siegel by her Chinese lover, Leon Ling, in New York City: "If Elsie Siegel had known the first principles of self-defense there would have been no Chinese murder to shock the world."[95] Siegel's murder generated a great deal of hysteria about the Yellow Peril threat of the Chinese sexual predator.[96] By tapping into those racialized fears, Glasgow hoped to garner support for her case about the necessity of women's self-defense. Besser, Gilman, and Glasgow all relied on racialized constructions of a sexually deviant stranger to make their point even as they innately understood that the real threat to women was not an "other" but their own husbands, suitors, fathers, and family members. They also noted that the oppression of and violence against women was related less to race and more to generations of male-imposed social, economic, and political inequality for women.

In these writers' minds, women's self-defense stood at least symbolically and often in reality as a powerful challenge to the oppressive status quo. These ideas were echoed in the writings of the popular press, which often simplified it as a battle between the sexes for supremacy in the home. In 1906, newspapers across the nation reprinted an article titled "Women as Boxers," which announced that "the woman who can box, really box like a man, not like other women who dabble in the manly art, is to be a feature in our homes." This newfound knowledge, the writer suggested, would free women from their subjugation inside and outside the home. "Knowing how to box successfully . . . she would be able to control matters at home and abroad in a forcible way that a former generation never dreamed of."[97]

Despite all the talk by radical self-defense advocates and predictions about a sex war by the press, most women who came face-to-face with violence in the home were not attempting to wage any kind of war against patriarchy. They were merely trying to survive. Abused women sought the assistance of law enforcement and the courts, only to find that these efforts often failed to solve the problem. Separation or divorce was not always a feasible option given women's economic dependence on men. Furthermore, abusive husbands frequently became more violent when confronted with the possibility of impending separation or divorce. Young women entirely dependent on fathers, male relatives, and family friends faced severely restricted options in seeking to escape a violent home life. With their backs against the wall and no other recourse, some women chose to fight back.

Twelve-year-old Lillian Ellis of New York City was caring for her younger siblings while her mother and father were out when one of her father's friends stopped by the home for a visit. The man tried to strangle Lillian and broke a vase over her head, fracturing her skull. For half an hour she fended off his attacks using jiu-jitsu holds and techniques. She twisted his fingers and attempted to gouge his eyes. She fought back and survived but was sent to the hospital to recover from the injuries she incurred in the battle.[98] Lillian did not articulate the significance of her use of self-defense, but her ability to resist the assault and the admiration of the public following the incident highlighted the importance of her fight.

Whether or not they had formally studied self-defense, and most women who fought back against abuse had not, their efforts to resist assault justified the arguments of self-defense advocates. For some women, with no connection to the middle- and upper-class women who promoted self-defense, the brutal experience with domestic violence affirmed their belief in the urgency and necessity of women's self-defense training. Mary Helen Lippitt filed for divorce in the Cook County Superior Court in August 1911, charging her husband, Alburn, with extreme and repeated cruelty. Mary testified that at one point she had been lying on the lounge in her home, recuperating from an illness, when her husband became angry and "got on her stomach and pounded her face." The beating left her covered in bruises for two weeks. On another occasion when she was also lying in bed ill, her husband demanded that she get up and get him breakfast. When she replied that she could not, he threw her from the bed unto the floor, causing severe bruising of her neck, back, and shoulder. Feeling sorry for what he had done, he tried to make up with her and attempted to kiss her. When Mary refused to kiss him in return, he grabbed her by the throat and slammed her head against the wall, trying to force her to do so. Mary's mother, Mrs. Millard, verified the story by testifying before the court that she saw Alburn slam Mary against the wall and saw the blood begin pouring from her daughter's nose. The assault also left bruises around Mary's neck where her husband had grabbed her. Marie Johnson, a family friend, testified as an additional witness to this incident, describing the bruising that she saw. Mary recounted to the court additional stories of abusive behavior, explaining that at one point Alburn had attempted to kill them both by turning on the gas when she was sleeping. Alburn immediately filed a cross-complaint, claiming that his wife had punched him on several occasions, at one point bloodying his nose and causing severe pain. In further testimony before the court and in interviews with local newspapers, Mary insisted that she had never used force against her husband except once in self-defense when she retaliated against his assault by punching him in the nose with the very same techniques he had taught her. A sympathetic judge sided with Mary, finding Alburn guilty of "extreme and repeated cruelty," and granted her request for a divorce.[99] The press was enamored with the story and especially with Mary's use of boxing to fight back against the assault. Mary used her moment in the spotlight to urge other women to learn boxing, just as she had, to protect themselves in the home against abusive husbands. Women like Mary Helen Lippitt, who fought back against abuse and sexual assault, physically asserted their right to protect themselves. Their action stood as a powerful symbol of their rejection of patriarchal authority and changing attitudes toward domestic violence even if they did not articulate it as such.[100]

## Conclusion

The idea of women studying self-defense as protection from attack by mashers on the street was less threatening than the radical idea of women practicing self-defense for political empowerment or protection against abuse in their homes. This in part explains why so many articles in popular periodicals focused on stranger attacks. Mary Odem argued that female moral reformers were less vocal about the issue of sexual assault in the home because "it was more acceptable for them to address public forms of sexual danger like prostitution and white slavery. But in the end, these campaigns may have diverted attention away from the more imminent sources of sexual harm facing young women and girls."[101] Yet individual women were increasingly asserting their own power by filing for divorce on the grounds of cruelty, pressing criminal charges against wife beaters, and sometimes even physically fighting back. Advocates of self-defense training tackled the issue head-on by focusing on empowering individual women. Dr. Maude Glasgow wrote that "women have been taught that they are not strong enough physically to fight for themselves and that they must not even try to do so, but this is untrue. . . . The artificial helplessness of women, carefully cultivated through the centuries, has made her the spoil of the strongest. Yet women are strong."[102] Self-defense practitioners rejected patriarchal notions of feminine weakness and male protectionism and insisted instead on their right to protect themselves from their so-called protectors. They believed in the potential of women's self-defense to provide this same sense of empowerment to all women.

Although self-defense was no magic cure-all for domestic violence, advocates recognized the importance of empowering women to identify signs of violence, remove themselves from dangerous situations, and, if necessary, physically defend themselves. At the very least, the public discussion of women's self-defense facilitated a more open discourse about the realities of violence against women. This discussion attempted to crack through the veneer of the myth of the dangerous stranger, to reveal the reality of violence against women. The women's self-defense movement symbolized the fight against gender oppression both in public and in private spaces.

# Conclusion

The woman's self-defense movement in the Progressive Era grew out of a number of sometimes contradictory and competing factors. The early twentieth-century physical culture movement sparked public interest in a number of athletic pursuits for men and women. Imperialistic concerns about the weakening of the nation fueled a national obsession with boxing and jiu-jitsu as a means of strengthening American men and women to compete on the international stage. Reformers' anxieties over the impacts of industrialization, urbanization, and the changing roles of women lent credence to arguments for the necessity of self-defense training to protect women from violent attacks by immigrants and nonwhite strangers on the street. These factors also coincided with campaigns for women's suffrage and broader campaigns for women's equality that rejected patriarchal notions of male protectionism and called for an end to men's oppression of women in the public and private spheres. These at times conflicting ideas came together to fuel the emergence of the first women's self-defense movement.

Despite its varied origins, the significance of this movement was profound. At its most basic level, it fostered a belief in the necessity of women's self-defense as a means of preparing women to protect themselves from violent attacks by strangers on the city streets. At the most radical level, women's self-defense represented a physical challenge to the existing patriarchal order and resistance to the political and personal subjugation of women. Although the reasons women pursued self-defense training may have varied dramatically, the very act of learning a traditionally male-dominated physical art contested gender stereotypes and stretched the boundaries of acceptable female behavior. Practitioners of self-defense attempted to create new social norms that challenged the idea of women as weak and in need of male protection, suggesting instead that women were powerful and capable of protecting themselves. Astute women's rights activists recognized the significance of the birth of the women's self-defense movement as a revolution of sorts as it represented the physical embodiment of feminist ideals.

Yet there were clear limits to this revolution. First, this was primarily a movement created by and for Anglo middle- and upper-class women. Courses in jiu-jitsu and boxing as offered by elite universities, athletic gymnasiums, and social clubs were available mostly to white society women. Working-class women's access to formal self-defense training was limited, and training was often provided by upper-class reformers only within the context of rescuing and uplifting the "less-civilized" classes. Progressive Era reformers promoted self-defense training for working-class women as a means of extending their own racialized and class-based notions of protectionism, moral policing, and social control. Even when it was somewhat accepted in the mainstream as a means of empowering women of all classes to protect themselves on the street, self-defense training was promoted primarily as a way to protect white women's bodies against assaults by foreigners and lower-class men of color. Anglo men acquiesced to women's self-defense training when it was presented as a way of preserving and protecting the physical bodies and purity of women of their own race and class from attacks by non-white, working-class men, especially as women moved into dangerous urban spaces. Nonwhite women were deemed less worthy of protection or empowerment.

The gendered dimensions of women's self-defense training also limited its effectiveness as a total revolution. Self-defense instructors increasingly taught women modified versions of the manly arts in an effort to avoid upsetting traditional class and gender roles. These modified courses taught exercises focused more on toning and shaping women's bodies into an appearance and size that conformed to an ideal of feminine beauty rather than preparing women to fight effectively. Furthermore, women's participation in boxing and jiu-jitsu was justified as a means of strengthening their bodies for their traditional roles as wives and mothers. Although women's rights leaders recognized the revolutionary potential of self-defense in disrupting the status quo and helping to end the subjugation of women, female advocates of self-defense quickly discovered the limits of their lofty ambitions. They attempted, relatively unsuccessfully, to create long-lasting, new social norms that recognized women as powerful and capable of protecting themselves.

Self-defense advocates, instead, increasingly found their ideas patronized, marginalized, or at worst completely rejected in the decades that followed.

The winning of suffrage and some social freedoms by the 1920s did not fully address women's liberation from their status as sexualized objects and victims of violence. Women's rights advocates hoped that once women had achieved the right to vote, they would proceed to pass laws to address relevant issues, including men's violence against women. Yet resistance to women's new political authority remained a formidable obstacle. Growing schisms in women's rights organizations about the most effective strategy moving forward also splintered the movement and impeded future progress. Changing attitudes toward conventions of sexual behavior further shifted the focus away from women as victims of sexual violence. The issue of violence against women would not become a major focus of the feminist movement again until the mid-twentieth century.[1]

The women's self-defense movement experienced a resurrection in the 1960s and 1970s paralleling the resurgence of what scholars have termed the second wave of the women's rights movement. The issue of violence against women would become a topic of public discussion and fuel the emergence of a much more widespread self-defense movement by a new generation of activists. Some feminists espousing women's liberation in the second wave embraced women's self-defense as another form of consciousness-raising that empowered women physically, psychologically, and politically. Patricia Searles and Ronald Berger, in examining the radical roots of the movement in the second wave, argued that the feminist self-defense movement offered "an alternative view of women as strong, capable, and self-reliant." The movement countered "the traditional patriarchal family structure that emphasizes women's passivity, deference, and dependence on men."[2] Firmly embedded in feminist discourse, this second era of women's self-defense would make even more explicit political connections regarding the physical embodiment of feminist politics. Self-defense practitioners of this era represented a more diverse range of women from a variety of racial and class backgrounds. They openly discussed the issue of rape in their courses and embraced a broader definition of self-defense that included not only teaching effective physical strategies but also equipping women with psychological tools to overcome barriers to self-protection. As astute instructors and practitioners contextualized their self-defense training within the broader framework of the women's movement, their physical training came to symbolize the feminist quest for liberation in the radical second wave.

Feminists in the 1980s and 1990s drew even more attention to the continuum of violence against women, including a broader discussion of harassment, sexual assault, and domestic violence. Self-defense seminars and classes offered through martial art studios and college campuses were accessible to a greater number of women than at any time in the past, and many of these courses continue to operate to this day. The classes that emerged in the second wave included a wide variety of approaches to women's self-defense, including a limited number of classes focused on adrenal stress training, in which women practiced defending themselves against larger-than-life, menacing opponents in padded attacker uniforms. As sociologist Martha McCaughey has argued, the women who took these courses learned to set clear verbal and physical boundaries to thwart their attacker, signifying their entry into the adult and very dangerous world of femininity. McCaughey's ethnographic study on women's self-defense, titled *Real Knockouts* (1997), showed that the physical work of self-defense training prompted in women a transformation of consciousness.[3] The women made "their aggression, and the femininity that prevents it, conscious. They develop a new self-image, a new understanding of what a female body can do." In this manner, much as with Progressive Era self-defense practitioners, the body "is not simply the locus of patriarchal power, ideology, or brutality; it is a potential locus of resistance."[4] By challenging the norms of femininity, self-defense practitioners developed an embodied knowledge of women as strong, powerful, and capable. Women who attended these classes did not necessarily do so with any feminist political intentions. Even so, scholars who have studied the women's self-defense movement argue that these women embodied a feminist resistance to the sexist norms of a rape culture.[5]

From the 1960s onward, more open conversations about physical and sexual violence against women helped bring greater visibility and urgency to the self-defense movement. However, the movement encountered severe limitations in ending violence against women as it was confronted with a powerful mainstream culture that continued to objectify, sexualize, and victimize women. Criticism from opponents of women's self-defense and disagreements about the most effective strategy to eliminate violence against women have led some to overlook the significance of women's self-defense even into the present day.

Progressive Era advocates of self-defense faced many of the same criticisms that modern women's self-defense proponents encounter. In the early twentieth century the majority of people denied that violence against women was a problem, preferring instead to ignore the extent of sexual harassment, sexual assault, and domestic violence perpetrated by men against women. Others blamed women for encouraging or inviting harassment or attacks. Similarities between the past and the present are clear in the ways in which a few modern individuals and policy makers continue to make statements or promote policies that essentially blame the victim. However, so much has changed since the Progressive Era. Violence against women is now widely recognized as a significant issue largely due to the efforts of second-wave feminists. Although victim blaming remains an issue, feminists have fought to keep responsibility for violence on the perpetrator and to focus conversations on the larger societal issues that contribute to a culture of violence against women.

During the Progressive Era, one common suggestion offered to address concerns about the harassment and violence that women encountered on the streets was that women should simply avoid going out in public by themselves. If women insisted on going out, they were told to make themselves invisible in public spaces by dressing modestly, avoiding eye contact, not speaking, and acting demurely to avoid attracting unwanted attention from dangerous men. Although today women are rarely advised to avoid going out in public, many of the other suggestions are echoed in modern women's safety seminars, especially the emphasis on trying to be less visible in public. The stated intent behind this advice is to provide women with strategies to remain safe, but the unintended effect is to suggest that women are intruders in the public arena and that as such they must try to make themselves invisible and take up less space. Earlier warnings about the dangers for women who ventured out into the streets reflected a general cultural backlash against the advances of feminism.[6] Progressive Era self-defense advocates, however, challenged these ideas, resisting women's confinement to the domestic sphere and insisting on their right to occupy public spaces. Second-wave self-defense advocates similarly made very public statements, such as through Take Back the Night rallies, about women's right to walk the streets at night free from fear. Self-defense instructors in the present era who embrace an empowerment self-defense (ESD) model are aware of this long history of the close association between women's self-defense training and their larger struggle for gender equality. Modern safety instructors without this awareness unwittingly risk reinforcing the very inequality they are attempting to help women resist.

Detractors of women's self-defense in the Progressive Era argued that training in boxing and jiu-jitsu would masculinize women. Although most of the arguments against the masculinizing effects of women's athletics and self-defense have lost sway in the modern era, many women's self-defense courses have been commodified and repackaged in a patronizing way that is far less threatening to the patriarchal order and less disruptive to existing gender boundaries. Some women's "self-defense" classes, for example, emphasize primarily cardio training and weight control, minimizing the emphasis on fighting per se. Instead, they focus on helping women achieve an unrealistic appearance focused on a distorted notion of ideal body shape and size that promotes thinness and limited muscular development. In the process, women's self-defense is visibly marked as different from, and by implication inferior to, men's self-defense courses. Unlike feminist empowerment self-defense courses, these commodified self-defense classes provide women with just enough knowledge to feel "empowered" but without enough real training to ensure that their techniques would be effective against a real assault. In this manner, women's self-defense is reconstructed as nonthreatening especially as presented by instructors who teach watered-down or ineffective techniques to women whom they perceive as incapable of learning "real" fighting techniques.[7] We saw a similar trend in the Progressive Era when some instructors presented more "feminine" versions of boxing and jiu-jitsu classes for women in an attempt to deflect criticism against the masculinizing effect of women's athletics and present instead an image of respectable femininity.[8] Focusing more on stretching, weight training, shadowboxing, and light bag work, these instructors insisted that their classes were intended to enhance the feminine beauty of practitioners. In earlier eras, in which the very concept of women's athletics and especially of women training in fighting was a radical idea, these modified classes helped to overcome objections to women's self-defense. However, in the past and even more so in the present, these watered-down courses reinforce patriarchal authority and minimize the significance and power of women's self-defense.

Deeply embedded beliefs about gender differences dating back to even before the Progressive Era have contributed to the idea that women are too weak to defend themselves against physically stronger men and instead must rely on factors outside themselves for protection. Just as women in the late nineteenth century were advised to avoid venturing out into public spaces without their male protector and encouraged to seek assistance from male relatives and authorities when confronted with dangerous situations, some modern approaches to addressing violence against women inadvertently tap into these early sexist notions of protectionism. Some safety seminars encourage women to protect themselves by relying primarily on male authorities, bystanders, or self-defense apps and gadgets. Although these approaches are useful in educating individuals on the variety of available options, when offered as the only means of defense for women they subsume and devalue the role of women as their own advocates. Progressive Era self-defense proponents insisted on the necessity of training women to protect themselves, countering Victorian ideas about innate feminine weaknesses. Feminist self-defense advocates in the past and the present have insisted on teaching women not to look to others for help but to depend on themselves for protection. These instructors focused less on protecting women's feminine grace and more on teaching women to overcome deeply gendered notions about female physical and emotional weaknesses. They taught women to use effective and, if necessary, deadly techniques to stop attackers.

Still, some detractors have insisted that it is too dangerous for women to fight back and that women must beware of further provoking an attacker. Recent research, however, has demonstrated that fighting back does not escalate the actions of the offender, nor does it increase a woman's risk of additional injury. "Fighting, fleeing and screaming" are effective strategies for preventing rape, whereas more passive strategies such as "begging, pleading and reasoning" usually are not.[9] Increased self-esteem and assertiveness gained through self-defense training also helps lessen anxiety and fear. Most important, studies have found both training in self-defense and enacting self-defense (whether or not one has received formal training) effective in helping women resist assault or avoid assault altogether.[10] Advocates of women's self-defense from the Progressive Era to the present day have argued that women who train in self-defense not only gain valuable verbal and physical self-defense strategies but also develop a sense of confidence that makes them more likely to recognize, avoid, report, and, when necessary, fight back against assault.

A few radical Progressive Era self-defense advocates suggested that the real roots of resistance to women training in self-defense were related to fears about unleashing women's violence. As Charlotte Perkins Gilman noted, some people feared that women would use their knowledge to fight back against their male oppressor, both in public and in private. Self-defense for women in the Progressive Era was justified primarily as providing middle- and upper-class white women with a means to protect themselves from sinister nonwhite strangers on the streets. Men agreed to the idea of women's self-defense only when framed as a temporary solution to protect the respectability of white women when civilized white men were not available to serve as protectors. Many Progressive Era self-defense advocates, however, insisted on women's right and ability to serve as their own defenders. Some took it a step further by challenging the notion of stranger danger and suggesting instead that the real threat to women was their so-called natural protectors. The discussion about women's self-defense in the Progressive Era opened a larger conversation about the reality of violence against women, especially in the form of intimate partner violence. Since the 1960s, feminists have helped make this issue even more public and have fought to initiate reforms to address the far-reaching causes and effects of domestic violence. Their struggle for recognition of these issues continues to this day.

Today, the relevance and significance of women's self-defense are perhaps more important than ever. Despite that fact that women now enjoy greater political and economic equality than at any point in U.S. history, sexual violence against women and intimate partner violence remain ever-present realities. According to the National Intimate Partner and Sexual Violence Survey, 19.3 percent of women have been raped in their lifetimes, and 43.9 percent of women have experienced other forms of sexual violence.[11] Courses today that promote an empowerment model of women's self-defense, espousing many of the ideas of the Progressive Era self-defense movement and the second-wave feminist self-defense movement, including the "radical" notion that women are fully capable of defending themselves, receive minimal funding and support.

Despite the continued significance and relevance of women's self-defense, feminists remain divided over the best way to combat the problem of sexual assault and violence against women. Advocating an approach that focuses primarily on government policy solutions and victim services, some feminists marginalize self-defense as a secondary strategy to combating violence against women or, worse, dismiss women's self-defense altogether. Other feminists strongly criticize self-defense as a victim-blaming approach that derails the conversation from focusing on the perpetrator and the larger rape culture. These critics are right to condemn women's self-defense courses that focus on a fear-based approach that encourages women to restrict their behavior or limit their free movement to avoid danger in public spaces. However, proponents of empowerment self-defense argue that self-defense courses based on a feminist model are not victim blaming or restrictive but instead focus on empowering women. In empowerment self-defense courses, women learn about their right to defend themselves and practice a variety of physical, verbal, and psychological tools to do so. Such courses have proved transformational and effective for women as a means of primary assault prevention.

Violence against women is a very serious cultural issue that requires a multifaceted solution. Traditional forms of gender socialization promote aggression in men and physical passivity in women, thereby creating a dangerous combination that contributes to the aggressor/victim dichotomy. A rape culture that associates masculinity with sexual conquest and condones violence against women while blaming women for their own victimization exacerbates the situation. Ending men's violence against women thus requires a concerted societal effort that includes mobilizing individuals to work together to address the extent of this deeply rooted cultural problem.

Parents who challenge their own binary definitions of gender and reconsider the ways in which they encode certain sexist behaviors and expectations in their male and female children promote a gender socialization that focuses on a less dichotomous approach to defining masculinity and femininity. In this manner, parents can also help to deconstruct powerful stereotypes about male aggression and female passivity while combating sexism. Many parents are becoming part of the solution by allowing their children to participate in a range of mixed-gender activities and exposing them to a combination of masculine- and feminine-stereotyped toys and activities. Parents increasingly enroll their daughters in empowerment self-defense classes to instill in them confidence in their abilities and provide them with knowledge of how to protect themselves in a variety of situations. Some parents promote gender equity by trying to model egalitarian gender roles at home, for example, with both parents taking on child care responsibilities and domestic duties. Others try to provide their children with role models in the community who counter dominant stereotypes. Openly discussing gender stereotypes may also help to challenge negative cultural influences.

Equipping both boys and girls with a variety of strategies that they need to be successful in life and especially in their relationships is crucial to combating multiple forms of violence. This includes educating young people about how to develop and maintain healthy relationships and how to recognize warning signs of potentially unhealthy or violent relationships. A proactive approach to preventing violence also requires a curriculum plan that focuses on social and emotional learning to help young people recognize and appropriately deal with their emotions, without resorting to harassment, bullying, physical assault, or sexual violence. Social and emotional learning emphasizes fostering greater emotional awareness, practicing techniques for managing emotions, developing interpersonal communication skills, and feeling empathy for others. The immediate goal is to help young people grow into happier, healthier, and more compassionate adults. The long-term goal is to foster a culture that promotes peaceful resolutions to personal conflicts and reduces bullying and violence. Cooperation, compassion, and empathy are also keys to building strong individuals and strong communities.[12] Empowerment self-defense courses incorporate these principles into their curriculum and help equip participants with the tools for developing these skills. Social and emotional learning and empowerment self-defense classes may help reduce bullying, sexual harassment, and dating violence. Sex education programs should likewise be revised to focus on helping young people develop the skills they need to build and maintain healthy interpersonal relationships and understand the meaning of sexual consent.

Women's self-defense is one part of the larger solution, especially because it focuses on dismantling stereotypes of female passivity by teaching women to explore the impact of gender socialization on their behavior and to disrupt that process in order to trust their own judgments, feelings, and physical abilities. Progressive Era self-defense advocates understood that physical training could help transform women's bodies and minds. Self-defense based on the empowerment model instills women with a sense of self-worth and confidence by helping them to identify their internal sources of psychological and physical power. They learn that they have the right and the ability to establish their own boundaries at the same time that they develop a sense of their physical power through technique training. Empowerment self-defense courses teach a range of verbal and physical strategies, providing women with the opportunity to envision their capacity to protect themselves while ultimately keeping responsibility on the perpetrators of violence against women. Participants work to overcome psychological barriers to self-protection and develop strategies that build confidence and assertiveness in resisting assaults. In the end, participants recognize that they have the ability and the right to defend themselves.[13] According to sociologist Martha E. Thompson, who has examined the empowerment self-defense model, this approach is especially important in "placing violence in a social context, holding perpetrators responsible for violence, centering embodiment, and offering a comprehensive self-defense toolbox."[14] In this manner, self-defense instructors provide participants with a broad understanding of the varied meanings and applications of the techniques they learn.

Sociologist Jocelyn A. Hollander has also extensively studied the women's self-defense movement in the present era and has argued that "women's empowerment-based self-defense training should be part of any sexual violence prevention effort."[15] Self-defense training remains a crucial element in the larger campaign to challenge sexism and violence against women. Progressive Era women long ago recognized the significance of women's physical empowerment to the larger struggle against gender inequality. They encountered resistance from critics who challenged the necessity of women's self-defense, relying on notions of male protectionism and fears about women's use of violence. Feminist self-defense advocates today can trace their lineage to the women who advocated and organized self-defense classes for women in the Progressive Era. Modern self-defense proponents may recognize many of the same criticisms that earlier advocates of women's self-defense faced. Then as now, women promoted self-defense as a powerful symbol of their resistance to existing social hierarchies and a set of tools for preventing their own victimization and oppression. In the end, they transformed themselves into empowered agents of change.

# NOTES

INTRODUCTION

1  A much earlier version of the ideas presented here was published by Rouse and Slutsky, "Empowering the Physical and Political Self," 470–499.

2  Robert Zeidel notes that "Anglo-Saxon" as it was used during the Progressive Era was never a "precise ethnic category." It was primarily used by nativists to distinguish themselves from immigrant others. To them the term "denoted Protestant whites whose ancestors had come to America before the immigrants of their own era, and who were, in some vaguely defined manner, of distinguished ethnic stock." I will be using the term "Anglo" in the same manner throughout this book and often interchangeably with the word "white." Zeidel, *Immigrants, Progressives, and Exclusion Politics,* 6.

3  "Anne Morgan Takes Peep into Circus 'Green Room,'" *Pittsburgh Post,* April 12, 1912, 1; "N.Y. Girls Will Learn to Jiu-Jitsu Mashers," *San Francisco Call,* April 13, 1912, 15; "Jiu-Jitsu for New York Society," *Winnipeg Tribune,* May 8, 1912, 6; "To Demonstrate Value of Jiu Jitsu," *Allentown Democrat,* April 26, 1913, 6.

4  "Learning to Smash 'Mashers,'" *Ogden Standard-Examiner,* August 6, 1920, 7.

5  Newman, *White Women's Rights,* 57, 87, 96.

6  Gorn, *The Manly Art,* 138.

7  The term "suffragist" here is generally used to refer to those in favor of women's right to vote. The term "suffragette" is used to describe members of the WSPU and other militant advocates of women's suffrage.

8  Searles and Berger, "The Feminist Self-Defense Movement," 79; McCaughey, "The Fighting Spirit"; McCaughey, *Real Knockouts,* 90. For more on corporeal feminism, see Grosz, *Volatile Bodies.*

9  A note on sources: I have consulted a diverse range of sources on this topic, from the records of women's rights organizations to the personal diaries and letters of women who studied self-defense. However, the richest source of information on this topic was uncovered in the newspapers and magazines of the era. The public discussion and debate about women's self-defense occurred primarily in the popular press, fueled both by the era of yellow journalism's obsession with sensational stories and by the increasing number of female journalists writing stories about women and of interest to women. I used national newspaper databases such as Chronicling America: Historic American Newspapers, Proquest Historical Newspapers, and Newspapers.com to locate articles related to the

topic. I also consulted regional and local databases such as the California Digital Newspaper Collection when available. Wherever possible, I have worked to flesh out the stories in the newspapers by researching the individual women mentioned as practitioners or advocates of self-defense. I have consulted census records, city directories, immigration files, university records, personal letters, and diaries in an effort to reconstruct these women's lives and to reveal more detailed information about their self-defense training. I have also examined police and court records where relevant to reveal further information about specific cases of street harassment against women. However, police and court records provided only minimal information, since the record books usually noted only the name of the offender, the charge, and the sentence. Little mention was made of the women who used self-defense to resist these men. When these records did yield additional information, I included details in the endnotes. Newspaper and magazine writers, on the other hand, provided detailed accounts of women training in and using self-defense to protect themselves. Periodicals further revealed the cultural tensions around the topic and hinted at the broader significance of women's self-defense. This study, then, depended on these sources to tease out the interesting story of the birth of the women's self-defense movement in the Progressive Era.

## CHAPTER 1. THE WOMANLY ART OF BOXING

1  Beard, *American Nervousness*.

2  Hall, *Adolescence*.

3  McLeod, *Building Character in the American Boy*; Putney, *Muscular Christianity*, 99–126; Kimmel, *Manhood in America*, 168–169; Rotundo, *American Manhood*, 241–242.

4  Segel, *Body Ascendant*, 3–6, 204–208.

5  Putney, *Muscular Christianity*, 1–4, 33.

6  Letter from Theodore Roosevelt to Edward Sandford Martin, November 26, 1900.

7  Gail Bederman explains that in the middle to late nineteenth century the term "manly" generally referred to a broader definition of manhood that idealized both physical abilities and moral integrity. In the early twentieth century, the terms "masculine" and "masculinity" came into popular usage and referred more generally to all the positive and negative characteristics of being a man. "Masculinity" gradually took on the more narrow meaning of physical strength, aggressiveness, and sexual virility, especially as Victorian notions of gender began to fade by the 1930s. During the era of the present study, both "manly" and "masculinity" were in popular usage. Bederman, *Manliness and Civilization*, 18–20.

8  Zeidel, *Immigrants, Progressives, and Exclusion Politics*, 8–10.

9  Spencer, *The Principles of Biology*; Omi and Winant, *Racial Formation in the United States*, 24; Jacobson, *Whiteness of a Different Color*, 78–80; Zeidel, *Immigrants, Progressives, and Exclusion Politics*, 105–107.

10  Roediger, *Working toward Whiteness*, 13–20; Zeidel, *Immigrants, Progressives, and Exclusion Politics*, 10, 100; Omi and Winant, *Racial Formation in the United States*, 24.

11 Grant, *The Passing of the Great Race*; Zeidel, *Immigrants, Progressives, and Ex-clusion Politics*, 10, 100; Jacobson, *Whiteness of a Different Color*, 78–90; Kevles, *In the Name of Eugenics*, 20, 46–47, 95; Larson, *Sex, Race, and Science*, 19–22, 29, 32–39.

12 Newman, *White Women's Rights*, 28.

13 Kimmel, *Manhood in America*, 90–91; Kevles, *In the Name of Eugenics*, 20, 74; Larson, *Sex, Race, and Science*, 19–22, 29.

14 Roosevelt, *The Strenuous Life*.

15 Kimmel, *Manhood in America*, 120.

16 Gorn, *The Manly Art*, 138.

17 Ibid., 56; Kim, "Fighting Men and Fighting Women," 105–109; Rotundo, *American Manhood*, 39–42, 225–226, 241; Hargreaves, "Women's Boxing and Related Activi-ties," 212; Woodward, *Boxing, Masculinity and Identity*.

18 Hall, *Adolescence*, 217–218.

19 "Box," *Pittsburgh Press*, January 4, 1915, 24.

20 Chauncey Thomas, *Outdoor Life*, reprinted in "America is Effeminate," *Los Angeles Times*, April 23, 1917, 18.

21 Gorn, *The Manly Art*; Gorn, "'Gouge and Bite, Pull Hair and Scratch,'" 18–43.

22 Putney, *Muscular Christianity*, 29; Kimmel, *Manhood in America*, 86–87, 121, 162–163.

23 Putney, *Muscular Christianity*, 144–161; Verbrugge, *Able-Bodied Womanhood*, 98–99.

24 Clarke, *Sex in Education or a Fair Chance for Girls*, 128.

25 Cahn, *Coming On Strong*, 8–9; Vertinsky, *The Eternally Wounded Woman*, 12, 51–55, 135, 157; Bittel, *Mary Putnam Jacobi and the Politics of Medicine*, 1, 116–153; Verbrugge, *Able-Bodied Womanhood*, 120–122; Smith-Rosenberg, *Disorderly Con-duct*, 187, 259; Lenskyj, *Out of Bounds*, 19–22.

26 Jacobi, "Mental Action and Physical Health," 255–306; Jacobi, *The Question of Rest for Women during Menstruation*. For more on Jacobi and her influence, see Bittel, *Mary Putnam Jacobi and the Politics of Medicine*, 1, 22–125; Vertinsky, *The Eternally Wounded Woman*, 141–143; Verbrugge, *Able-Bodied Womanhood*, 123; Smith-Rosenberg, *Disorderly Conduct*, 262.

27 Brackett, "The Education of American Girls," 48.

28 Putney, *Muscular Christianity*, 29, 48; Vertinsky, *The Eternally Wounded Woman*, 21, 150, 171–191.

29 Newman, *White Women's Rights*, 7–10, 19–20, 23, 52–53.

30 Smith, *A History of Women's Boxing*, 39; Putney, *Muscular Christianity*, 48–49; Vertinsky, *The Eternally Wounded Woman*, 80; Verbrugge, *Able-Bodied Woman-hood*, 42–43; Cahn, *Coming On Strong*, 14; Lenskyj, *Out of Bounds*, 27–30.

31 "Those College Girls," *St. Paul Globe*, November 20, 1903, 6. A similar argument was made by a writer in the *New York Tribune* who noted that "decent people take no interest in such furious and violent struggles among members of the graceful and gentle sex. Women boxers, women ballplayers, women wrestlers and women

in long continued professional bicycle contests in cheap halls are alike intoler-able." "A Bicycle Contest," *New York Tribune*, November 22, 1900, 8.

32 Sargent, "What Athletic Games, If Any, Are Injurious for Women in the Form in Which They Are Played by Men?," 180–181.

33 Cahn, *Coming On Strong*, 7–30.

34 de Koven, "The Athletic Woman," 150–151. De Koven's reference to the tomboy here is important for its hinting at expanding gender constructions. For more on the tomboy and athleticism in American culture, see Abate, *Tomboys*.

35 Kim, "Fighting Men and Fighting Women," 109–114. Residents of Waltham, Mas-sachusetts, banned female students from attending boxing matches among boys at the local high school. "Girls Barred from Bouts," *New York Times*, January 7, 1915, 14. Women were barred from watching a wrestling and jiu-jitsu match in Los Angeles in 1913 "on the ground that the match promises to be far too strenuous for the fair sex" and that the jiu-jitsu match "is likely to end in injuries." "Women Barred in Wrestling," *Los Angeles Times*, March 3, 1913, 3.

36 Kim, "Fighting Men and Fighting Women," 116.

37 Smith, *A History of Women's Boxing*, 23–28.

38 Cahn, *Coming On Strong*, 2–3, 165–166.

39 "Emphasizes Opposition to Athletics for Women," *St. Louis Republic*, June 24, 1901.

40 See also "Football, Boxing, Cycling Harmful to Women, *Washington Post*, Novem-ber 20, 1921, 68; "As a Woman Thinks," *Tulsa Daily World*, July 31, 1920, 6.

41 "Ban on Boxing of High School Girls," *San Francisco Call*, December 28, 1911, 11.

42 Smith, *A History of Women's Boxing*, 28–32.

43 "Woman Boxer Is Put Out of Ring in Harlem after First Round," *Evening World*, March 1, 1916, 12; "This Woman Boxer Weighs 105 and She Has Boxed Two Champs," *Tacoma Times*, November 27, 1917, 6.

44 Krafft-Ebing, *Psychopahia Sexualis*, 399.

45 Ellis, *Studies in the Psychology of Sex*, 144.

46 Cahn, *Coming On Strong*, 166–168, 180–181; Smith-Rosenberg, *Disorderly Con-duct*, 275–282.

47 Lafferty and McKay, "'Suffragettes in Satin Shorts?,'" 249–255.

48 Smith, *A History of Women's Boxing*, 30; Kim, "Fighting Men and Fighting Women," 117–119.

49 "'I'm No Ladies Man,' Says Dempsey; 'Put Me Down for Fighting Guy!,'" *Bismarck Tribune*, April 28, 1921, 6.

50 Antrim, "The Masculization of Girls," 565.

51 For more on this issue of the racialization of athletic women and especially of "tomboys," see Abate, *Tomboys*, xxv–xxvi, 4, 73, 83.

52 "Never Was Kissed," *St. Paul Daily Globe*, June 4, 1895, 3; Smith, *A History of Women's Boxing*, 50–53.

53 Antrim, "The Masculization of Girls," 565–566.

54 Fitzsimmons, *Physical Culture and Self-Defense*, 47–50.

55  Abate, *Tomboys*, 74. Interestingly, Lafferty and McKay noted a similar trend in female boxers in the present day: "For example, in order to counter pervasive charges that they are lesbians, heterosexual women boxers often wear long hair, pink colors, and make-up, accentuate their domestic and maternal traits, and deny that they want to be like men." Lafferty and McKay, "'Suffragettes in Satin Shorts?,'" 254. Jennifer Hargreaves argues that "in sports, as in other areas of public life, the construction of heterosexual femininity is a powerful form of control." Hargreaves, *Sporting Females*, 169. See also Lenskyj, *Out of Bounds*, 56–57.

56  "Girl Athlete Says Boxing Is Valuable for Protection," *Toronto World*, February 18, 1918, 5. See also "Orpheum Theatre: Roehm's Athletic Girl," *South Bend News-Times*, December 25, 1913, 2.

57  "This Female Boxer Wields Wicked Left," *Pittsburgh Press*, March 27, 1919, 28.

58  "Health, Beauty Perfect Figure for Every Woman."

59  "Girl Athlete Says Boxing Is Valuable for Protection," 5.

60  Cahn, *Coming On Strong*, 4, 29. For more on the emphasis on femininity by physical educators, see Verbrugge, *Active Bodies*, 23–32, 55–58.

61  "Boxing Girl Arrives," *Washington Post*, October 30, 1904, S4; originally published in the *New York Times*.

62  "Boxing Has Become a Fashionable Fad of New York Women," *Evening Bulletin*, November 29, 1902, 12.

63  "The Maid and the Mitts," *San Francisco Call*, December 2, 1906, 9.

64  Patterson, *The American New Woman Revisited*, 4.

65  Nixola Greeley-Smith, "New York Women Pay $25 Apiece for Boxing Lessons—It's a Craze," *Tacoma Times*, March 8, 1915, 2.

66  "'Ware the Woman with the Wicked Jolt," *San Francisco Chronicle*, April 6, 1913, 5.

67  "Box," *Pittsburgh Press*, January 4, 1915, 24.

68  Cahn, *Coming On Strong*, 14–18.

69  "Student's Reception to Tulane Faculty," *Times-Picayune*, July 14, 1915, 6; "She Wins in Third," *Anaconda Standard*, August 26, 1915, 7; "Vigorous 3-Round Bout Fought by College Girls," *Daily News*, July 21, 1915, 4.

70  "Society Girls Become Boxers," *Reading Eagle*, July 20, 1915, 13; "Girls Await Gong but Bout's Barred," *Plain Dealer*, July 16, 1915, 1; "Women in the News," *Miami Herald*, August 9, 1915, 2.

71  "New Orleans Item," July 18, 1915, 11, Tulane University Archives files.

72  "Better Than Some Things," *Day Book*, August 17, 1915, 9.

73  Greeley-Smith, "New York Women Pay $25 Apiece for Boxing Lessons," 2.

74  "'Ware the Woman with the Wicked Jolt," 5.

75  "Champion Woman Boxer," *Washington Times*, December 31, 1905, 11.

76  "Wins on a Faint," *Kansas City Journal*, May 29, 1898, 6.

77  "An Uppercut from the Fair Fighters Fist," *Hartford Herald*, May 1, 1912, 8.

78  Greeley-Smith, "New York Women Pay $25 Apiece for Boxing Lessons," 2.

79  "Girl Boxer Dons Mitts with Man and Defeats Him," *Evening World*, February 27, 1915, 2.

80 "Girl Boxer Lands on Pugilist's Chin," *Washington Times*, February 27, 1915, 7.

81 Kathy Peiss has argued that working-class women pioneered new mores and manners, especially with regard to leisure during this era. However, Peiss also suggests that "the lines of cultural transmission travel in both directions." This is especially important to keep in mind in examining women's participation in the fighting arts. Upper-class college women pursued athletic fighting sports with vigor at the same time that working-class women were making headway into competitive boxing. See Peiss, *Cheap Amusements*, 8.

82 Vertinsky, *The Eternally Wounded Woman*, 16.

83 Cahn, *Coming On Strong*, 14.

84 "Never Was Kissed," 3; Smith, *A History of Women's Boxing*, 50–53.

85 "Women Boxers Invade Prize Ring," *Norwich Bulletin*, November 15, 1918, 3.

86 "Women Boxers Meet in Classy Six-Round Engagement at Tulsa," *Leader*, January 22, 1911, 3.

87 "When a Woman Dons the Gloves," *Wichita Daily Eagle*, August 17, 1893, 2.

88 "Won Her with His Fists," *Helena Independent*, November 16, 1891, 6.

89 For more on the sexualization of female boxers, see Kim, "Fighting Men and Fighting Women," 117, 119; Hargreaves, "Women's Boxing and Related Activities," 215; Hargreaves, *Sporting Females*, 158–169.

90 See the concept of problem bodies described in Sears, *Arresting Dress*.

91 "Plays and Players," *Indianapolis Journal*, April 29, 1900, 14.

92 "Mrs. Parker Will Box," *Salt Lake Herald*, August 27, 1901, 3.

93 "Exercises for Women," *San Francisco Call*, April 5, 1903, 18.

94 "Woman Boxer Is Put Out of Ring in Harlem after First Round," *Evening World*, March 1, 1916, 12.

95 "Girls Biffed Each Other," *Police Gazette*, September 27, 1890, reprinted in Boddy, *Boxing*, 163–164.

96 Hargreaves, *Sporting Females*, 162–163.

97 Lafferty and McKay, "'Suffragettes in Satin Shorts?,'" 249–255, 273; Kim, "Fighting Men and Fighting Women," 118; Hargreaves, "Women's Boxing and Related Activities," 215.

CHAPTER 2. JIU-JITSU, GENDER, AND THE YELLOW PERIL

1 An earlier and condensed version of this chapter was originally published by the Pacific Coast Branch of the American Historical Association and the University of California Press. See Rouse, "Jiu-Jitsuing Uncle Sam," 448–477.

2 Akihiko Hirose and Kay Kei-ho Pih compared and contrasted Western and Eastern models of ideal masculinity in the modern sport of mixed martial arts (MMA). Their study suggested that the modern debates about the superiority of striking arts such as boxing versus submission arts such as jiu-jitsu revealed the interactive boundaries between hegemonic and marginalized masculinities. The authors suggested, however, that white hegemonic forms of masculinity selectively appropriate Asian masculinities, reconstructing them as feminized, exotic,

and useful to reinforce the dominance of white masculinity. Modern MMA tends to favor Western martial arts such as boxing that emphasize aggressive punching and kicking (and therefore Western masculinity). Asian martial arts that rely on submission techniques, such as judo or jiu-jitsu, are often seen as more passive and less aggressive (and therefore less masculine). Western audiences preferred the knockout to the tap-out as the more masculine way to win a fight. However, the effectiveness and efficiency of Japanese jiu-jitsu threatened the reputation of Western martial arts, and to enhance their skills, many modern fighters have begun cross-training in both striking and submission arts. Hirose and Pih suggest that this does not reflect an admission to the superiority of Asian martial arts or culture but rather an appropriation of selective aspects of Asian martial arts that further bolsters and ensures the dominance of Western masculinity. In this sense "exotic elements . . . are now authorized to remain as a familiar and domesticated other." I borrow from this theoretical framework to argue here that this process of domesticating aspects of Japanese martial arts began even earlier than Hirose and Pih suggested in their analysis of modern MMA. Hirose and Pih, "Men Who Strike and Men Who Submit," 190–209.

3  For historic context on the anti-Chinese movement and Chinese exclusion, see Lee, *At America's Gates*; Sayler, *Laws Harsh as Tigers*; Sandmeyer, *The Anti-Chinese Movement in California*; McClain, *In Search of Equality*; Pfaelzer, *Driven Out*.

4  Daniels, *The Politics of Prejudice*, 68; Tchen and Yeats, *Yellow Peril!*, 12–14.

5  Daniels, *The Politics of Prejudice*, 1, 6–7; Daniels, *Guarding the Golden Door*, 40–41; Takaki, *Strangers from a Different Shore*, 179–180.

6  Daniels, *Guarding the Golden Door*, 40–41; Zeidel, *Immigrants, Progressives, and Exclusion Politics*, 26.

7  "Japanese Invasion the Problem of the Hour for the United States," *San Francisco Chronicle*, February 23 1905, 1

8  Daniels, *The Politics of Prejudice*, 25–28.

9  Ibid., 38.

10  Ibid., 41–45; Chan, *Asian Americans*, 55, 59; Daniels, *Guarding the Golden Door*, 40–45; Takaki, *Strangers from a Different Shore*, 200–203.

11  Dalton, *Theodore Roosevelt*, 285–286.

12  Bederman, *Manliness and Civilization*, 18–20.

13  Letter from Theodore Roosevelt to Senator Philander Chase Knox, February 8, 1909.

14  Roger Daniels discusses Roosevelt's relationship toward the Japanese and concludes that, despite his statements to the contrary, "if anything about the first Roosevelt is clear," it is that he was "a convinced racist." Daniels, *The Politics of Prejudice*, 36. For a detailed analysis of Roosevelt's racial thinking, see Dyer, *Theodore Roosevelt and the Idea of Race*.

15  London, "The Yellow Peril," 269–289.

16  For further reading on Asian American masculinities, see Chan, *Chinese American Masculinities*; Chan, "Contemporary Asian American Men's Issues," 93–102;

Cheng, "'We Choose Not to Compete,'" 177–200; Chua and Fujino, "Negotiating New Asian-American Masculinities," 391–413; Lui, *The Chinatown Trunk Mystery*, 178–180; Lee, *Orientals*, 116–117; Tchen and Yeats, *Yellow Peril!*

17 Bederman, *Manliness and Civilization*, 171.

18 Roosevelt, *The Strenuous Life*, 8–9.

19 Wertheim, "Reluctant Liberator," 500.

20 Letter from William Sturgis Bigelow to Theodore Roosevelt, January 3, 1902.

21 Letter from Theodore Roosevelt to William Sturgis Bigelow, March 19, 1902; letter from John J. O'Brien to George B. Cortelyou, March 10, 1902; "Roosevelt Now Jujutsu Expert," *Chicago Daily Tribune*, March 20, 1902, 1.

22 Letter from Theodore Roosevelt to William Sturgis Bigelow, March 19, 1902.

23 Letter from Theodore Roosevelt to William Sturgis Bigelow, April 1, 1902.

24 "Transcript of Telephone Call with Charles Laurie McCawley," December 3, 1903, Theodore Roosevelt Papers, Manuscripts Division, Library of Congress, Theodore Roosevelt Digital Library, Dickinson State University, www.theodorerooseveltcenter.org; Svinth, "Professor Yamashita Goes to Washington," 52; "Jap Pigmy, Yamashita, Plays with a Giant," *Washington Times*, January 2, 1905, 8; "A Japanese Woman Teaching American Girls," *San Francisco Chronicle*, June 5, 1904, 5.

25 Letter from Theodore Roosevelt to Kermit Roosevelt, March 5, 1904.

26 It is important to note that Yamashita taught Roosevelt judo, which was a derivative of Japanese jiu-jitsu created by Jigoro Kano in 1882. "Jiu-jitsu" refers to a wide range of weaponless fighting systems that developed in Japan over centuries. Kodokan judo, as developed by Kano in the late nineteenth century, emphasized the philosophical aspects of martial arts training, with a focus on the improvement of self and society. Kano also revised many jiu-jitsu techniques to improve upon their effectiveness and efficiency. When judo and jiu-jitsu were introduced to the United States in the early twentieth century, most Americans made no distinction between the two. Throughout this book, I refer generically to the Japanese martial arts introduced in United States as jiu-jitsu, although sometimes the specific practitioners and techniques were actually teaching and sharing the art of judo. Rarely did contemporaries make this distinction. Also, note that there are multiple spellings for "jiu-jitsu" (with "jujutsu" being the preferred modern spelling). However, I have chosen to use "jiu-jitsu" in this book, since this was the most common spelling used in American newspapers and periodicals in the early twentieth century. For an overview of the history of judo and jiu-jitsu, see Green and Svinth, *Martial Arts of the World*.

27 Letter from Theodore Roosevelt to Kermit Roosevelt, February 24, 1905.

28 For more on Orientalism and Asian cultures, see Said, *Orientalism*.

29 "Society's Open Door for the Japanese," *New York Times*, March 20, 1904, 24.

30 John F. McDonald, "Jiu-Jitsu," in O'Brien, *A Complete Course of Jiu-Jitsu and Physical Culture*, 1–2.

31 Yai Kichi Yabe, Monroe County, Rochester, New York State Census 1905; "Japan's Beloved Emperor," *St. Paul Globe*, January 31, 1904, 1. By 1906, Yabe had appar-

ently returned to Japan, according to the *Rochester Directory for the Year Beginning July 1, 1906*, 962.

32  "The Yabe School of Jiu-Jitsu: Jiu-Jitsu Will Be Taught in Our Schools and Colleges," *Sun*, October 9, 1904, 7. Yabe was not the only Japanese American to establish a martial arts dojo in the United States. Japanese immigrants and their Nisei children established schools in Japanese American communities throughout the West Coast in the early twentieth century. For more information, see Svinth, *Getting a Grip*; Svinth, "Tokugoro Ito"; Green and Svinth, *Martial Arts in the Modern World*; Green and Svinth, *Martial Arts of the World*.

33  "Have You Had My Free Lesson in Jiu-Jitsu?," *St. Louis Republic*, February 26, 1905, magazine section, 17.

34  Benesch, *Inventing the Way of the Samurai*, 1–4; Hancock, *Physical Training for Children by Japanese Methods*, 7. For more on nineteenth-century romanticized notions of martial virtue in American popular culture, see Lears, *No Place of Grace*, 98–139.

35  "Jiu-Jitsu, Art of Self-Defense," *Times-Dispatch*, April 2, 1905, 2A.

36  "Japan's Athletics," *Evening Star*, September 16, 1904, 14; "Jiu-Jitsu, Art of Self-Defense," 2A; "Have You Had My Free Lesson in Jiu-Jitsu?," 17.

37  "How Seattle's Sons of Old Japan Practice Jiu-Jitsu," 1. Svinth adds in a footnote that this is actually Kodokan judo.

38  "Jap Bests Three Thugs by Jujutsu," *Evening Public Ledger*, June 5, 1922, 2.

39  Philadelphia, Ward 20, U.S. Bureau of the Census, Fourteenth Census of the United States, 1920.

40  Svinth, "The Circle and the Octagon," 64–65.

41  "Jiu-Jitsu School," *San Francisco Call*, February 20, 1905, 9

42  "A Japanese Girl Fells a Masher," *Times-Dispatch*, October 12, 1905, 11.

43  "Jiu Jitsu in Court, by Little Jap Girl," *Minneapolis Journal*, October 12, 1905, 2; "Jiu-Jitsu in Court," *Los Angeles Herald*, October 27, 1905, 2.

44  "Girls Who Know Jiu-Jitsu Bid Defiance to Mashers," *Daily Missoulian*, August 7, 1914, 8; "Girls, Here's How to Break a Masher's Wrist by 'Jiu-Jitsu,'" *Seattle Star*, August 19, 1912, 8; "Jiu Jitsu Girl Tells American Women How to Handle Masher or Street Thug," *Evening World*, November 21, 1913, 3; "Self-Defence Against Mashers by a Girl Jiu Jitsu Expert," *Pittsburgh Press*, November 30, 1913, 56.

45  "Jiu Jitsu Girl Tells American Women How to Handle Masher or Street Thug," 3. In a similar story a Japanese girl named "Little Koyama" shocked an audience at the Marquam Grand Theatre in Portland, Oregon, when she overenthusiastically applied her submission technique to her "husky Japanese assailant," thereby causing her partner to slip into unconsciousness. "She Knew Jiu-Jitsu," 7.

46  "The Jiu Jitsu Fake," *Daily Capital Journal*, April 22, 1905, 2.

47  Ibid.; "The Danger in Jiu-Jitsu," *Arizona Republican*, September 11, 1905, 7; "We Need Not Fear Jiu-Jitsu," *Salt Lake Tribune*, February 19, 1905, 2.

48  Hoganson, *Fighting for American Manhood*, 134.

49  "The Other Side of Jiu Jitsu," *Columbian*, March 16, 1905, 2.

50 Lewis, *The New Science*, 9.
51 "Can't Drop Jiu Jitsu," *Times-Dispatch*, August 6, 1906, 8.
52 "The Danger in Jiu-Jitsu," 7.
53 "Jiu-Jitsu to Be Avoided," *Perrysburg Journal*, May 19, 1905, 7.
54 "We Need Not Fear Jiu-Jitsu," 2.
55 "Jolts from John L.," *San Francisco Call*, June 4, 1905, 8.
56 Yamagata, "Jiu-Jitsu, the Art of Self-Defense," 95, 96.
57 Hancock, *Physical Training for Women by Japanese Methods*.
58 "Jolt for Jiu-Jitsu," *Salt Lake Herald*, March 9, 1905, 7.
59 "Not True Athletics," *Daily Press*, February 10, 1907, 10.
60 Svinth notes that this was actually a school of Kodokan judo operated by Iitaro Kano, who arrived in 1903 and began teaching judo in Seattle. "How Seattle's Sons of Old Japan Practice Jiu-Jitsu," 1.
61 Hedrick, "Some Echoes of the Week," 6.
62 "Jiu-Jitsu Fails to Retain Hold," *Los Angeles Herald*, October 8, 1906, 6.
63 Nixola Greeley-Smith, "How a Girl Can Repel a Masher's Attack," *Evening World*, January 3, 1905, magazine section, 15.
64 Yamagata, "Jiu-Jitsu, the Art of Self-Defense," 93.
65 "Editorial Comment: A New Idea from Japan," 828.
66 Yet it should be noted that Japanese women were far from equals in dojos in Japan. For more on the gendered dimensions of Japanese martial art training in the early twentieth century, see Miarka, Marques, and Franchini, "Reinterpreting the History of Women's Judo in Japan," 1016–1029.
67 Lillian Lauferty, "Beauty: Mlle Dazie Tells How to Mould Beautiful Shoulders and Points Out the Value of Poise," *El Paso Herald*, August 2, 1913, 7A. For a photograph of Dazie performing jiu-jitsu onstage, see Wolf, "'Mlle. Dazie's Jiu-Jitsu Dance.'"
68 "Jiu-Jitsu Practiced by Women Gives Slim Waists," *Sun*, March 26, 1905, 5; "Eating on the Jiu-Jitsu Plan, *Sun*, April 9, 1905, 5.
69 Hancock, *Jiu-Jitsu Combat Tricks*; Hancock, *Physical Training for Children by Japanese Methods*; Hancock, *Physical Training for Women by Japanese Methods*.
70 Hancock, *Physical Training for Women by Japanese Methods*, xi, 1.
71 Ibid., xi.
72 "Jiu-Jitsu Taught," *New York Times*, October 17, 1904, 13.
73 *How Girls Can Help Their Country*, 8.
74 "Peace Scouting for Girls," *Marlborough Express*, November 29, 1909, 5.
75 "Barnard Field Day," *Sun*, May 22, 1908, 12; "College Women in Athletic Club," *Sun*, April 26, 1916, 4; "Jiu-Jitsu for College Girls," *Sun*, April 11, 1915, 8. Jiu-jitsu appeared to be on the list of activities into the 1920s; see "Intercollegiate Alumnae Athletic Association," 88.
76 "Japanese Will Meet American at Jiu-Jitsu," *Los Angeles Herald*, January 4, 1910, 12; "Japanese Wins Wrestling Bout," *Los Angeles Herald*, January 5, 1910, 12.
77 "A Japanese Woman Teaching American Girls," 5; "Jiu-Jitsu, Boxing, and Wrestling Are to Be Introduced in the Army," *Rock Island Argus*, March 31, 1905, 1;

"To Teach Jiu-Jitsu," *Walla Walla Statesman*, December 30, 1904, 1; "Jiu-Jitsu at Annapolis," *Evening Star*, February 4, 1905, 11.

78  "Will Jiu-Jitsu Uncle Sam," *San Francisco Call*, April 1, 1905, 8.

79  Hancock, *Jiu-Jitsu Combat Tricks*, v.

80  "Japanese System of 'Jiu-Jitsu,'" *San Francisco Call*, February 28, 1904, 7.

81  "Editorial: The Manly Art of Self-Defense," *Argonaut*, April 10, 1905, 1.

82  "To Teach Jiu-Jitsu," 1; "Jiu-Jitsu at Annapolis," *Evening Star*, 11; "Jiu Jitsu at Chase's," *Washington Post*, April 23, 1905, B6.

83  "Jiu-Jitsu, Boxing, and Wrestling Are to Be Introduced in the Army," 1.

84  Svinth, "Professor Yamashita Goes to Washington," 59.

85  "How Philadelphia 'Strong-Arm' Policemen Are Trained," 14–15; "Rookie Policemen Being Taught Jiu Jitsu in Central Park," *Sun*, August 26, 1917, magazine section, 18.

86  "Subduing the Most Dangerous of Criminals with the Twist of the Wrist," *Ogden Standard*, November 8, 1913, magazine section, 22.

87  "Cannon May Kill," 808–809.

88  Marriott, *Hand-to-Hand Fighting*, 6–7.

89  Edna Egan, "Every Woman Her Own Bodyguard," *Ogden Standard*, July 14, 1917, magazine section, 23.

90  Winship, "Looking About," 431.

91  "This Woman Boxer Weighs 105 and She Has Met Two Champions," *Tacoma Times*, November 27, 1917, 6.

92  Jensen, *Mobilizing Minerva*, xi.

93  "These Girls Won't Have to Use Rolling Pins," *Norwich Bulletin*, May 15, 1918, 3.

94  Kimberley Jensen has argued that World War I mobilized women to fight against violence on a variety of fronts. See Jensen, *Mobilizing Minerva*.

95  "Moose to Hold Classes under Ireland, Plan," *Weekly Journal-Miner*, April 13, 1921, 5; H. C. Hamilton, "Athletic Activities at Camp Lewis," *Oswego Daily Times*, December 24, 1917, 7.

96  "Learn Expert Wrestling and Physical Culture," 48.

97  "Gotch Ridicules Jiu Jitsu System," *St. Paul Globe*, January 16, 1905, 5; "Gotch Talks of Jiu-Jitsu," *Scranton Republican*, January 15, 1905, 3.

98  Smith, *The Secrets of Jujitsu*; Bowen, "Some Background on Captain Allan Corstorphin Smith."

99  "Black Belt Is Coveted Prize for Jiu Jitsu Men," *Indiana Evening Gazette*, February 26, 1916, 3.

100  "How I Learned JuJitsu in 30 Minutes," 167.

101  This idea of the necessity of self-defense training for the purpose of defending one's manliness can also be seen in an article in the *Seattle Star*, where Les Darcy, an Australian middleweight champion boxer, argues that "every American should know the rudiments of self-defense! If he is single he owes it to himself and if married to his family." "Les Darcy, Australian Boxing Marvel, Gives Pointers on How to Defend Yourself in Street," *Seattle Star*, January 19, 1917, 13.

102 "Boy Scouts, Can You Defend Yourselves?," 36.

103 "Brave but Helpless," 126; "Who Wants to Learn Boxing?," 126; "Can You Play a Man's Part?," 112.

104 "Brave but Helpless," 126.

105 Smith, *The Secrets of Jujitsu.*

106 For similar studies dealing with imperialism, Orientalism, and consumption, see Yoshihara, *Embracing the East*; Hoganson, "Cosmopolitan Domesticity," 55–83; Hoganson, *Consumers' Imperium.*

107 "The Danger in Jiu-Jitsu," 7.

## CHAPTER 3. SELF-DEFENSE AND CLAIMING PUBLIC SPACE

1 "Girl Whose Skill in Jiu Jitsu Enabled Her to Overcome Robber," *Chicago Daily Tribune*, April 5, 1909, 3; Girl's Wit and Jiu Jitsu Land Masher on His Back," *Chicago Daily Tribune*, April 4, 1909, 3; "She Routed a Footpad, but Not Cupid," *Chicago Daily Tribune*, June 24, 1912, 7; "Wilma M. Berger," Chicago, Cook County, U.S. Bureau of the Census, Thirteenth Census of the United States, 1910.

2 "Social Sets of Other Cities," *Washington Post*, September 10, 1909, 7. After Berger successfully thwarted the attacker, disbelieving policemen asked for a demonstration. Much to their amusement, Berger offered a brief tutorial of her technique on Detective Frank Gard, as a few reporters watched in astonishment. Berger even received letters from adoring male admirers who offered proposals of marriage. She politely declined these requests. Berger married Raymond Ackley on June 22, 1912, in Chicago. "Wilma H. Berger," in *Cook County, Illinois, Marriages Index, 1871–1920.*

3 "Doubt If Women Boxers Will Ever Be Numerous," *Chicago Daily Tribune*, August 26, 1909, 11.

4 Sewell, *Women and the Everyday City*, xxiii; see also Walkowitz, "Going Public," 1–30.

5 Welter, "The Cult of True Womanhood," 151–174; Cott, *The Bonds of Womanhood*; Ryan, *Cradle of the Middle Class*; Mintz and Kellogg, *Domestic Revolutions*; Kessler-Harris, *Out to Work*, 90.

6 Newman, *White Women's Rights*, 7–10, 32; Hine, "'We Specialize in the Wholly Impossible,'" 70–93.

7 Odem, *Delinquent Daughters*, 22–23.

8 Ibid., 2–3; Sewell, *Women and the Everyday City*, 2; Peiss, *Cheap Amusement*, 5–7; Kessler-Harris, *Out to Work*, 90.

9 Sewell, *Women and the Everyday City*, xxiii.

10 Ibid., 2–4; Hickey, "From Civility to Self-Defense," 80–81; Walkowitz, "Going Public," 7; Herman Schuettler, "Police Are Handicapped by Unwillingness of Women to Appear in Court against Mashers," *Chicago Daily Tribune*, January 27, 1907, F3; "To Drive the Mashers Out of Chicago," *Chicago Daily Tribune*, January 27, 1907, F3.

11 Odem, *Delinquent Daughters*, 24, 53; Walkowitz, "Going Public," 18–19.

12 Freedman, *Redefining Rape*, 191, 196; Segrave, *Beware the Masher*, 8–9.

13  "What Can Be Done to Rid the Palmer House of Mash," *Chicago Daily Tribune*, February 4, 1906, F2; Alice M. Johnson, "The Truth about Mashing," *Chicago Daily Tribune*, January 18, 1914, D13.

14  "Woman's Fists Land on Masher," *Evening World*, December 3, 1903, 2.

15  Marguerite Mooers Marshall, "Girls with R.S.V.P. Eyes Invite Mashers; Three Rules to Help Others Dodge Them," *Evening World*, October 21, 1914, 3.

16  Esther Andrews, "New York Women Start 'Smash Masher' Crusade," *Tacoma Times*, September 19, 1906, 5.

17  "Judge Fines the Mashers: 'Baby Doll' Costs 'Em $20," *Tacoma Times*, May 12, 1913, 4.

18  See, for example, "Slashed Masher's Ear, She Says," *Sun*, January 1, 1903, 3.

19  Nixola Greeley-Smith, "Flirtation Squad of Girl Detectives Will Clear All the Peacock Alley of the Hotel Mashers of Both Sexes," *Evening World*, January 2, 1917, 3.

20  Freedman, *Redefining Rape*, 10, 89–124; Donovan, *White Slave Crusades*, 12–15, 43, 48, 52; Pliley, *Policing Sexuality*, 2, 24–25, 30.

21  This analysis is based on a review of a search of three newspapers (the *Chicago Daily Tribune*, *San Francisco Chronicle*, and *Evening World*) for the term "masher" between 1900 and 1919. The search was completed through Proquest Historical Newspaper Database and Newspapers.com. A total of 462 articles specifically discussed the arrest or prosecution of mashers. The *Chicago Daily Tribune* search generated more than 800 hits, with 297 specifically discussing the arrest or prosecution of mashers. The *Evening World* revealed 462 hits, with 133 specific articles, and the *San Francisco Chronicle* revealed 252 hits, with 32 articles describing the arrest or prosecution of mashers.

22  "Woman's Fists Land on Masher," 2.

23  "She Smashed Masher with Her White Fists," *Albuquerque Evening Citizen*, August 29, 1905, 2; "Mutilates Masher on Street," *Alexandria Times*, September 20, 1905, 6.

24  Freedman, *Redefining Rape*, 204–205.

25  Gross, *Colored Amazons*, 73–74; Hicks, *Talk with You Like a Woman*, 14, 36–37, 54, 64.

26  Hine, "Rape and the Inner Lives of Black Women," 912–920; Hine, "We Specialize in the Wholly Impossible," 70–93.

27  Gross, *Colored Amazons*, 75.

28  Herman Schuettler, "Police Are Handicapped by Unwillingness of Women to Appear in Court against Mashers," *Chicago Daily Tribune*, January 27, 1907, F3; "Leading Women Hope to Arouse Sentiment That Will Put an End to the Growing Evil," *Chicago Daily Tribune*, February 4, 1906, F3; "Woman's Fists Out of Chicago," *Chicago Daily Tribune*, January 27, 1907, F3.

29  Hine, "Rape and the Inner Lives of Black Women," 912–920; Hine, "Black Migration to the Urban Midwest," 130, 138.

30  Hine, "Lifting the Veil, Shattering the Silence," 223–249.

31  "Bold Flirt Is Taken to Jail," *Chicago Defender*, April 12, 1924, 3.

32  Freedman, *Redefining Rape*, 205.

33  "Girls Whip White Mashers," *Pittsburgh Courier*, October 27, 1928, A7.

34  Freedman, *Redefining Rape*, 208.

35  White, *Too Heavy a Load*, 60–71; Hicks, *Talk with You Like a Woman*, 56–57.

36  "Smashing the Masher Newest Aim of Police," *Washington Times*, July 10, 1910, 2; Clarence L. Cullen, "Special Cop Squads," *Evening Star*, March 2, 1907, pt. 3, 2.

37  "Heiresses Join Ranks of Policewomen," *Ogden Standard*, July 24, 1915, magazine section; "You'd Better Make Your Eyes Behave!," *Ogden Standard*, October 23, 1915, magazine section; "Policewomen Apt Pupils with Pistols and Jiu Jitsu," *Chicago Daily Tribune*, March 10, 1914, 15; "Police Women to Wrestle," *New York Times*, March 8, 1914, C5.

38  "Ten New Policewomen Appointed by Enright," *New York Tribune*, May 28, 1919, 13.

39  "Policewomen Badly Needed," *Chicago Defender*, June 13, 1914, 1; "Death on Mashers," *Chicago Defender*, January 29, 1927, A3.

40  Odem, *Delinquent Daughters*, 111.

41  "Women Police Grapple with the Masher Evil," *New York Times*, March 23, 1924, XX11.

42  Peiss, *Cheap Amusements*, 53–55, 107–110.

43  Nixola Greeley-Smith, "Says More Policewomen Will Rid Streets of Mashers Who Pester Young Girls," *Day Book*, February 10, 1914, 9.

44  Nixola Greeley-Smith, "'Mashers' Pictured by New York Girls in Language That's Terse and Accurate," *Evening World*, July 24, 1912, 3.

45  "You'd Better Make Your Eyes Behave."

46  Stamp, *Movie-Struck Girls*, 51.

47  Pliley, *Policing Sexuality*, 2, 24–25, 30.

48  Zeidel, *Immigrants, Progressives, and Exclusion Politics*, 10, 12, 55, 109.

49  McCoy, "Claiming Victims," xii, 24, 166, 194.

50  Donovan, *White Slave Crusades*, 43, 48, 52, 127–129; Freedman, *Redefining Rape*, 192; Rosen, *The Lost Sisterhood*, 116–119.

51  Adler, *First in Violence, Deepest in Dirt*.

52  "Girl Smashes 'Masher,'" *Daily Press*, October 6, 1906, 1.

53  "Plucky Phone Girl Fights a Masher," *Seattle Star*, June 22, 1912, 1.

54  "'Masher' Hit Her Is Charge of Girl," *Washington Times*, August 21, 1919, 2.

55  "Masher Slashes Girl," *New York Tribune*, December 15, 1913, 2.

56  "Feeney Has a Rival at Robbing Women," *St. Paul Globe*, December 19, 1898, 2; "Another Assault," *St. Paul Globe*, June 29, 1899, 8; "Beat Off the Terror," *St. Paul Globe*, July 22, 1899, 8.

57  "Bullets in His Body," *St. Paul Globe*, July 23, 1899, 2; "Paltry Ninety Days," *St. Paul Globe*, October 31, 1899, 2.

58  "Police Round Up Henry Slipka," *St. Paul Globe*, May 23, 1903, 2; "Slipka Sentenced," *Minneapolis Journal*, June 19, 1903, 7.

59  Frankenberg, *White Women, Race Matters*, 76–77; Bederman, *Manliness and Civilization*, 46–76; Freedman, *Redefining Rape*, 27, 89–111, 124, 192; Donovan, *White Slave Crusades*, 12–15.

60  Larson, *The Devil in the White City*.

61  Berrington and Jones, "Reality vs. Myth," 307.

62  "What Can Be Done to Rid the Palmer House of Mash," F2. See also Johnson, "The Truth about Mashing," D13; "Leading Women Hope to Arouse Sentiment That Will Put an End to the Growing Evil," *Chicago Daily Tribune*, February 4, 1906, F3; "Woman's Fists Out of Chicago," F3.

63  Freedman, *Redefining Rape*, 198–199; "Murder Rife in Chicago," *Abbeville Press and Banner*, February 7, 1906, 2.

64  Nixola Greeley-Smith, "Street Masher Is Really a Timid Sort, Disposed of with a Word by Woman of Wits," *Evening World*, August 7, 1912, 3.

65  Greeley-Smith, "'Mashers' Pictured by New York Girls in Language That's Terse and Accurate," 3.

66  "Victims of 'Flirty Bosses' Who Seek Miss Libbey's Advice by Mail," *Chicago Daily Tribune*, September 29, 1912, G7.

67  *Final Report and Testimony of the U.S. Commission on Industrial Relations*, 3:2343.

68  *Report on Condition of Woman and Child Wage-Earners in the United States*, 3:179–180.

69  Odem, *Delinquent Daughters*, 79; Jensen, *Mobilizing Minerva*, 9, 10.

70  "Women Who Find the Streets Safe," *Washington Post*, November 5, 1905, SM7.

71  Marshall, "Girls with R.S.V.P. Eyes Invite Mashers," 3.

72  Blount, Speech before National American Convention of 1910, 5: 295.

73  Hickey, "From Civility to Self-Defense," 80–81.

74  Marshall, "Girls with R.S.V.P. Eyes Invite Mashers," 3.

75  "Smash the Street Masher," *St. Paul Daily Globe*, August 9, 1885, 2.

76  Greeley-Smith, "Street Masher Is Really a Timid Sort," 3.

77  Cullen, "Special Cop Squads," pt. 3, 2.

78  "Not Always the Men," *Los Angeles Herald*, November 20, 1892, 3.

79  "The Judge and the Mashers," *Hawaiian Star*, July 8, 1911, 13.

80  Greeley-Smith, "Street Masher Is Really a Timid Sort," 3.

81  Marshall, "Girls with R.S.V.P. Eyes Invite Mashers," 3.

82  "The Season of Flirting Is Now at Its Dizziest Height," *Washington Times*, July 13, 1902, 7.

83  Peiss, *Cheap Amusements*, 186–187; Odem, *Delinquent Daughters*, 24, 39, 53.

84  Peiss, *Cheap Amusements*, 187.

85  Nixola Greeley-Smith, "New York Mashers, Their Insulting Tricks and the Different Brands of the Pests," *Evening World*, July 13, 1912, 3.

86  Greeley-Smith, "Street Masher Is Really a Timid Sort," 3.

87  Nixola Greeley-Smith, "Ravenous Police Dogs Protect New York Girls from Mashers," *Day Book*, January 19, 1914, 28.

88 Greeley-Smith, "Street Masher Is Really a Timid Sort," 3.

89 Greeley-Smith, "'Mashers' Pictured by New York Girls in Language That's Terse and Accurate," 3.

90 Esther Andrews, "New York Women Start 'Smash Masher' Crusade," *Tacoma Times*, September 19, 1906, 5.

91 "Girl Stenographer Uses Glove on Masher," *Bisbee Daily Review*, June 17, 1909, 8.

92 Other scholars have examined the various ways that women claimed public space in the urban environment. See Deutsch, *Women and the City*; Peiss, *Cheap Amusements*; Ryan, *Women in Public*; Sewell, *Women and the Everyday City*; Spain, *How Women Saved the City*; Stansell, *City of Women*.

93 "Athletic Women," *Los Angeles Times*, April 28, 1889, 6.

94 "Girls Should Be Boxers," *Seattle Star*, May 28, 1901, 3. Bates was an actress who apparently also later studied jiu-jitsu extensively under Professor Higashi. De Montaigu, "What Women Are Doing in America," 179.

95 "Smashers of Mashers to Escape Punishment," *Washington Herald*, May 27, 1913, 2.

96 "Women Must Fight Back at Mashers, Is Advice," *Seattle Star*, September 11, 1911, 1.

97 "Mashers and Thugs Beware! Girls Plan Jiu-Jitsu Club," *Los Angeles Herald*, April 29, 1906, 17.

98 "Fifty Girls of Spokane Train to Whip Mashers," *Washington Post*, December 26, 1914, 4.

99 See, for example, discussions of boxing classes for women in high schools in Wharton, New Jersey, and Los Angeles, California. "Boxing Made Safe," *Day Book*, May 29, 1913, 19; "Ban on Boxing of High School Girls," *San Francisco Call*, December 28, 1911, 11.

100 "Notice to Highway Men" and "Clever in the Art of Jujutsu," *Evening Public Ledger*, May 10, 1920, night extra, 26; "Barnard College Girls Becoming Experts in Jiu-Jitsu Art," *Allentown Leader*, February 9, 1916, 10; "Girls Practice Wrestling," *Cincinnati Enquirer*, February 6, 1916, 14 "Co-eds Must Take Lessons in Boxing," *Los Angeles Herald*, October 20, 1906, 8.

101 "Ultra Smart Boston Club," *Richmond Climax*, April 27, 1904, 3.

102 "Girls of Philly Have Boxing Club All of Their Own," *San Francisco Chronicle*, February 17, 1920, 14.

103 "Women to Study Jiu Jitsu," *Chicago Daily Tribune*, February 25, 1906, 10.

104 "Learning to Smash 'Mashers,'" 7.

105 "Safe from Attack."

106 Skinner, *Jiu-Jitsu*, 7.

107 Hancock, *Jiu-Jitsu Combat Tricks*; Hancock, *Physical Training for Children by Japanese Methods*; Hancock, *Physical Training for Women by Japanese Methods*.

108 "Girl Athlete Says Boxing Is Valuable for Protection," *Toronto World*, February 18, 1918, 5.

109 MacDonald, "Motion Picture Educator," 1773.

110 "Mashers and Thugs Beware! Girls Plan Jiu-Jitsu Club."

111 "How to Defend Yourself," *San Francisco Call*, August 21, 1904, 11.

112 "Safe from Attack."

113 Edna Egan, "Everywoman Her Own Bodyguard," *Ogden Standard*, July 14, 1917, magazine section, 23.

114 "How to Defend Yourself," 11.

115 Ruth Helen Lang, "How I Thrash the Mashers," *Spokesman-Review*, April 29, 1911.

116 "Woman Grabs Highwayman," *New York Times*, October 21, 1905, 1.

117 "Judge Fines the Mashers: 'Baby Doll' Costs 'Em $20," 4.

118 "The Parasol Broke," *Los Angeles Herald*, August 26, 1893, 8.

119 Newman, *White Women's Rights*, 57, 86, 96.

120 Faderman, *To Believe in Women*, 140, 148–149.

121 Dudley and Kellor, *Athletic Games in the Education of Women*, 110.

122 Hollister, *The Woman Citizen*, 117.

123 Ibid., 127.

124 "Anne Morgan Takes Peep into Circus 'Green Room,'" 1; "N.Y. Girls Will Learn to Jiu-Jitsu Mashers"; "Jiu-Jitsu for New York Society," 6; "To Demonstrate Value of Jiu Jitsu," 6.

125 Thompson, "Vacation Savings Movement," 257.

126 Ibid., 259.

127 "Masher Laid Out by Woman," *San Francisco Chronicle*, June 27, 1905, 13.

128 "Miss Anne Morgan . . . ," 1.

129 Sewell, *Women and the Everyday City*, 127; Freedman, *Redefining Rape*, 191–192.

CHAPTER 4. SELF-DEFENSE IN THE ERA OF SUFFRAGE AND THE NEW WOMAN

1 Gammel, "Lacing Up the Gloves," 371–372.

2 Griswold, "Divorce and the Legal Redefinition of Victorian Manhood," 96–101.

3 Harper, *The Life and Work of Susan B. Anthony*, 390–392.

4 Hancock, *Jiu-Jitsu Combat Tricks*, 146.

5 Stanton, "Impunity in Crime," 362.

6 Blackwell, "Sparring for Women," 100.

7 Ibid.

8 "Girl Knocks Out Masher," *Chicago Daily Tribune*, May 22, 1905, 5.

9 For more on gender performativity, see Butler, *Gender Trouble*.

10 Bederman, *Manliness and Civilization*, 193; Watts, *Rough Rider in the White House*, 46–47; Hoganson, *Fighting for American Manhood*, 143–145.

11 Svinth, "Editor's Notes," in "Jiu jitsu for Women." See also "Woman Smashes Riding Records," *Burlington Free Press*, July 28, 1910, 6.

12 Svinth, "Professor Yamashita Goes to Washington," 52; Svinth, "The Evolution of Women's Judo."

13 "A Japanese Woman Teaching American Girls," 5; see also Looser, "Radical Bodies and Dangerous Ladies," 3–19.

14 Smith College Yearbook, Class of 1903, 78–79, 82–82.

15 Letter from Blanche Butler Ames to Blanche Ames Ames, March 18, 1904.

16  Clark, "My Dear Mrs. Ames."
17  Thomas went to work as a writer for the D'Arcy Advertising Company in 1918. She lived with her mother and grandfather in St. Louis, Missouri. "Louise Le Noir Thomas," St. Louis, Missouri, U.S. Bureau of the Census, Fourteenth Census of the United States, 1920; "The Co-ed Cane," *Mexico Weekly Ledger*, March 18, 1915, 4; "Louise Lenoir Thomas," 155; "Suffrage League to Give Tea Tomorrow," *St. Louis Post-Dispatch*, April 25, 1919, 12; "Seventy Years of Age," *Washington Post*, February 16, 1890, 2; Anthony and Harper, *The History of Woman Suffrage*, 4:175; Johnson, *Notable Women of St. Louis*, 230–234.
18  Louise Le Noir Thomas, "How a Woman Can Protect Herself upon the Street," *Ogden Standard*, April 14, 1917, magazine section, 1.
19  "Smashing Cures Mashing Says Ethel Intropodi," *Tacoma Times*, September 9, 1912, 2; "Ethel Intropidi [sic]," Manhattan, New York, U.S. Bureau of the Census, Fourteenth Census of the United States, 1920.
20  Wilson, *With All Her Might*, 54–55; Purvis, "Emmeline Pankhurst (1858–1928) and Votes for Women," 122; Kent, *Sex and Suffrage in Britain*, 101, 173–175; Morrell, *"Black Friday" and Violence against Women in the Suffragette Movement*.
21  "Miss Sylvia Pankhurst's Account," 120–121.
22  Pankhurst, *The Suffragette*, 502.
23  Wilson, *With All Her Might*, 88–89.
24  Purvis, "'Deeds, Not Words,'" 138–139; Winslow, *Sylvia Pankhurst*, 34; Kent, *Sex and Suffrage in Britain*, 173–175.
25  See also Mayhall, *The Militant Suffrage Movement*; Parkins, "Protesting Like a Girl," 59–78.
26  Pankhurst, "Title Deeds of Political Liberty," 441.
27  Kent, *Sex and Suffrage in Britain*, 48–49.
28  Mulvey-Roberts, "Militancy, Masochism or Martyrdom?," 170–171.
29  Wilson, *With All Her Might*, 49–51, 105–106, 123; Purvis, "'Deeds, Not Words,'" 135–158; "What Happens in Holloway," 99.
30  Wilson, *With All Her Might*, 131–132.
31  "Ju-Jutsu for Suffragettes," 56, 49; "Jiu-Jitsu for Suffragettes," 675; "Ju-Jutsu for Suffragette Self-Defence," 667. See also Garrud, "The World We Live In," 355.
32  Svinth, "The Evolution of Women's Judo"; "Woman Physically Militant: Suffragette, Learns Jiu-Jitsu to Eject Male Intruders," *Washington Post*, July 3, 1910; 4; "Militant for Ballot: English Suffragettes Learning Art of Jiu-Jitsu," *Washington Post*, July 18, 1910, 3.
33  "A New Jujutsu School," 222; "Jujitsu for Policewomen," 747.
34  Mary Wilson, "Boston Girl Shows Muscles to London," *Indianapolis Star*, May 21, 1911, 13; "Women and Sport," *Mercury*, May 17, 1911, 6.
35  "'Justice' at the Old Bailey," 62–63; "Our Prisoners," 81; "A Visit to Mrs. Chapin," 111; "Alison Neilans' Release," 182–183; Hilary Frances, "'Dare to Be Free!,'" 181–202.

36  The Women's Freedom League broke off from the Women's Social and Political Union in 1907. Frances, "'Dare to Be Free!,'" 181–202; Eustance, "Meanings of Militancy," 51–64.

37  "The 'Physical Force' Fallacy," 425.

38  "Suffragettes Train for New Campaign," *San Francisco Chronicle*, August 7, 1910, 43.

39  "Jiu-Jitsu for Militants," *New York Times*, August 20, 1913, 4.

40  "The Suffragette Athlete," *Daily Mail*, June 27, 1910, 9.

41  "Victory Is Assured," 397.

42  Wilson, *With All Her Might*, 140–141; see also Purvis, "Emmeline Pankhurst (1858–1928) and Votes for Women," 127.

43  Murray, "Glasgow's Shame," 343–344.

44  Wilson, *With All Her Might*, 148–151.

45  Ibid.; "Government's War on Women," 361.

46  Murray, "Glasgow's Shame," 343–344.

47  "King Looks on from Palace as Women Fight," *Toledo Blade*, May 28, 1914, 3.

48  "Echoes of the Deputation to the King," 547.

49  "The New Year," 228.

50  Pankhurst, "Why We Are Militant"; "Victory Is Assured," 397.

51  Winslow, *Sylvia Pankhurst*, 56–59; Kent, *Sex and Suffrage in Britain*, 109.

52  Pankhurst, "Why We Are Militant."

53  Winslow, *Sylvia Pankhurst*, 34, 44–45, 54, 70; "Miss Emerson Is Charming Woman," *Spartanburg Herald*, May 4, 1913, 7; "The Second Demonstration" and "Suffragists in Prison in Holloway Gaol," 300: "Miss Emerson Released," 424.

54  "Militant Troops Study Jiu Jitsu," *Chicago Examiner*, November 18, 1913, 1.

55  "British Suffragettes Are Going to Take Up Art of Self-Defense," *Milwaukee Sentinel*, April 15, 1911, 14; Nixola Greeley-Smith, "Suffragettes Will Cultivate Muscles and Fight Like Amazons for Her Ballot," *Evening World*, April 11, 1911, 3.

56  "Hopes Women Will Train Muscles," *Oklahoma City Daily Pointer*, April 11, 1911, 1.

57  Allen, *The Feminism of Charlotte Perkins Gilman*; Bederman, *Manliness and Civilization*, 121–169. Despite her overt feminism and resistance to sexist theories of biological determinism, Gilman was also very much a product of her time, insisting on appropriately gendered exercises for women. Gilman, *The Man-Made World or Our Androcentric Culture*, 153.

58  Gilman, "Should Women Use Violence?"; Allen, *The Feminism of Charlotte Perkins Gilman*, 153–154.

59  Jensen, *Mobilizing Minerva*, 6–8, 10, 40–41.

60  *Suffrage Parade*, 31.

61  Ibid., 52.

62  Jensen, *Mobilizing Minerva*, 10.

63  "Boxing Lessons Now a Fad for Suffragists," *Leavenworth Times*, March 20, 1913, 3.

64  "Boxing Lessons for Women in Germany," *Anaconda Standard*, January 21, 1910, 2.

65  Louise Bodecker, in *Gould's St. Louis Directory for 1913*, 356. She applied for an emergency passport to return to Germany for four months in August 1914. Ac-

cording to the passport, she had lived in St. Louis since her immigration to the United States in 1900. Louise Von Decker, Emergency Passport Application.

66 "Badger Notes," *Kennewick Courier*, July 18, 1913, 4.

67 Frank J. Gilbert and Alta M. Hyde, marriage license; "Frank and Alta Gilbert," Cleveland, Ohio, U.S. Bureau of the Census, Thirteenth Census of the United States, 1910; "Frank J. Gilbert," in *Cleveland Directory for the Year Ending August 1906*, 495. "Frank J. Gilbert," in *Classified Business and Director's Directory of Cleveland*, 570.

68 "Woman Who Knocked Down Masher Wants Society for the Suppression of Ilk," *Chicago Daily Tribune*, August 26, 1905, 2; "She Smashed Masher with Her White Fists," 2; "Mutilates Masher on Street," 6.

69 "Ohio Suffragists," *Lima Daily News*, October 19, 1913, 14; "Aha!," *Cincinnati Enquirer*, October 21, 1913, 3; "New Suffrage Party," *Chronicle-Telegram*, January 14, 1914, 8; "Suffrage March on Church Called Off," *Tennessean*, June 5, 1914, 7; "Wives of Union Men to March," *Leavenworth Times*, June 4, 1914, 1. Gilbert's Socialist Party membership is deduced from a short excerpt from a Girard, Kansas, Socialist newspaper she apparently subscribed to: "'Enclosed find my renewal. The Appeal is the best paper printed. I have read it ten years and have never detected an attempt to deceive the public.'—Comrade Alta H. Gilbert, Ohio." "Enclosed," *Appeal to Reason*, July 29, 1917, 2.

70 Putnam, "Women and Democracy," 113–114.

71 "Boxing Classes for Women," *New York Tribune*, November 2, 1922, 14.

72 "The Pugilists," *Evening Star*, May 25, 1905, 4.

73 "The Washboard Method," *Gazette Times*, April 8, 1911, 4.

74 Chauncey Thomas, *Outdoor Life*, reprinted in "America Is Effeminate," *Los Angeles Times*, April 23, 1917, 18.

75 "Do Girls Wish They Were Boys?," *Evening World*, July 1, 1904, 8.

76 Nixola Greeley-Smith, "Girls, Develop Muscles, Speed and a Punch," *Pittsburgh Press*, April 18, 1911, 10.

77 Nixola Greeley-Smith, "Jiu-Jitsu for the Masher," *Evening World*, January 2, 1905, 10.

78 See, for example, Greeley-Smith, "How a Girl Can Repel a Masher's Attack," 15; Nixola Greeley-Smith, "How a Girl Can Foil a Pickpocket," *Evening World*, magazine section, January 4, 1905; Nixola Greeley-Smith, "Jiu-Jitsu Lesson for Girls," *Evening World*, magazine section, January 5, 1905.

79 Smith-Rosenberg, *Disorderly Conduct*, 176.

80 Patterson, *The American New Woman Revisited*, 11–12.

81 Smith-Rosenberg, *Disorderly Conduct*, 176–178.

82 Patterson, *The American New Woman Revisited*, 1–2.

83 "'Ware the Woman with the Wicked Jolt," 5.

84 "And Now It's Athletic Championships the Ladies Want," *Ogden Standard-Examiner*, July 2, 1922, 4.

85 "Wrestling and Jiu-Jitsu for Women," *Milwaukee Sentinel*, April 30, 1911, 20.

86 "Suffrage Here to Stay," *New York Tribune*, November 28, 1918, 15. A similar point was also made in the article "Women's Rights May Not Stop with the Successful Passage of the Suffrage Amendment," *Charlotte News*, December 26, 1920, 16.

87 "What Chance Has a Burglar against Girls Like These?," *San Francisco Chronicle*, magazine section, June 11, 1922, 3.

88 Vertinsky, *The Eternally Wounded Woman*, 214–215.

89 Kent, *Sex and Suffrage in Britain*.

## CHAPTER 5. SELF-DEFENSE IN THE DOMESTIC SPHERE

1 Frankenberg, *White Women, Race Matters*, 76–77; Odem, "Cultural Representations and Social Contexts of Rape in the Early Twentieth Century," 363; Bederman, *Manliness and Civilization*, 46–76; Freedman, *Redefining Rape*, 27, 89–111, 192; Donovan, *White Slave Crusades*, 12–15, 43, 48, 52, 127–129; Pliley, *Policing Sexuality*, 2, 24–25, 30; Siegel, "'The Rule of Love,'" 2139.

2 Jensen, *Mobilizing Minerva*, 22.

3 Gordon, *Heroes of Their Own Lives*, 21–22; Odem, "Cultural Representations and Social Contexts of Rape in the Early Twentieth Century," 353–367.

4 Odem, "Cultural Representations and Social Contexts of Rape in the Early Twentieth Century," 363.

5 Berrington and Jones, "Reality v. Myth," 309–310.

6 "Chicago Enduring a Reign of Terror from Criminals," *New York Tribune*, January 29, 1906, 3.

7 "Women Killed; Record of Year," *Chicago Tribune*, January 21, 1906, 3.

8 "Murder Rife in Chicago," 2.

9 Analysis based on seventeen women listed in "Chicago Enduring a Reign of Terror from Criminals," 3; "Murder Rife in Chicago," 2. Further information gathered on the individual cases from "Women Killed; Record of Year," 3; "Chicago Woman Murdered," *Evening Statesman*, January 6, 1906, 1; "24 Women Slain in a Year in Chicago," *Minneapolis Journal*, January 21, 1906, 2; "Gets a Life Sentence," *Palatine Enterprise*, September 27, 1907, 6; "On Deadly Rampage," *Morning Post*, October 11, 1905, 1; "Woman Is Slain for Her Money," *Alton Evening Telegraph*, April 22, 1905, 7; "Citizens to End Murder Carnival," *Inter Ocean*, January 14, 1906, 2.

10 These data were collected by first extracting a list of the murders of women from the "Homicide in Chicago, 1870–1930" database (based on the records of the Chicago Police Department). I followed up by researching individual cases in the newspapers to verify the victim's relationship with the perpetrator and the location of the murder.

11 Twenty-four individual cases of women killed are listed in other newspaper articles from around the same time, and an analysis of these cases reveals similar results. Of the twenty-four women, sixteen (67%) were killed by a known assailant (intimate partner, male relative, or boarder). The same number, sixteen (67%), were killed in their own home, room, or place of employment. See original ar-

ticles: "Women Killed; Record of Year," 3; "24 Women Slain in a Year in Chicago," 2. Further information gathered on the individual cases from "Gets a Life Sentence," 6; "Murder Rife in Chicago," 2; "Chicago Enduring a Reign of Terror from Criminals," 3; "Woman Is Slain for Her Money," 7; "On Deadly Rampage," 1.

12  Odem, *Delinquent Daughters*, 58–60. See also Odem, "Cultural Representations and Social Contexts of Rape in the Early Twentieth Century," 353–367.

13  Pleck, *Domestic Tyranny*, 4.

14  "A Husband Attempts to Kill His Wife," *New York Daily Tribune*, January 18, 1870, 2.

15  Case File 1107, *Eva Chester v. Frank C. Chester*.

16  Bowman and Altman, "Wife Murder in Chicago," 774–779; Gordon, *Heroes of Their Own Lives*, 10, 265–271; Adler, *First in Violence, Deepest in Dirt*, 53, 66–67, 74.

17  Griswold, "Divorce and the Legal Redefinition of Victorian Manhood," 96–101.

18  Adler, *First in Violence, Deepest in Dirt*, 53, 66–67, 74, 117–118.

19  "Threatened to Kill Her," *Democratic Banner*, May 2, 1916, 6.

20  "Jealous, He Shoots Wife," *Inter Ocean*, October 5, 1905, 9.

21  Adler, *First in Violence, Deepest in Dirt*, 46, 100.

22  Bowman and Altman, "Wife Murder in Chicago," 739–740.

23  Ibid., 779; Adler, *First in Violence, Deepest in Dirt*, 61, 72.

24  "Wife's Charges," *Evening Star*, June 23, 1899, 8

25  "Crime of Drink Crazed Husband," *Mattoon Morning Star*, January 12, 1905, 3.

26  "Moving Picture Show Causes Fatal Shooting," *Los Angeles Herald*, August 6, 1910, 11.

27  "Marry Me or I'll Kill You," *Evening World*, December 31, 1904, 2.

28  "Politics Causes Downfall," *Nebraska State Journal*, May 26, 1902, 1.

29  "Old Man Rapes Girl," *Wichita Daily Eagle*, August 16, 1902, 1.

30  Gordon, *Heroes of Their Own Lives*, 8–12.

31  Jones, *Labor of Love, Labor of Sorrow*, 96.

32  Bowman and Altman, "Wife Murder in Chicago," 739–790; see also Adler, "'I Wouldn't Be No Woman If I Wouldn't Hit Him,'" 14–36; Gross, *Colored Amazons*, 89.

33  Hine, "Rape and the Inner Lives of Black Women," 912–920; Hine, "Black Migration to the Urban Midwest," 130, 138.

34  Gordon, *Heroes of Their Own Lives*, 11; Bowman and Altman, "Wife Murder in Chicago," 739–790; Adler, *First in Violence, Deepest in Dirt*, 50.

35  Tsu, "Sex, Lies, and Agriculture," 171–209.

36  Siegel, "'The Rule of Love,'" 2139–2140.

37  Edwards, "Women and Domestic Violence in Nineteenth-Century North Carolina," 127.

38  Egemonye, "Treat Her Like a Lady," 283–290; Newman, *White Women's Rights*, 7–10, 32.

39  "Hard on Parson Lott," *Daily Ardmoreite*, October 5, 1909, 1.

40  "Mrs. Novak Seeks Divorce," *Omaha Daily Bee*, June 23, 1913, 1.

41  Pleck, *Domestic Tyranny*, 4.

42  Gordon, *Heroes of Their Own Lives*, 4.

43  Gordon and Dubois, "Seeking Ecstasy on the Battlefield," 10–11; Marilley, *Woman Suffrage and the Origins of Liberal Feminism in the United States*, 100–123; Pleck, *Domestic Tyranny*, 49–66.

44  Pleck, *Domestic Tyranny*, 69–87.

45  Ibid., 95–98; Gordon, *Heroes of Their Own Lives*, 6–7.

46  Edwards, "Women and Domestic Violence in Nineteenth-Century North Carolina," 129–130.

47  "Disagree over Whipping Post," *Lake Shore News*, August 8, 1912, 9.

48  According to Pleck, whipping post laws were passed in Maryland in 1882, Delaware in 1901, and Oregon in 1905. Pleck, *Domestic Tyranny*, 108–109.

49  Pleck, *Domestic Tyranny*, 6, 57–66, 101–103; Gordon, *Heroes of Their Own Lives*, 254; Bourke, "Sexual Violence, Marital Guidance, and Victorian Bodies," 419–436; Hasday, "Contest and Consent," 1373–1505; Freedman, *Redefining Rape*, 54.

50  Pleck, *Domestic Tyranny*, 99–103; Pleck, "Feminist Responses to 'Crimes against Women' 1868–1896," 458, 470.

51  U.S. Bureau of the Census, *Special Reports: Marriage and Divorce, 1867–1906*, pt. 1, 26.

52  This is based on a search for the terms "wife-beater" and "wife-beating" in Newspapers.com, a digitized database of more than 3,000 newspapers. See the similar findings of Elizabeth Katz in "Judicial Patriarchy and Domestic Violence," 405–406.

53  Fahs, *Out on Assignment*, 117–121, 272; Abramson, *Sob Sister Journalism*, 117–119.

54  Nixola Greeley-Smith, "Favors Whipping Post for Wife Beaters, but No State Support for Their Victims," *Evening World*, January 20, 1912, 3.

55  See, for example, Greeley-Smith, "How a Girl Can Foil a Pickpocket"; Greeley-Smith, "Jiu-Jitsu Lesson for Girls"; Greeley-Smith, "How a Girl Can Repel a Masher's Attack," 15.

56  Pleck, *Domestic Tyranny*, 5.

57  For scholarship that questions the conclusions of these previous studies, see more recent research by legal historians such as Ramsey, "Public Responses to Intimate Violence," 460–463; Katz, "Judicial Patriarchy and Domestic Violence," 379–471.

58  Pleck, *Domestic Tyranny*, 125–144; Gordon, *Heroes of Their Own Lives*, 21–22.

59  "A Fad for Fighting," *St. Paul Daily Globe*, July 10, 1892, 12.

60  "President Roosevelt's Desire to Punish Wife-Beaters . . . ," *St. Louis Republic*, January 22, 1905, 2.

61  "Woman Wrestler Thinks Strength More Necessary Than Ballast for Her Sex," *Wichita Eagle*, March 12, 1911, 7.

62  "Down with the Male Boss," *Hawaiian Star*, May 7, 1912, 4.

63  Frank G. Menke, "Claims Boxing Cures Girls' Bad Tempers," *El Paso Herald*, January 27, 1915, sport and classified section.

64  "May Slap Back Says the Judge," *St. Paul Globe*, March 25, 1905, 7.

65  "Subduing the Most Dangerous of Criminals with the Twist of the Wrist," 22.

66  "Wants All Women to Box So Murders May Decrease," *Inter Ocean*, August 25, 1909, 1.

67  "Ju-Jutsu as a Husband-Tamer," 339.

68  Looser, "Radical Bodies and Dangerous Ladies," 11.

69  "Get Out, Get Under."

70  "Who Said Divorce?"

71  "Is Marriage a Failure?"

72  "Boxing—The Newest Womanly Art," *Chicago Daily Tribune*, October 6, 1911, 5.

73  Kathleen Fox, "Taming My Husband," *Washington Herald*, April 28, 1919, 1.

74  Ibid.

75  Kathleen Fox, "Taming My Husband," *Washington Herald*, August 20, 1919, 8.

76  Kathleen Fox, "Taming My Husband," *Washington Herald*, August 21, 1919, 4.

77  Kathleen Fox, "Taming My Husband," *Washington Herald*, August 22, 1919, 8.

78  Gilman, "Joan's Defender," 295.

79  Ibid., 296.

80  Kimmel and Aronson, "Introduction to the 1998 Edition," xvi.

81  Gilman, "Should Women Use Violence?," 11.

82  Kimberley Jensen makes a similar point in her analysis of women physicians, nurses, and soldiers in World War I. They "challenged the traditional gender bargain of men as the Protectors and women as the Protected: women armed to defend the state could defend themselves against violence of invasion and also domestic violence." She further argues that "for some women, claiming the right of preparedness was also an assertion of their right to defend themselves against male violence, whether in the contest of war or in a broader definition of 'home defense' against domestic violence or other assault." Jensen, *Mobilizing Minerva*, ix, 40.

83  Gilman, "Should Women Use Violence?," 11.

84  "Boxing for Girls Favored by Club," *San Francisco Call*, February 21, 1909, 33; "Pugilistic Girls," *Los Angeles Herald*, February 21, 1909, 3.

85  "Catharine Gouger Waugh McCulloch"; Freedman, *Redefining Rape*, 199.

86  "Boxing for Girls Favored by Club," 33; "Pugilistic Girls," 3.

87  Catharine Waugh McCulloch, "Let Women Vote in Self Defense," *Chicago Daily Tribune* April 1, 1906, pt. 3, editorial, 5.

88  McCulloch, "Woman Is Held in Savagery," 349.

89  "When a Woman Dons the Gloves," *Wichita Daily Eagle*, August 17, 1893, 2.

90  "May Slap Back Says the Judge," 7.

91  "When a Woman Dons the Gloves," 2.

92  Gilman, "Should Women Use Violence?," 11. Gail Bederman has described Gilman as having a "lukewarm opposition to lynching." Bederman, *Manliness and Civilization*, 158.

93  "When a Woman Dons the Gloves," 2.

94  Gilman, "Should Women Use Violence?," 11. There are contradictory scholarly readings of Gilman's racial thinking. Some scholars have suggested that Gilman's feminism was grounded in racism and label Gilman as a eugenic feminist. Gail Bederman, for example, has argued that Gilman's "feminism

was inextricably rooted in the white supremacism of 'civilization.'" Louise M. Newman followed with a similar reading of Gilman's racist feminism. Other scholars such as Judith Allen have contested that narrow reading of Gilman's work and prefer to examine Gilman within the context of her time existing in an era where most people believed in a natural racial hierarchy. Allen avoids going so far as to label Gilman a racist and instead points to her rejection of Jim Crow racism as evidence of the complexity of her racial thinking. For the two extremes of the argument see Bederman, *Manliness and Civilization*, 121–169; Newman, *White Women's Rights*, 132–157; Allen, *The Feminism of Charlotte Perkins Gilman*, 335–349.

95  "Wants All Women to Box So Murders May Decrease," 1.

96  For more detail on the Elsie Siegel murder and Leon Ling, see Lui, *The Chinatown Trunk Mystery*.

97  From the *Boston Transcript* but published in "Women as Boxers," *Butler Weekly Times*, January 25, 1906, 8.

98  "Girl Uses Jiu-Jitsu in Fight with Crook," *Sun and New York Herald*, June 9, 1920, 22.

99  Lippitt, Mary Helen vs. Lippitt, Alburn. See also "Boxing—The Newest Womanly Art," 5; "Wife Who Urges Fiancées to Learn Boxing," *Chicago Daily Tribune*, October 4, 1911, 5; "Taught Wife Boxing; Sorry," *Oshkosh Daily Northwestern*, September 30, 1911, 2; "Teaches Wife to Box; Rues It," *Chicago Daily Tribune*, September 30, 1911, 9.

100  Adler, *First in Violence, Deepest in Dirt*, 102–107.

101  Odem, *Delinquent Daughters*, 62.

102  "Wants All Women to Box So Murders May Decrease," 1.

## CONCLUSION

1  Freedman, *Redefining Rape*, 52.

2  Searles and Berger, "The Feminist Self-Defense Movement," 79. On women's empowerment through radical feminism in the 1960s and 1970s, see Echols, *Daring to Be Bad*; Evans, *Personal Politics*; Bevacqua, "Reconsidering Violence against Women"; Bevacqua, *Rape on the Public Agenda*; Rosen, *The World Split Open*.

3  McCaughey, *Real Knockouts*.

4  McCaughey, "The Fighting Spirit," 281.

5  Ibid., McCaughey, *Real Knockouts*, 90; Jocelyn A. Hollander, "'I Can Take Care of Myself,'" 205–235.

6  Hickey, "From Civility to Self-Defense," 88.

7  Mankins, "Why Women Need Self-Defense Classes of Their Own."

8  Cahn, *Coming On Strong*, 2–4, 29; Verbrugge, *Active Bodies*, 23–32, 55–58.

9  Ullman, "Reflections on Researching Rape Resistance," 343–350. See also Ullman, "Does Offender Violence Escalate When Rape Victims Fight Back?," 179–192; Ullman and Knight, "Fighting Back," 31–43; Tark and Kleck, "Resisting Rape," 270–292.

10  Hollander, "Does Self-Defense Training Prevent Sexual Assault against Women?,"
    252–269; Hollander, "'I Can Take Care of Myself,'" 205–235; Senn et al., "Efficacy of
    a Sexual Assault Resistance Program for University Women," 2326–2335.
11  Breiding et al., "Prevalence and Characteristics of Sexual Violence, Stalking, and
    Intimate Partner Violence Victimization."
12  "What Is SEL?"; see also Bridgeland, Bruce, and Hariharan, *The Missing Piece*;
    Durlak et al., "The Impact of Enhancing Students' Social and Emotional Learn-
    ing," 405–432.
13  Gidycz and Dardis, "Feminist Self-Defense and Resistance Training for College
    Students," 322–333.
14  Thompson, "Empowering Self-Defense Training," 352.
15  Hollander, "The Importance of Self-Defense Training for Sexual Violence Preven-
    tion," 208.

# BIBLIOGRAPHY

PRIMARY SOURCES

"Alison Neilans' Release." *Vote* 1, no. 16 (February 12, 1910): 182–183.

Anthony, Susan B., and Ida Husted Harper. *The History of Woman Suffrage.* Vol. 4. Indianapolis, IN: Hollenbeck Press, 1902.

Antrim, Minna Thomas. "The Masculization of Girls." *Lippincott's Magazine* 88 (October 1911): 564–566.

Blackwell, Alice Stone. "Sparring for Women." *Woman's Journal* 28, no. 13 (March 26, 1887): 100.

Blount, Dr. Anna E. Speech before National American Convention of 1910. In *The History of Woman Suffrage,* edited by Ida Husted Harper, 5:295. National American Woman Suffrage Association. New York: J. J. Little and Ives, 1922.

"Boy Scouts, Can You Defend Yourselves?" *Boys' Life* 3, no. 1 (March 1913): 36.

Brackett, Anna C. "The Education of American Girls." In *The Education of American Girls,* edited by Anna C. Brackett, 11–114. New York: G. P. Putnam's Sons, 1874.

"Brave but Helpless." *Popular Science* 96, no. 2 (February 1920): 126.

"Cannon May Kill." *Popular Science* 92, no. 6 (June 1918): 808–809.

"Can You Play a Man's Part?" *Popular Science* 97, no. 5 (November 1920): 112.

Case File 1107. *Eva Chester v. Frank C. Chester.* Superior Court of the State of Washington, Mason County, October 21, 1910. Washington, Mason County Divorce Records. Ancestry.com.

*Classified Business and Director's Directory of Cleveland.* Cleveland, OH: Penton Press, 1913.

*Cleveland Directory for the Year Ending August 1906.* Cleveland, OH: Cleveland Directory Company, 1905.

*Cook County, Illinois, Marriages Index, 1871–1920* [database online]. Provo, UT: Ancestry.com Operations, 2011.

"Could You Hold Your Own?" *Popular Science Monthly* 98, no. 1 (January 1921): 104.

de Koven, Anna. "The Athletic Woman." *Good Housekeeping* 55, no. 2 (August 1912): 148–157.

De Montaigu, Comtesse. "What Women Are Doing in America." *Womanhood Magazine* 14, no. 80 (July 1905): 179.

Dudley, Gertrude, and Frances A. Kellor. *Athletic Games in the Education of Women.* New York: Henry Holt, 1909.

"Echoes of the Deputation to the King." *Votes for Women* 7, no. 326 (June 5, 1914): 547.

"Editorial Comment: A New Idea from Japan." *Harper's Bazaar* 38, no. 8 (August 1904): 828.

Ellis, Havelock. *Studies in the Psychology of Sex: Sexual Inversion.* Philadelphia: F. A. Davis, 1901.

*Final Report and Testimony of the U.S. Commission on Industrial Relations.* Vol. 3. Senate Doc. No. 21, 64th Cong., 1st sess. (1916): 2343.

Fitzsimmons, Robert. *Physical Culture and Self-Defense.* Philadelphia: Drexel Biddle, 1901.

Frank J. Gilbert and Alta M. Hyde. Marriage license, Cuyahoga County, Ohio, April 9, 1902. *Cuyahoga County, Ohio, Marriage Records and Indexes, 1810–1973* [database online]. Provo, UT: Ancestry.com Operations, 2010.

Garrud, Edith. "The World We Live In." *Votes for Women* 3, no. 104 (March 4, 1910): 355.

"Get Out, Get Under." Catherine H. Palczewski Postcard Archive. University of Northern Iowa, Cedar Falls, Iowa.

Gilman, Charlotte Perkins. "Joan's Defender." In *The Yellow Wall-Paper, Herland, and Selected Writings*, edited by Denise D. Knight, 289–296. New York: Penguin Books, 1999.

———. *The Man-Made World or Our Androcentric Culture.* New York: Charlton, 1911.

———. "Should Women Use Violence?" *Pictorial Review* 14 (November 1912): 11, 78–79.

"Giving Him the Jiu-Jitsu." *American Monthly Review of Reviews* 29, no. 3 (March 1904): 262.

*Gould's St. Louis Directory for 1913.* St. Louis, MO: Gould Directory Company, 1913.

"Government's War on Women." *Votes for Women* 7, no. 314 (March 13, 1914): 361.

Grant, Madison. *The Passing of the Great Race: Or, the Racial Basis of European History.* New York: Charles Scribner's Sons, 1916.

Hall, G. Stanley. *Adolescence: Its Psychology and Its Relations to Physiology, Anthropology, Sociology, Sex, Crime, Religion and Education.* 2 vols. New York: D. Appleton, 1904.

Hancock, Harrie Irving. *Jiu-Jitsu Combat Tricks: Japanese Feats of Attack and Defence in Personal Encounter.* New York: G. P. Putnam's Sons, 1904.

———. *Physical Training for Children by Japanese Methods.* New York: G. P. Putnam's Sons, 1904.

———. *Physical Training for Women by Japanese Methods.* New York: G. P. Putnam's Sons, 1905.

Harper, Ida Husted. *The Life and Work of Susan B. Anthony.* Indianapolis, IN: Bowen-Merrill, 1899.

"Health, Beauty Perfect Figure for Every Woman." *Physical Culture* 27, no. 3 (March 1922).

Hedrick, T. K. "Some Echoes of the Week: A Bow for the Japomaniacs." *Wetmore's Weekly* 1, no. 29 (March 24, 1905): 6.

Hollister, Horace Adelbert. *The Woman Citizen: A Problem in Education.* New York: D. Appleton, 1918.

*How Girls Can Help Their Country: Handbook for Girl Scouts.* 1913. Reprint, New York: Cosimo Books, 2010.

"How I Learned JuJitsu in 30 Minutes." *Illustrated World* 36, no. 2 (October 1921): 167.

"How Philadelphia 'Strong-Arm' Policemen Are Trained." *Popular Science* 93, no. 1 (July 1918): 14–15.

"How Seattle's Sons of Old Japan Practice Jiu-Jitsu." *Seattle Times*, March 10, 1907, magazine section, 1. Reprinted in *Journal of Combative Sport* 1 (December 1999). www.ejmas.com.

*The Inside of the White Slave Traffic.* Moral Feature Film Company, 1913.

"Intercollegiate Alumnae Athletic Association." *Smith Alumnae Quarterly* 12, no. 1 (November 1920): 88.

"Is Marriage a Failure?" Glasgow and London: Millar and Lang, Ltd., Art Publishers, ca. 1910.

Jacobi, Mary Putnam. "Mental Action and Physical Health." In *The Education of American Girls*, edited by Anna C. Brackett, 255–305. New York: G. P. Putnam's Sons, 1874.

———. *The Question of Rest for Women during Menstruation.* New York: G. P. Putnam's Sons, 1877.

Johnson, Mrs. Charles P., ed. *Notable Women of St. Louis.* St. Louis, MO, 1914. www.archive.org.

"Jujitsu for Policewomen." *Votes for Women* 7, no. 342 (September 25, 1914): 747.

"Jiu-Jutsu for Suffragettes." *The Vote* 3, no. 56 (November 19, 1910): 56, 49.

"Jiu-Jitsu for Suffragettes." *Votes for Women* 3, no. 122 (July 8, 1910): 675.

"Ju-Jutsu as a Husband-Tamer: A Suffragette Play with a Moral." *Health and Strength*, April 8, 1911, 339. Reprinted in *Journal of Non-lethal Combatives* 1 (December 1999). www.ejmas.com.

"Ju-Jutsu for Suffragette Self-Defence." *Women's Franchise* 2, no. 53 (July 1, 1909): 667.

"'Justice' at the Old Bailey." *Vote* 1, no. 6 (December 2, 1909): 62–63.

Krafft-Ebing, Richard. *Psychopahia Sexualis: With Especial Reference to the Antipathic Sexual Instinct, a Medico-Forensic Study.* New York: Rebman, 1906.

"Learn Expert Wrestling and Physical Culture." *Popular Mechanics* 24 (December 1915): 48.

Letter from Blanche Butler Ames to Blanche Ames Ames, March 18, 1904. Box 39, Folder 1. Ames Family Papers, Sophia Smith Collection, Smith College, Northampton, Massachusetts.

Letter from William Sturgis Bigelow to Theodore Roosevelt, January 3, 1902. Theodore Roosevelt Papers, Manuscripts Division, Library of Congress. Theodore Roosevelt Digital Library, Dickinson State University. www.theodorerooseveltcenter.org.

Letter from John J. O'Brien to George B. Cortelyou, March 10, 1902. Theodore Roosevelt Papers, Manuscripts Division, Library of Congress. Theodore Roosevelt Digital Library, Dickinson State University. www.theodorerooseveltcenter.org.

Letter from Theodore Roosevelt to William Sturgis Bigelow, March 19, 1902. Theodore Roosevelt Papers, Manuscripts Division, Library of Congress. Theodore Roosevelt Digital Library, Dickinson State University. www.theodorerooseveltcenter.org.

Letter from Theodore Roosevelt to William Sturgis Bigelow, April 1, 1902. Theodore Roosevelt Papers, Manuscripts Division, Library of Congress. Theodore Roosevelt Digital Library, Dickinson State University. www.theodorerooseveltcenter.org.

Letter from Theodore Roosevelt to Senator Philander Chase Knox, February 8, 1909. Papers of Theodore Roosevelt, Manuscript Division, Library of Congress.

Letter from Theodore Roosevelt to Edward Sandford Martin, November 26, 1900. Theodore Roosevelt Collection. MS Am 1863 (378). Houghton Library, Harvard University, Theodore Roosevelt Digital Library, Dickinson State University. www.theodorerooseveltcenter.org.

Letter from Theodore Roosevelt to Kermit Roosevelt, March 5, 1904. Theodore Roosevelt Collection. MS Am 1541 (75). Houghton Library, Harvard University, Theodore Roosevelt Digital Library, Dickinson State University. www.theodorerooseveltcenter.org.

Letter from Theodore Roosevelt to Kermit Roosevelt, February 24, 1905. Theodore Roosevelt Collection. MS Am 1541 (107). Houghton Library, Harvard University, Theodore Roosevelt Digital Library, Dickinson State University. www.theodorerooseveltcenter.org.

Lewis, Frank S. *The New Science: Weaponless Defense*. Los Angeles: Frank S. Lewis, 1906.

*Lippitt, Mary Helen vs. Lippitt, Alburn*, General No. 288023. Term No. 10870. 1911–1912. Superior Court of Cook County, Illinois.

Longhurst, Percy. "The Secret Lock: A Splendid Yarn of Jiu-Jitsu." *Boys' Life* 1, no. 6 (August 1911): 16.

"Louise Lenoir Thomas." *Smith Alumnae Quarterly* 6, no. 2 (February 1920): 155.

Louise Von Decker, Emergency Passport Application, 07702, August 12, 1914. National Archives and Records Administration (NARA), Washington, DC. NARA Series: Emergency Passport Applications, Argentina thru Venezuela, 1906–1925. Box 4585, Vol. 174: Germany.

MacDonald, Margaret I. "Motion Picture Educator." *Moving Picture World* 34, no. 12 (December 22, 1917): 1773.

Marriott, Arthur Elmer. *Hand-to-Hand Fighting: A System of Personal Defense for the Soldier*. New York: Macmillan, 1918.

McCulloch, Catherine Waugh. "Woman Is Held in Savagery." *Ohio Journal of Commerce* 5, no. 23 (June 8, 1912): 349.

"Miss Anne Morgan . . . ." *Weekly People* 22, no. 4 (April 27, 1912): 1.

"Miss Emerson Released." *Suffragette* 6, no. 266 (April 11, 1913): 424.

"Miss Sylvia Pankhurst's Account." *Votes for Women* 4, no. 142 (November 25, 1910): 120.

Murray, Eunice G. "Glasgow's Shame." *Vote* 9, no. 230 (March 20, 1914): 343–344.

"A New Jujutsu School." *Votes for Women* 6, no. 253 (January 10, 1913): 222

"The New Year." *Votes for Women* 4, no. 148 (January 6, 1911): 228.

New York State Census. 1905.

"Our Prisoners." *Vote*. 1, no. 7 (December 9, 1909): 81.

Pankhurst, Christabel. "Title Deeds of Political Liberty." *Votes for Women* 1, no. 27 (September 10, 1908): 441.

Pankhurst, Emmeline. "Why We Are Militant." A Speech Delivered by Mrs. Pankhurst in New York, October 21, 1913. London: Women's Press, 1914.

Pankhurst, E. Sylvia. *The Suffragette: The History of the Women's Militant Suffragette Movement, 1905–1910.* Boston: Woman's Journal, 1911.

"The 'Physical Force' Fallacy." *Votes for Women* 2, no. 53 (March 12, 1909): 425.

Putnam, Emily James. "Women and Democracy." *The Fiftieth Anniversary of the Opening of Vassar College, October 10 to 13, 1915: A Record,* 109–125. Poughkeepsie, NY: Vassar College, 1916.

*Report on Condition of Woman and Child Wage-Earners in the United States.* 19 vols. Senate Doc. No. 645, 61st Cong., 2nd sess. (1911): 3:179–180.

*Rochester Directory for the Year Beginning July 1, 1906.* Rochester, NY: Drew Allis, 1906.

Roosevelt, Theodore. *The Strenuous Life.* New York: Review of Reviews, 1900.

"Safe from Attack." *Cosmopolitan* 39, no. 6 (October 1905). Advertising section.

Sargent, Dudley Allen. "What Athletic Games, If Any, Are Injurious for Women in the Form in Which They Are Played by Men?" *American Physical Education Review* 11, no. 3 (March 1906): 174–181.

"The Second Demonstration" and "Suffragists in Prison in Holloway Gaol." *Votes for Women* 6, no. 259 (February 21, 1913): 300.

Smith, Allan Corstorphin. *The Secrets of Jujitsu: A Complete Course in Self-Defense.* Columbus, GA: Stahara Publishing, 1920.

Smith College Yearbook. Class of 1903. Sophia Smith Collection, Smith College Archives, Northampton, Massachusetts.

"She Knew Jiu-Jitsu." *National Police Gazette,* January 21, 1905, 7.

Skinner, Harry H. *Jiu-Jitsu.* New York: Baker and Taylor, 1904.

Stanton, Elizabeth Cady. "Impunity in Crime." *Revolution* 3, no. 23 (June 10, 1869): 362.

*Suffrage Parade: Hearings before a Subcommittee of the Committee on the District of Columbia United States Senate.* Sixty-Third Congress, Special Session of the Senate under S. Res. 499, pt. 1, March 6–17, 1913. Washington, DC: Government Printing Office, 1913.

"The Suffragette That Knew Jiu-Jitsu." *Punch* 139 (July 6, 1910): 9.

Thompson, Hugh. "Vacation Savings Movement." *Munsey's Magazine* 49, no. 2 (May 1913): 257.

*Traffic in Souls.* Independent Moving Pictures Company of America. 1913.

U.S. Bureau of the Census. Fourteenth Census of the United States. 1920.

———. *Special Reports: Marriage and Divorce, 1867–1906.* Pt. 1. Washington, DC: Government Printing Office, 1909.

———. Thirteenth Census of the United States, 1910.

———. Twelfth Census of the United States, 1900.

"Victory Is Assured." *Suffragette* 70, no. 2 (February 13, 1914): 397.

"A Visit to Mrs. Chapin." *Vote.* 1, no. 10 (December 30, 1909): 111.

"What Happens in Holloway." *Vote* 1, no. 9 (December 23, 1909): 99.

"Who Said Divorce?" New York: Bamforth and Co. Publishers, 1910. Catherine H. Palczewski Postcard Archive. University of Northern Iowa, Cedar Falls, Iowa.

"Who Wants to Learn Boxing?" *Popular Science* 95, no. 4 (October 1919): 126.

Winship, A. E. "Looking About." *Journal of Education* 85, no. 16 (April 19, 1917): 431.

Wolf, Tony. "'Mlle. Dazie's Jiu-jitsu Dance.'" The Baritsu Society (blog), October 4, 2010. www.bartitsu.org.
Yamagata, Teiichi. "Jiu-Jitsu, the Art of Self-Defense." *Leslie's Monthly* 59, no. 1 (November 1904): 91–100.


*Newspapers*
*Abbeville Press and Banner* (Abbeville, SC)
*Albuquerque Evening Citizen* (Albuquerque, NM)
*Alexandria Times* (Alexandria, VA)
*Allentown Democrat* (Allentown, PA)
*Allentown Leader* (Allentown, PA)
*Alton Evening Telegraph* (Alton, IL)
*Anaconda Standard* (Anaconda, MT)
*Appeal to Reason* (Girard, KS)
*Argonaut* (San Francisco, CA)
*Arizona Republican* (Phoenix, AZ)
*Belvidere Daily Republican* (Belvidere, IL)
*Bisbee Daily Review* (Bisbee, AZ)
*Bismarck Tribune* (Bismarck, ND)
*Boston Post* (Boston, MA)
*Burlington Free Press* (Burlington, VT)
*Butler Weekly Times* (Butler, MO)
*Charlotte News* (Charlotte, NC)
*Chicago Daily Tribune* (Chicago, IL)
*Chicago Defender* (Chicago, IL)
*Chicago Eagle* (Chicago, IL)
*Chicago Examiner* (Chicago, IL)
*Chicago Tribune* (Chicago, IL)
*Chronicle-Telegram* (Elyria, OH)
*Cincinnati Enquirer* (Cincinnati, OH)
*Columbian* (Bloomsburg, PA)
*Daily Ardmoreite* (Ardmor, OK)
*Daily Capital Journal* (Salem, OR)
*Daily Mail* (London)
*Daily Missoulian* (Missoula, MT)
*Daily News* (Batavia, NY)
*Daily Press* (Newport News, VA)
*Day Book* (Chicago, IL)
*Democratic Banner* (Mt. Vernon, OH)
*El Paso Herald* (El Paso, TX)
*Evening Bulletin* (Honolulu, HI)
*Evening News* (San Jose, CA)
*Evening Public Ledger* (Philadelphia, PA)

*Evening Star* (Washington, DC)
*Evening Statesman* (Walla Walla, WA)
*Evening Times* (Washington, DC)
*Evening World* (New York, NY)
*Gazette Times* (Pittsburgh, PA)
*Hartford Herald* (Hartford, CT)
*Hawaiian Star* (Honolulu, HI)
*Helena Independent* (Helena, MT)
*Humboldt Union* (Humboldt, KS)
*Indiana Evening Gazette* (Indiana, PA)
*Indianapolis Journal* (Indianapolis, IN)
*Indianapolis Star* (Indianapolis, IN)
*Inter Ocean* (Chicago, IL)
*Kansas City Journal* (Kansas City, MO)
*Kennewick Courier* (Kennewick, WA)
*Lake Shore News* (Chicago, IL)
*Leader* (Guthrie, OK)
*Leavenworth Times* (Leavenworth, KS)
*Lima Daily News* (Lima, OH)
*Los Angeles Herald* (Los Angeles, CA)
*Los Angeles Times* (Los Angeles, CA)
*Marlborough Express* (Fairfax, New Zealand)
*Mattoon Morning Star* (Mattoon, IL)
*Mercury* (Hobart, Tasmania)
*Mexico Weekly Ledger* (Mexico, MO)
*Miami Herald* (Miami, FL)
*Milwaukee Sentinel* (Milwaukee, WI)
*Minneapolis Journal* (Minneapolis, MN)
*Morning Post* (Raleigh, NC)
*Nebraska State Journal* (Lincoln, NE)
*New Castle News* (New Castle, PA)
*New York Amsterdam News* (New York, NY)
*New York Daily Tribune* (New York, NY)
*New York Times* (New York, NY)
*New York Tribune* (New York, NY)
*Norwich Bulletin* (Norwich, CT)
*Ogden Standard* (Ogden City, UT)
*Ogden Standard-Examiner* (Ogden, UT)
*Oklahoma City Daily Pointer* (Oklahoma City, OK)
*Omaha Daily Bee* (Omaha, NE)
*Oregon Daily Journal* (Portland, OR)
*Oshkosh Daily Northwestern* (Oshkosh, WI)
*Oswego Daily Times* (Oswego, NY)

*Palatine Enterprise* (Palatine, IL)
*Perrysburg Journal* (Perrysburg, OH)
*Philadelphia Tribune* (Philadelphia, PA)
*Pittsburgh Courier* (Pittsburgh, PA)
*Pittsburgh Post* (Pittsburgh, PA)
*Pittsburgh Press* (Pittsburgh, PA)
*Plain Dealer* (Cleveland, OH)
*Reading Eagle* (Reading, PA)
*Richmond Climax* (Richmond, KY)
*Rock Island Argus* (Rock Island, IL)
*Salt Lake Herald* (Salt Lake City, UT)
*Salt Lake Tribune* (Salt Lake City, UT)
*San Francisco Call* (San Francisco, CA)
*San Francisco Chronicle* (San Francisco, CA)
*Scranton Republican* (Scranton, PA)
*Seattle Star* (Seattle, WA)
*South Bend News-Times* (South Bend, IN)
*Spartanburg Herald* (Spartanburg, SC)
*Spokesman-Review* (Spokane, WA)
*St. Louis Post-Dispatch* (St. Louis, MO)
*St. Louis Republic* (St. Louis, MO)
*St. Paul Daily Globe* (St. Paul, MN)
*St. Paul Globe* (St. Paul, MN)
*Sun* (Philadelphia, PA)
*Sun and New York Herald* (New York, NY)
*Tacoma Times* (Tacoma, WA)
*Tennessean* (Nashville, TN)
*Times-Dispatch* (Richmond, VA)
*Times-Picayune* (New Orleans, LA)
*Toledo Blade* (Toledo, OH)
*Toronto World* (Toronto, ON)
*Tulsa Daily World* (Tulsa, OK)
*Virginia Enterprise* (Virginia, MN)
*Walla Walla Statesman* (Walla Walla, WA)
*Washington Herald* (Washington, DC)
*Washington Post* (Washington, DC)
*Washington Times* (Washington, DC)
*Weekly Journal-Miner* (Prescott, AZ)
*Wichita Daily Eagle* (Wichita, KS)
*Winnipeg Tribune* (Manitoba, Canada)

*Archival Collections*

Ames Family Papers. Sophia Smith Collection, Smith College Archives, Northampton, Massachusetts.

Catherine H. Palczewski Postcard Archive. University of Northern Iowa, Cedar Falls, Iowa.

Harry M. Rhoads photograph collection, Denver Public Library, Western History Collection.

Lillian Schoedler Papers, 1891–1963, MC 273. Schlesinger Library. Radcliffe Institutes for Advanced Study, Harvard University, Cambridge, Massachusetts.

Smith College Yearbooks. Sophia Smith Collection, Smith College Archives, Northampton, Massachusetts.

University Records and Archives Collection, Tulane University Archives, New Orleans, Louisiana.

William M. Van der Weyde Collection. George Eastman Museum, Rochester, New York.

Women's Library Suffrage Collection. London School of Economics and Political Science Library.

Yoshiaki Yamashita Photograph Album (PH 006). Special Collections and University Archives, University of Massachusetts Amherst Libraries.

SECONDARY SOURCES

Aaltonen, Emilia. "Punching Like a Girl: Embodied Violence and Resistance in the Context of Women's Self-Defense." *Journal of International Women's Studies* 13, no. 2 (March 2012): 51–65.

Abate, Michelle Ann. *Tomboys: A Literary and Cultural History*. Philadelphia: Temple University Press, 2008.

Abramson, Phyllis Leslie. *Sob Sister Journalism*. Westport, CT: Greenwood Press, 1990.

Adler, Jeffrey. *First in Violence, Deepest in Dirt: Homicide in Chicago, 1875–1920*. Cambridge, MA: Harvard University Press, 2006.

———. "'I Wouldn't Be No Woman If I Wouldn't Hit Him': Race, Patriarchy, and Spousal Homicide in New Orleans, 1921–1945." *Journal of Women's History* 27, no. 3 (Fall 2015): 14–36.

Allen, Judith A. *The Feminism of Charlotte Perkins Gilman: Sexualities, Histories, Progressivism*. Chicago: University of Chicago Press, 2009.

Anderson, Kristin L., and Debra Umberson. "Gendering Violence: Masculinity and Power in Men's Accounts of Domestic Violence." *Gender and Society* 15, no. 3 (June 2001): 358–380.

Banyard, Victoria L., Mary M. Moynihan, and Elizabeth G. Plante. "Sexual Violence Prevention through Bystander Education: An Experimental Evaluation." *Journal of Community Psychology* 35, no. 4 (May 2007): 463–481.

Beard, George M. *American Nervousness: Its Causes and Consequences*. New York: G. P. Putnam's Sons, 1881.

Bederman, Gail. *Manliness and Civilization: A Cultural History of Gender and Race in the United States, 1880–1917*. Chicago: University of Chicago Press, 1995.

Benesch, Oleg. *Inventing the Way of the Samurai: Nationalism, Internationalism, and Bushidō in Modern Japan*. Oxford: Oxford University Press, 2014.

Berrington, Eileen, and Helen Jones. "Reality vs. Myth: Constructions of Women's Insecurity." *Feminist Media Studies* 2, no. 3 (2002): 307–323.

Bevacqua, Maria. *Rape on the Public Agenda: Feminism and the Politics of Sexual Assault*. Boston: Northeastern University Press, 2000.

——. "Reconsidering Violence against Women: Coalition Politics in the Antirape Movement." In *Feminist Coalitions: Historical Perspectives on Second-Wave Feminism in the United States*, edited by Stephanie Gilmore and Sara Evans, 163–177. Urbana: University of Illinois Press, 2008.

Boddy, Kassia. *Boxing: A Cultural History*. London: Reaktion Books, 2008.

Bourke, Joanna. "Sexual Violence, Marital Guidance, and Victorian Bodies: An Aesthesiology." *Victorian Studies* 50, no. 3 (Spring 2008): 419–436.

Bowman, Cynthia Grant, and Ben Altman. "Wife Murder in Chicago: 1910–1930." *Journal of Criminal Law and Criminology* 92, no. 3 (Spring–Summer 2002): 739–790.

Bittel, Carla. *Mary Putnam Jacobi and the Politics of Medicine in Nineteenth-Century America*. Chapel Hill: University of North Carolina Press, 2009.

Bowen, Richard. "Some Background on Captain Allan Corstorphin Smith." *Journal of Non-lethal Combatives* (June 2003). www.ejmas.com

Brailsford, Dennis. *Bareknuckles: A Social History of Prize-fighting*. Cambridge: Lutterworth Press, 1989.

Breiding, Matthew J., Sharon G. Smith, Kathleen C. Basile, Mikel L. Walters, Jieru Chen, and Melissa T. Merrick. "Prevalence and Characteristics of Sexual Violence, Stalking, and Intimate Partner Violence Victimization—National Intimate Partner and Sexual Violence Survey, United States, 2011." *Morbidity and Mortality Weekly Report* 63, no. SS-8. Atlanta, GA: Centers for Disease Control and Prevention, September 5, 2014. www.cdc.gov.

Bridgeland, John, Mary Bruce, and Arya Hariharan. *The Missing Piece: A National Teacher Survey on How Social and Emotional Learning Can Empower Children and Transform Schools*. Chicago: Collaborative for Academic, Social, and Emotional Learning, 2013.

Butler, Judith. *Gender Trouble: Feminism and the Subversion of Identity*. New York: Routledge, 1990.

Cahn, Susan K. *Coming On Strong: Gender and Sexuality in Women's Sport*. 2nd ed. Urbana: University of Illinois Press, 2015.

"Catharine Gouger Waugh McCulloch." Women Working, 1800–1930. Harvard University Library Open Collections Program. www.ocp.hul.harvard.edu.

Chan, Jachinson W. *Chinese American Masculinities: From Fu Manchu to Bruce Lee*. New York: Routledge, 2001.

——. "Contemporary Asian American Men's Issues." In *Teaching Asian America: Diversity and the Problem of Community*, edited by Lane Ryo Hirabayashi, 93–102. Lanham, MD: Rowman and Littlefield, Publishers 1998.

Chan, Sucheng. *Asian Americans: An Interpretive History*. New York: Twayne, 1991.

Cheng, Cliff. "'We Choose Not to Compete': The 'Merit' Discourse in the Selection Process, and Asian and Asian American Men and Their Masculinity." In *Masculinities in Organizations*, edited by Cliff Cheng, 177–200. Thousand Oaks, CA: Sage, 1996.

Chua, Peter, and Dune C. Fujino. "Negotiating New Asian-American Masculinities: Attitudes and Gender Expectations." *Journal of Men's Studies* 7, no. 3 (1999): 391–413.

Clark, Anne Biller. "My Dear Mrs. Ames: A Study of the Life of Suffragist, Cartoonist and Birth Control Reformer, Blanche Ames Ames, 1878–1969." PhD diss., University of Massachusetts Amherst, 1996.

Clarke, Edward H. *Sex in Education or a Fair Chance for Girls.* Boston: Houghton, Mifflin, 1884.

Cott, Nancy F. *The Bonds of Womanhood: "Woman's Sphere" in New England, 1778–1835.* New Haven, CT: Yale University Press, 1973.

———. *Public Vows: A History of Marriage and the Nation.* Cambridge, MA: Harvard University Press, 2002.

Dalton, Kathleen. *Theodore Roosevelt: A Strenuous Life.* New York: Vintage Books, 2004.

Daniels, Roger. *Guarding the Golden Door: American Immigration Policy and Immigrants since 1882.* New York: Hill and Wang, 2004.

———. *The Politics of Prejudice: The Anti-Japanese Movement in California and the Struggle for Japanese Exclusion.* Berkeley: University of California Press, 1962.

Deutsch, Sarah. *Women and the City: Gender, Space, and Power in Boston, 1876–1940.* Oxford: Oxford University Press, 2000.

Dobash, R. Emerson, and Russell Dobash. *Violence against Wives: A Case against the Patriarchy.* New York: Free Press, 1979.

Donovan, Brian. *White Slave Crusades: Race, Gender and Anti-vice Activism, 1887–1917.* Urbana: University of Illinois Press, 2006.

DuBois, Ellen Carol, and Richard Candida Smith. *Elizabeth Cady Stanton, Feminist as Thinker: A Reader in Documents and Essays.* New York: New York University Press, 2007.

Durlak, Joseph A., Roger P. Weissberg, Allison B. Dymnicki, and Kriston B. Schellinger. "The Impact of Enhancing Students' Social and Emotional Learning: A Meta-analysis of School-Based Universal Interventions." *Child Development* 82, no. 1 (January/February 2011): 405–432.

Dyer, Thomas. *Theodore Roosevelt and the Idea of Race.* Baton Rouge: Louisiana State University Press, 1992.

Echols, Alice. *Daring to Be Bad: Radical Feminism in America, 1967–1975.* Minneapolis: University of Minnesota Press, 1989.

Edwards, Laura F. "Women and Domestic Violence in Nineteenth-Century North Carolina." In *Lethal Imagination: Violence and Brutality in American History*, edited by Michael A. Bellesiles, 115–136. New York: New York University Press, 1999.

Egemonye, Uche. "Treat Her Like a Lady: Judicial Paternalism and the Justification for Assaults against Black Women, 1865–1910." In *Lethal Imagination: Violence and*

*Brutality in American History*, edited by Michael A. Bellesiles, 283–292. New York: New York University Press, 1999.

Elias, Maurice J., Joseph E. Zins, and Roger P. Weissberg. *Promoting Social and Emotional Learning: Guidelines for Educators*. Alexandria, VA: Association for Supervision and Curriculum Development, 1997.

Eustance, Claire. "Meanings of Militancy: The Ideas and Practice of Political Resistance in the Women's Freedom League, 1907–14." In *The Women's Suffrage Movement: New Feminist Perspectives*, edited by Maroula Joannou, 51–64. Manchester: Manchester University Press, 1998.

Evans, Sara. *Personal Politics: The Roots of Women's Liberation in the Civil Rights Movement and the New Left*. New York: Vintage Books, 1980.

Faderman, Lillian, *To Believe in Women: What Lesbians Have Done for America—A History*. Boston: Houghton Mifflin, 1999.

Fahs, Alice. *Out on Assignment: Newspaper Women and the Making of Modern Public Space*. Chapel Hill: University of North Carolina Press, 2011.

Frances, Hilary. "'Dare to Be Free!': The Women's Freedom League and Its Legacy." In *Votes for Women*, edited by June Purvis and Sandra Stanley Holton, 181–202. London: Routledge, 2000.

Frankenberg, Ruth. *White Women, Race Matters: The Social Construction of Whiteness*. Minneapolis: University of Minnesota Press, 1993.

Freedman, Estelle. *Redefining Rape: Sexual Violence in the Era of Suffrage and Segregation*. Cambridge, MA: Harvard University Press, 2013.

Gammel, Irene. "Lacing Up the Gloves: Women, Boxing and Modernity." *Cultural and Social History* 9, no. 3 (2012): 369–389.

Gidycz, Christine A., and Christina M. Dardis. "Feminist Self-Defense and Resistance Training for College Students: A Critical Review and Recommendations for the Future." *Trauma, Violence and Abuse* 15, no. 4 (October 2014): 322–333.

Gordon, Linda. *Heroes of Their Own Lives: The Politics and History of Family Violence, Boston 1880–1960*. Urbana: University of Illinois Press, 1988.

Gordon, Linda, and Ellen Carol Dubois. "Seeking Ecstasy on the Battlefield: Danger and Pleasure in Nineteenth-Century Feminist Sexual Thought." *Feminist Studies* 9, no. 1 (Spring 1983): 7–25.

Gorn, Elliott J. "'Gouge and Bite, Pull Hair and Scratch': The Social Significance of Fighting in the Southern Backcountry." *American Historical Review* 90, no. 1 (February 1985): 18–43.

———. *The Manly Art: Bare-Knuckle Prize Fighting in America*. Ithaca, NY: Cornell University Press, 2010.

Graham, Sara Hunter. *Woman Suffrage and the New Democracy*. New Haven, CT: Yale University Press, 1996.

Green, Thomas A., and Joseph R. Svinth, eds. *Martial Arts in the Modern World: Transmission, Change and Adaptation*. Westport, CT: Praeger, 2003.

———. *Martial Arts of the World: An Encyclopedia of History and Innovation*. Santa Barbara, CA: ABC-CLIO, 2010.

Griswold, Robert L. "Divorce and the Legal Redefinition of Victorian Manhood." In *Meanings for Manhood: Constructions of Masculinity in Victorian America*, edited by Mark C. Carnes and Clyde Griffen, 96–110. Chicago: University of Chicago Press, 1990.

Gross, Kali N. *Colored Amazons: Crime, Violence, and Black Women in the City of Brotherly Love, 1880–1910.* Durham, NC: Duke University Press, 2006.

Grosz, Elizabeth. *Volatile Bodies: Toward a Corporeal Feminism.* Bloomington: Indiana University Press, 1994.

Hargreaves, Jennifer. *Sporting Females: Critical Issues in the History and Sociology of Women's Sports.* New York: Routledge, 1994.

———. "Women's Boxing and Related Activities: Introducing Images and Meanings." In *Martial Arts in the Modern World: Transmission, Change and Adaptation*, edited by Thomas A. Green and Joseph R. Svinth, 209–228. Westport, CT: Praeger, 2003.

Hasday, Jill. "Contest and Consent: A Legal History of Marital Rape." *California Law Review* 88, no. 5 (October 2000): 1373–1505.

Hickey, Georgina. "From Civility to Self-Defense: Modern Advice to Women on the Privileges and Dangers of Public Space." *Women's Studies Quarterly* 39, nos. 1–2 (Spring/Summer 2011): 77–94.

Hicks, Cheryl D. *Talk with You Like a Woman: African American Women, Justice, and Reform in New York, 1890–1935.* Chapel Hill: University of North Carolina Press, 2010.

Hine, Darlene Clark. "Black Migration to the Urban Midwest: The Gender Dimension, 1915–1945." In *The Great Migration in Historical Perspectives*, edited by Joe W. Trotter, 127–146. Bloomington: Indiana University Press, 1991.

———. "Lifting the Veil, Shattering the Silence: Black Women's History in Slavery and Freedom." In *The State of Afro-American History: Past, Present and Future*, edited by Darlene Clark Hine, 223–249. Baton Rouge: Louisiana State University Press, 1986.

———. "Rape and the Inner Lives of Black Women: Thoughts on the Culture of Dissemblance." *Signs* 14, no. 4 (Summer 1989): 912–920.

———. "'We Specialize in the Wholly Impossible': The Philanthropic Work of Black Women." In *Lady Bountiful Revisited: Women, Philanthropy, and Power*, edited by Kathleen D. McCarthy, 70–95. New Brunswick, NJ: Rutgers University Press, 1990.

Hirose, Akihiko, and Kay Kei-ho Pih. "Men Who Strike and Men Who Submit: Hegemonic and Marginalized Masculinities in Mixed Martial Arts." *Men and Masculinities* 13, no. 2 (November 2010): 190–209.

Hoganson, Kristin L. *Consumers' Imperium: The Global Production of American Domesticity, 1865–1920.* Chapel Hill: University of North Carolina Press, 2007.

———. "Cosmopolitan Domesticity: Importing the American Dream, 1865–1920." *American Historical Review* 107, no. 1 (2002): 55–83.

———. *Fighting for American Manhood: How Gender Politics Provoked the Spanish-American and Philippine-American Wars.* New Haven, CT: Yale University Press, 1998.

Hollander, Jocelyn A. "Does Self-Defense Training Prevent Sexual Violence against Women?" *Violence against Women* 20, no. 3 (March 2014): 252–269.

———. "'I Can Take Care of Myself': The Impact of Self-Defense Training on Women's Lives." *Violence against Women* 10, no. 3 (March 2004): 205–235.

———. "The Importance of Self-Defense Training for Sexual Violence Prevention." *Feminism and Psychology* 26, no. 2 (May 2016): 207–226.

———. "The Roots of Resistance to Women's Self-Defense." *Violence against Women* 15, no. 5 (May 2009): 574–594.

———. "Vulnerability and Dangerousness: The Construction of Gender through Conversation about Violence." *Gender and Society* 15, no. 1 (February 2001): 83–109.

———. "Why Do Women Take Self-Defense Classes?" *Violence against Women* 16, no. 4 (April 2010): 459–478.

"Homicide in Chicago, 1870–1930." Northwestern University School of Law. www.homicide.northwestern.edu.

Jacobson, Matthew Frye. *Whiteness of a Different Color: European Immigrants and the Alchemy of Race*. Cambridge, MA: Harvard University Press, 1998.

Jensen, Kimberly. *Mobilizing Minerva: American Women in the First World War*. Urbana: University of Illinois Press, 2008.

Jones, Jacqueline. *Labor of Love, Labor of Sorrow: Black Women, Work and the Family from Slavery to the Present*. New York: Basic Books, 2010.

Katz, Elizabeth. "Judicial Patriarchy and Domestic Violence: A Challenge to the Conventional Family Privacy Narrative." *William and Mary Journal of Women and the Law* 21, no. 2 (Winter 2015): 378–471.

Kent, Susan Kingsley. *Sex and Suffrage in Britain, 1860–1914*. Princeton, NJ: Princeton University Press, 1987.

Kessler-Harris Alice. *Out to Work: A History of Wage-Earning Women in the United States*. New York: Oxford University Press, 1982.

Kevles, Daniel J. *In the Name of Eugenics: Genetics and the Uses of Human Heredity*. Cambridge, MA: Harvard University Press, 1985.

Kim, Jeonguk. "Fighting Men and Fighting Women: American Prizefighting and the Contested Gender Order in the Late Nineteenth and Early Twentieth Centuries." *Sport History Review* 43, no. 2 (November 2012): 103–127.

Kimmel, Michael. *Manhood in America: A Cultural History*. New York: Free Press, 1996.

Kimmel, Michael, and Amy Aronson. "Introduction to the 1998 Edition." In Charlotte Perkins Gilman, *Women and Economics: A Study of the Economic Relation between Men and Women as a Factor in Social Evolution*. Berkeley: University of California Press, 1998. www.ark.cdlib.org.

Lafferty, Yvonne, and Jim McKay. "'Suffragettes in Satin Shorts?' Gender and Competitive Boxing." *Qualitative Sociology* 27, no. 3 (Fall 2004): 249–276.

Larson, Edward J. *Sex, Race, and Science: Eugenics in the Deep South*. Baltimore: Johns Hopkins University Press, 1995.

Larson, Erik. *The Devil in the White City: Murder, Magic, and Madness at the Fair That Changed America*. New York: Crown, 2003.

Lears, T. J. Jackson. *No Place of Grace: Antimodernism and the Transformation of American Culture, 1880–1920*. Chicago: University of Chicago Press, 1981.

Lee, Erika. *At America's Gates: Chinese Immigration during the Exclusion Era, 1882–1943*. Chapel Hill: University of North Carolina Press, 2003.

Lee, Robert G. *Orientals: Asian Americans in Popular Culture*. Philadelphia: Temple University Press, 1999.

Lenskyj, Helen. *Out of Bounds: Women, Sport and Sexuality*. Toronto: Women's Press, 1986.

Leovy, Jennifer. "Chicago Pioneer Got Women onto Courts, Fields for Variety of Competitive Athletics." *University of Chicago Chronicle* 18, no. 4 (November 12, 1998). www.chronicle.uchicago.edu.

London, Jack. "The Yellow Peril." June 1904. In *Revolution, and Other Essays*. New York: Macmillan, 1910.

Looser, Diana. "Radical Bodies and Dangerous Ladies: Martial Arts and Women's Performance, 1900–1918." *Theatre Research International* 36, no. 1 (March 2010): 3–19.

Lui, Mary Ting Yi. *The Chinatown Trunk Mystery: Murder, Miscegenation, and Other Dangerous Encounters in Turn-of-the-Century New York City*. Princeton, NJ: Princeton University Press, 2005.

Mankins, Meg. "Why Women Need Self-Defense Classes of Their Own." *Vice Magazine*, October 18, 2015. www.vice.com.

Marilley, Suzanne M. *Woman Suffrage and the Origins of Liberal Feminism in the United States, 1820–1920*. Cambridge, MA: Harvard University Press, 1997.

Mayhall, Laura Nym. *The Militant Suffrage Movement: Citizenship and Resistance in Britain, 1860–1930*. New York: Oxford University Press, 2003.

McCaughey, Martha. "The Fighting Spirit: Women's Self-Defense Training and the Discourse of Sexed Embodiment." *Gender and Society* 12, no. 3 (June 1998): 277–300.

———. *Real Knockouts: The Physical Feminism of Women's Self-Defense*. New York: New York University Press, 1997.

McCaughey, Martha, and Jill Cermele. "Changing the Hidden Curriculum of Rape Prevention Education: Women's Self-Defense as a Key Protective Factor for a Public Health Model of Prevention." *Trauma, Violence, and Abuse* (October 2015). Advance online publication. www.tva.sagepub.com.

———. "Guest Editors' Introduction." *Violence against Women* 20, no. 3 (March 2014): 247–251.

McClain, Charles J. *In Search of Equality: The Chinese Struggle against Discrimination in Nineteenth-Century America*. Berkeley: University of California Press, 1994.

McCoy, Kelli Ann. "Claiming Victims: The Mann Act, Gender, and Class in the American West, 1910–1930s." PhD diss., University of San Diego, 2010.

McGerr, Michael. *A Fierce Discontent: The Rise and Fall of the Progressive Movement in America, 1870–1920*. New York: Oxford University Press, 2005.

McLeod, David. *Building Character in the American Boy: The Boy Scouts, the YMCA, and Their Forerunners, 1870–1920*. Madison: University of Wisconsin Press, 2004.

Meyerowitz, Joanne. *Women Adrift: Independent Wage Earners in Chicago, 1880–1930*. Chicago: University of Chicago Press, 1988.

Miarka, Bianca, Juliana Bastos Marques, and Emerson Franchini. "Reinterpreting the History of Women's Judo in Japan." *International Journal of Sport History* 28, no. 7 (May 2011): 1016–1029.

Miller, Elizabeth, Daniel J. Tancredi, Heather L. McCauley, Michele R. Decker, Maria Catrina D. Virata, Heather A. Anderson, Nicholas Stetkevich, Ernest W. Brown, Feroz Moideen, and Jay G. Silverman. "'Coaching Boys into Men': A Cluster-Randomized Controlled Trial of a Dating Violence Prevention Program." *Journal of Adolescent Health* 51 no. 5 (November 2012): 431–438.

Mintz, Steven, and Susan Kellogg. *Domestic Revolutions: A Social History of American Family Life*. New York: Free Press, 1988.

Morrell, Caroline. *"Black Friday" and Violence against Women in the Suffragette Movement*. London: Women's Research and Resources Centre Publications, 1980.

Mulvey-Roberts, Marie. "Militancy, Masochism or Martyrdom? The Public and Private Prisons of Constance Lytton." In *Votes for Women*, edited by June Purvis and Sandra Stanley Holton, 159–180. London: Routledge, 2000.

Newman, Louise Michelle. *White Women's Rights: The Racial Origins of Feminism in the United States*. New York: Oxford University Press, 1999.

O'Brien, John J. *A Complete Course of Jiu-Jitsu and Physical Culture*. Boston: Physicians' Publishing, 1905.

Odem, Mary E. "Cultural Representations and Social Contexts of Rape in the Early Twentieth Century." In *Lethal Imagination: Violence and Brutality in American History*, edited by Michael A. Bellesiles, 353–372. New York: New York University Press, 1999.

———. *Delinquent Daughters: Protecting and Policing Adolescent Female Sexuality in the United States, 1885–1920*. Chapel Hill: University of North Carolina Press, 1995.

Omi, Michael, and Howard Winant. *Racial Formation in the United States: From the 1960s to the 1990s*. 3rd ed. New York: Routledge, 2015.

Parkins, Wendy. "Protesting Like a Girl: Embodiment, Dissent and Feminist Agency." *Feminist Theory*. 1, no. 1 (2000): 59–78.

Pascoe, Peggy. *Relations of Rescue: The Search for Female Moral Authority in the American West, 1874–1939*. New York: Oxford University Press, 1993.

Patterson, Martha H. *The American New Woman Revisited, A Reader, 1894–1930*. New Brunswick, NJ: Rutgers University Press, 2008. Kindle edition.

Peiss, Kathy. *Cheap Amusements: Working Women and Leisure in Turn-of-the-Century New York*. Philadelphia: Temple University Press, 1986.

Pfaelzer, Jean. *Driven Out: The Forgotten War against Chinese Americans*. New York: Random House, 2007.

Pleck, Elizabeth. *Domestic Tyranny: The Making of American Social Policy against Family Violence from Colonial Times to the Present*. New York: Oxford University Press, 1987.

———. "Feminist Responses to 'Crimes against Women' 1868–1896." *Signs* 8, no. 3, Women and Violence (Spring 1983): 451–470.

Pliley, Jessica R. *Policing Sexuality: The Mann Act and the Making of the FBI.* Cambridge, MA: Harvard University Press, 2014.

Purvis, June "'Deeds, Not Words': Daily Life in the Women's Social and Political Union in Edwardian Britain." In *Votes for Women*, edited by June Purvis and Sandra Stanley Holton, 135–158. London: Routledge, 2000.

———. "Emmeline Pankhurst (1858–1928) and Votes for Women." In *Votes for Women*, edited by June Purvis and Sandra Stanley Holton, 109–134. London: Routledge, 2000.

Putney, Clifford. *Muscular Christianity: Manhood and Sports in Protestant America, 1880–1920.* Cambridge, MA: Harvard University Press, 2001.

Ramsey, Carolyn B. "Public Responses to Intimate Violence: A Glance at the Past." *Public Health Reports* 121, no. 4 (July–August 2006): 460–463.

Roediger, David R. *Working toward Whiteness: How America's Immigrants Became White: The Strange Journey from Ellis Island to the Suburbs.* New York: Basic Books, 2005.

Rosen, Ruth. *The Lost Sisterhood: Prostitution in America, 1900–1918.* Baltimore: Johns Hopkins University Press, 1982.

———. *The World Split Open: How the Modern Women's Movement Changed America.* Rev. ed. New York: Penguin Books, 2006.

Rotundo, E. Anthony. *American Manhood: Transformations in Masculinity from the Revolution to the Modern Era.* New York: Basic Books, 1993.

Rouse, Wendy. "Jiu-Jitsuing Uncle Sam: The Unmanly Art of Jiu-Jitsu and the Yellow Peril Threat in the Progressive Era United States." *Pacific Historical Review* 84, no. 4 (November 2015): 448–477.

Rouse, Wendy, and Beth Slutsky. "Empowering the Physical and Political Self: Women and the Practice of Self-Defense, 1890–1920." *Journal of the Gilded Age and Progressive Era* 13, no. 4 (September 2014): 470–499.

Ryan, Mary P. *Cradle of the Middle Class: The Family in Oneida County, New York, 1790–1865.* New York: Cambridge University Press, 1981.

———. *Women in Public: Between Banners and Ballots, 1825–1880.* Baltimore: Johns Hopkins University Press, 1990.

Said, Edward W. *Orientalism.* New York: Cambridge University Press, 1978.

Sandmeyer, Elmer Clarence. *The Anti-Chinese Movement in California.* Urbana: University of Illinois Press, 1991.

Sayler, Lucy E. *Laws Harsh as Tigers: Chinese Immigrants and the Shaping of Modern Immigration Law.* Chapel Hill: University of North Carolina Press, 1995.

Searles, Patricia, and Ronald J. Berger. "The Feminist Self-Defense Movement: A Case Study." *Gender and Society* 1, no. 1 (March 1987): 61–84.

Sears, Clare. *Arresting Dress: Cross-Dressing, Law, and Fascination in Nineteenth-Century San Francisco.* Durham, NC: Duke University Press, 2015.

Segel, Harold B. *Body Ascendant: Modernism and the Physical Imperative.* Baltimore: Johns Hopkins University Press, 1998.

Segrave, Kerry. *Beware the Masher: Sexual Harassment in American Public Places, 1880–1930*. Jefferson, NC: McFarland, 2014.

Senn, Charlene, Misha Eliasziew, Paula C. Barata, Wilfreda E. Thurston, Ian R. Newby-Clark, Lorraine Radtke, and Karen L. Hobden. "Efficacy of a Sexual Assault Resistance Program for University Women." *New England Journal of Medicine* 372 (June 2015): 2326–2335.

Sewell, Jessica Ellen. *Women and the Everyday City: Public Space in San Francisco, 1890–1915*. Minneapolis: University of Minnesota Press, 2011.

Siegel, Reva B. "'The Rule of Love': Wife Beating as Prerogative and Privacy." Faculty Scholarship Series. Yale Law School Faculty Scholarship. Paper 1092 (January 1996): 2117–2207. www.digitalcommons.law.yale.edu.

Smith, Malissa. *A History of Women's Boxing*. Lanham, MD: Rowman and Littlefield, 2014. Kindle edition.

Smith-Rosenberg, Carroll. *Disorderly Conduct: Visions of Gender in Victorian America*. New York: Oxford University Press, 1985.

Spain, Daphne. *How Women Saved the City*. Minneapolis: University of Minnesota Press, 2001.

Spencer, Herbert. *The Principles of Biology*. London: Williams and Norgate, 1864.

Speidel, Lisa. "Exploring the Intersection of Race and Gender in Self-Defense Training." *Violence against Women* 20, no. 3 (March 2014): 309–325.

Stamp, Shelley. *Movie-Struck Girls: Women and Motion Picture Culture after the Nickelodeon*. Princeton, NJ: Princeton University Press, 2000.

Stansell, Christine. *City of Women: Sex and Class in New York, 1789–1860*. Urbana: University of Illinois Press, 1987.

Svinth, Joseph R. "The Circle and the Octagon: Maeda's Judo and Gracie's Jiu-Jitsu." In *Martial Arts in the Modern World: Transmission, Change and Adaptation*, edited by Thomas A. Green and Joseph R. Svinth, 61–70. Westport, CT: Praeger, 2003.

———, ed. "Editor's Notes," in "Jiu jitsu for Women." *InYo: Journal of Alternative Perspective* (August 2000). www.ejmas.com.

———. "The Evolution of Women's Judo." *InYo: Journal of Alternative Perspectives* (February 2001). www.ejmas.com.

———. *Getting a Grip: Judo in the Nikkei Communities of the Pacific Northwest, 1900–1950*. Guelph, ON: Electronic Journals of the Martial Arts and Sciences, 2003.

———. "Professor Yamashita Goes to Washington." In *Martial Arts in the Modern World: Transmission, Change and Adaptation*, edited by Thomas A Green and Joseph R. Svinth, 47–60. Westport, CT: Praeger, 2003.

———. "Tokugoro Ito." *InYo: Journal of Alternative Perspectives* (July 2006). www.ejmas.com.

Takaki, Ronald. *Strangers from a Different Shore*. Boston: Little, Brown, 1998.

Tark, Jongyeon, and Gary Kleck. "Resisting Rape: The Effects of Victim Self-Protection on Rape Completion and Injury." *Violence against Women* 20, no. 3 (March 2014): 270–292.

Tchen, John Kuo Wei, and Dylan Yeats. *Yellow Peril! An Archive of Anti-Asian Fear*. New York: Verso, 2014.

Thompson, Martha E. "Empowering Self-Defense Training." *Violence against Women* 20, no. 3 (March 2014): 351–359.

Tobin, Christopher P. *Nixola of the New York World*. Christchurch, New Zealand: C. P. Tobin, 2013.

Tsu, Cecilia M. "Sex, Lies, and Agriculture: Reconstructing Japanese Immigrant Gender Relations in Rural California, 1900–1913." *Pacific Historical Review* 78, no. 2 (May 2009): 171–209.

Ullman, Sarah E. "Does Offender Violence Escalate When Rape Victims Fight Back?" *Journal of Interpersonal Violence*, 13, no. 2 (April 1998): 179–192.

———. "Reflections on Researching Rape Resistance." *Violence against Women* 20, no. 3 (March 2014): 343–350.

Ullman, Sarah E., and Raymond A. Knight. "Fighting Back: Women's Resistance to Rape." *Journal of Interpersonal Violence* 7, no. 1 (March 1992): 31–43.

Verbrugge, Martha. *Able-Bodied Womanhood: Personal Health and Social Change in Nineteenth-Century Boston*. New York: Oxford University Press, 1988.

———. *Active Bodies: A History of Women's Physical Education in Twentieth-Century America*. New York: Oxford University Press, 2012.

Vertinsky, Patricia A. *The Eternally Wounded Woman: Women, Doctors, and Exercise in the Late Nineteenth Century*. Urbana: University of Illinois Press, 1994.

Walkowitz, Judith R. "Going Public: Shopping, Street Harassment, and Streetwalking in Late Victorian London." *Representations* 62 (Spring 1998): 1–30.

Watts, Sarah. *Rough Rider in the White House: Theodore Roosevelt and the Politics of Desire*. Chicago: University of Chicago Press, 2003.

Welter, Barbara. "The Cult of True Womanhood: 1820–1860." *American Quarterly* 18, no. 2 (Summer 1966): 151–174.

Wertheim, Stephen. "Reluctant Liberator: Theodore Roosevelt's Philosophy of Self-Government and Preparation for Philippine Independence." *Presidential Studies Quarterly* 39, no. 3 (September 2009): 494–518.

"What Is SEL?" Collaborative for Academic, Social and Emotional Learning. 2015. www.casel.org.

White, Deborah Gray. *Too Heavy a Load: Black Women in Defense of Themselves, 1894–1994*. New York: Norton, 1999.

Wilson, Gretchen. *With All Her Might: The Life of Gertrude Harding Militant Suffragette*. New York: Holmes and Meier, 1996.

Winslow, Barbara. *Sylvia Pankhurst: Sexual Politics and Political Activism*. London: Routledge, 1996.

Wolf, Tony. "The Jujitsuffragettes: Jujitsu and Feminism in Early 1900s England." www.bullshido.net.

Woloch, Nancy. *Women and the American Experience*. Boston: McGraw Hill, 2006.

Woodward, Kath. *Boxing, Masculinity and Identity: The "I" of the Tiger*. New York: Routledge, 2007.

Yoshihara, Mari. *Embracing the East: White Women and American Orientalism*. New York: Oxford University Press, 2003.

Zeidel, Robert F. *Immigrants, Progressives, and Exclusion Politics: The Dillingham Commission, 1900–1927.* DeKalb: Northern Illinois University Press, 2004.

Ziegler, Kathryn A. "'Formidable-Femininity': Performing Gender and Third Wave Feminism in a Women's Self Defense Class." PhD diss., Southern Illinois University Carbondale, 2008.

Zins, Joseph E. *Building Academic Success on Social and Emotional Learning: What Does the Research Say?* Williston, VT: Teachers College Press, 2004.

# INDEX

## ABOUT THE AUTHOR

Wendy L. Rouse teaches U.S. history and social science teacher preparation at San Jose State University. Her research interests include childhood, family, and gender history during the Progressive Era.